NAPOLEON'S
EVERYDAY GOURMET BURGERS

NAPOLEON

GOURMET GRILLS

NAPOLEON'S
EVERYDAY
GOURMET
BURGERS

INSPIRED RECIPES
BY CHEF **TED READER**

KEY PORTER BOOKS

Library and Archives Canada Cataloguing in Publication

Reader, Ted
   Napoleon's everyday gourmet burgers : inspired recipes / by Ted Reader ; photographs by Mike McColl.

ISBN 978-1-55470-261-9

   1. Cookery (Meat). 2. Hamburgers. 3. Barbecue cookery.
I. Napoleon Appliance Corporation II. Title. III. Title: Everyday gourmet burger grilling.

TX749.R39 2010   641.6'6   C2009-905844-8

ONTARIO ARTS COUNCIL
CONSEIL DES ARTS DE L'ONTARIO

The publisher gratefully acknowledges the support of the Canada Council for the Arts and the Ontario Arts Council for its publishing program. We acknowledge the support of the Government of Ontario through the Ontario Media Development Corporation's Ontario Book Initiative.

We acknowledge the financial support of the Government of Canada through the Book Publishing Industry Development Program (BPIDP) for our publishing activities.

Key Porter Books Limited
Six Adelaide Street East, Tenth Floor
Toronto, Ontario
Canada M5C 1H6

www.keyporter.com

Design: Martin Gould
Electronic formatting: Alison Carr and Martin Gould
Photography: Mike McColl www.generalchefery.com

Printed and bound in China

10 11 12 13 14 6 5 4 3 2 1

As the largest family-owned hearth and grill manufacturer in North America, Napoleon maintains strong family values that carry through in every aspect of the organization. Since 1976, Napoleon has grown from a small manufacturing operation to a large private corporation instilling the same solid values that it began with. Napoleon products are found in homes around the globe and have become the preferred brand choice worldwide.

TABLE OF CONTENTS

FOREWORD

Burgers, burgers and more burgers!

The traditional and most often-cooked meal on the grill inspired us to go all out from a traditional beef burger to an out of this world recipe such as a stuffed chicken-wing burger with blue cheese celery salad. So start flipping through this exciting book, start your list, grab your favorite tongs and spark up the grill, you'll be the neighborhood burger champion!

NAPOLEON APPLIANCE CORPORATION

DEDICATION

To all my fans—this book of chin-dripping burger recipes is for you. Thanks for all your great support. I grill for you. Real Food for Real People.

Cheers, and make every day a delicious grilling day.

TED READER

For all the grilling enthusiasts out there who want to dazzle their friends with a different burger recipe every Saturday and Sunday for the entire year!

Burger fanatics, your time has come!

NAPOLEON APPLIANCE CORPORATION

ACKNOWLEDGMENTS

Ted and his gang of grill meisters who invent these mouth-watering masterpieces.

Mike McColl for making them come alive in the book with stunning photography and Jordan's staff from Key Porter Books who bring it all together.

Last but not least, everyone at Napoleon Appliance Corporation who gives their all to build the best grills in the world!

THE SCHROETER FAMILY

Pamela: My best friend, my true love, my delicious everything!

Layla and Jordan—my new taste testers: Lots of love to you, my children, you are my greatest inspirations. Love, your Daddy.

The Schroeter Family—Ingrid, Wolfgang, Christopher and Stephen: Thank you for all your support and encouragement over the past years. Your grills are the best, they make my food sing!

Napoleon Appliance Corporation: Thank you to all those involved at Napoleon in creating the best grills in the world. Your support, talent and dedication to the Ted Reader team is greatly appreciated.
Napoleongrills.com

David Coulson: Thank you for your dedication to my team and I. Your support is greatly appreciated, your BBQ style is inspirational and I can't wait to taste your next backyard creation!

Greg Cosway and Les Murray: My friends and business partners in Ted's World Famous BBQ. Thanks for all your hard work and awesome support. I am looking forward to more exciting and delicious adventures with you both. Cheers!
Tedreader.com

Key Porter Books—Jordan, Michael, Martin, Tom and the entire gang at Key Porter: Thank you for your support. Your belief in Ted Reader is awesome. Thanks again!
Keyporter.com

Stephen Murdoch: Stephen, thank you for all of your awesome support. You're a world-class publicist—promotion in motion! You rock and I love ya!

Mike McColl: Thank you for your passionate artistry; once again the photography is stunning. You truly have found your calling. Cheers to our next adventure!
generalchefery.com

Caiti McLelland and the "girls" in the office: Caiti, you and your team are a blessing. Thanks for all the hard work and support. Without you, chaos!

Ralph James—My agent at the "The Agency Group": The best agent any BBQ dude could ask for. Ralph, thanks for believing in me as your first non Rock 'n' Roll client. Cheers!
Theagencygroup.com

Mia Bachmaier—Principal Food Stylist: Thank you for all your hard work on this cookbook. Your artistry with the food styling makes the recipes look truly delicious.

Peter Gorka—Chef's Assistant: Thanks for your hard work and new found friendship.

Bryn Clarke—Chef's Assistant: Thanks for your hard work and dedication.

Brown Forman: Producer of fine-quality spirits such as Southern Comfort, Jack Daniel's, Gentleman Jack, Finlandia Vodka, Chambord and El Jimador Tequila. Thank you for your support on this book.
Brown-forman.com

Lindemans Wines: The joys of Australian wines . . . just exceptional flavors . . . fantastic with any of my burgers!
Lindemans.com

Guelph Toyota—Barry Dohms and Michael Taverese: I love my Tundra. The official wicked, awesome road machine of Ted's World Famous BBQ!
Guelphtoyota.com

Metro Grocery Stores—Gillian Kerr and Lori Falvo: Thanks for your ongoing support. *For Food at its Best Shop Metro!*
Metro.ca

Canadian Tire Corporation and Tony LaGuardia: Thanks for all your support in my world of BBQ and across the Great White North.
Canadiantire.ca

Honeyman's Beef Purveyors: Will Wallace, thank you for your great support of my endeavors. Your meats rock the grill!
Honeymansbeef.com

Black Angus Meats: Thank you for your support—your meats got game!
Blackangusmeat.com

Caledon Propane: Hugh Sr. and Jr. thank you for your support—you guys are a real gas! I grill hot because of you.
caledonpropane.com

Varsity Tents—Graham Bauckham a.k.a "The Professor": Thanks for turning my backyard into a grilling Oasis for without your services it would have been a very wet and cold photo shoot.
varsitytents.com

TED READER

INTRODUCTION

Is your love life dull or non-existent? Is the economic crisis getting you down? Are you feeling blue?

I have the answer to your woes.

A burger!

A burger that is thick, mouth-watering and chin-dripping with tastiness. A burger that gives you complete belly satisfaction and makes you smile from ear to ear with sheer pleasure. A burger that makes you want to shake, rattle and roll.

That's what a burger *should* do!

That piece of dried-up shoe leather on a stale bun? That's not a burger. That's a burger *nightmare*, and food nightmares are not what you want. You want deliciousness. A burger so delectable that it gushes goodness when you take that first bite. A burger so moist that the juices run down your chin and the bun gets a little soggy and the burger becomes a bit of a mess in your sticky fingers—and with every bite you crave more.

That's how a burger *should* be!

Hamburgers are my favorite food. There is little more satisfying to me than a big juicy burger, grill-fired and topped just the way I like it, and my love of the hamburger is what inspired this book.

This love of burgers started with my mom. She's not the best cook in the world, but I have fond memories of a number of truly outstanding recipes of hers. Her peanut-butter balls—made only during the holidays—are yummy, but her hamburgers are out of sight.

My mom, the ever-classy Astrida Reader, has a simple philosophy about burgers: the more garlic and onions, the better the burger. Mom takes ground beef and adds a big handful of chopped garlic and a diced white onion. Then she adds more garlic just to be safe, and a little more onion. She throws in a good portion of salt and pepper and mix everything up. That is it. No measuring, and no fussing with the patties. She never flattens her burgers; they are always like big meatballs, round and puffy.

Mom fries the burgers in butter in a well-seasoned cast-iron pan. (Now and then, she'd give the burgers to Dad to grill over a charcoal grill. A long time ago our grill was a wheelbarrow loaded with charcoal; we only had grilled burgers on special occasions.) The outside of the burgers would get crispy and golden brown. Because Mom never squishes her burgers, they come out moist and juicy. She serves the burgers on simple, white, small hamburger buns also fried in butter until they were golden. Topped with a stack of thinly sliced raw onions and some sliced garden fresh tomatoes, and you had burger heaven.

This memory of her burgers will live with me forever, proof that a burger can truly change your life. It does mine. It is part of my culinary history. It is a component of my passion for food and love for the world of barbecue and grilling.

Over the years, I have traveled the globe and eaten many a hamburger. Not a difficult thing to do. Hamburgers are made and eaten *everywhere!*

How did this burger phenomenon get started? Many people claim to have invented the hamburger, but where and how did it really originate? Some say that the birth of the hamburger dates back to England in the 1700s. The fourth Earl of Sandwich was the first to be credited with the creation while at a popular gentleman's club in London. But was this creation the burger or just the sandwich?

A burger is a sandwich, but for me the hamburger is an American invention.

Back in the 1800s, ground beef was expensive and was reserved for the upper class. The burger may have started out as a simple meat patty on a plate, served with mashed potatoes, fried onions and gravy and eaten with a knife and fork.

That didn't last. Burgers jumped from plate to bun, and an American icon was born. The hamburger offered the working class a hot alternative to sliced-meat sandwiches. And so began the American burger revolution.

A number of places in the United States of America claim to be the birthplace of the hamburger. Which of them was? That will be an ongoing argument forever, but here is what I know.

In November 2006, the Texas State Legislature designated Athens, Texas, as the Original Home of the Hamburger. Fletcher Davis is said to have invented the hamburger at his lunch counter in Athens sometime during the 1880s. But in 2007, the Wisconsin State Legislature passed a resolution saying that Charlie Nagreen invented the hamburger in the Wisconsin town of Seymour. Other competitors for the honor hail from Connecticut, New York and Massachusetts. To whoever invented the hamburger, I wish to say, "Thank you." Your invention has rocked the food world and made the hamburger the most popular sandwich ever.

It took many years for the hamburger to evolve into the cheeseburger. Adding cheese would seem to be a simple thing, but not until sometime between 1924 and 1926 did a Pasadena, California, chef named Lionel Sternberger top the mighty burger with cheese. Others have also laid claim. In Louisville, Kentucky, Kaelin's Restaurants professes to have invented the cheeseburger in 1934; and in 1935, a trademark for the name cheeseburger was given to Louis Ballast of the Humpty Dumpty Drive-In in Denver, Colorado. I don't know who first added cheese to the hamburger, but I do know that whoever did was brilliant. He invented the Great American Cheeseburger. See my version of The Great American Cheeseburger on page 48.

For me, the hamburger is a way of life. I am forever searching for the Ultimate Hamburger. I have traveled to many places all around the world and the search is unending. I have had many memorable hamburgers. Some so juicy you would have needed a mop and bucket to clean up the mess; others so dried out they resembled old-shoe leather.

But I won't tell you about those—just about my favorites.

I've mentioned my mom's mouth-watering burgers. Here are some places where equally extraordinary burgers can be had.

In-N-Out Burger, the original drive-thru hamburger chain, is based in California and a favorite of many celebrity chefs, including Emeril, Gordon Ramsay, Bobby Flay, Charlie Trotter and Thomas Keller. I love their burgers so much I've included an In-N-Out Burger recipe in this book (p. 55). Check them out at www.innoutburger.com. Any time I am in California, an In-N-Out hamburger is a must-have.

Then there is Shaggy's Burgers in Swanton, Vermont. Proprietor Shaggy looks just like the Shaggy character in *Scooby Doo*. He makes the juiciest burgers in Vermont—and I have had many burgers in Vermont. Shaggy's are freshly ground and griddle-fried. Topped with cheese and bacon, they are chin-dripping good.

Another of my favorites is Dan's Drive-In in Traverse City, Michigan. You need a basket of napkins to eat their moist and juicy burger. (They also have the ultimate milk shakes, so thick they can cause a stroke from having to suck so hard to drink them. Forget the straw and use a spoon.)

And then there is the Vortex in Atlanta. I like my Vortex burger done medium-rare because they use freshly ground sirloin. And I like it topped with cheese, bacon, lots of raw red onions, mayonnaise, a fried egg and a corn dog. Yup, a corn dog! You see, there are no rules about what you can put on your burger, so at the Vortex anything goes.

I have had a burger in every city that I have been to in the United States and Canada in my ongoing search for the Ultimate Hamburger. I've had mini-slider burgers from White Castle Hamburgers after a good night of partying. I've had my fill of Big Macs from McDonald's (they used to be much better), Whoppers from Burger King, the Baconator from Wendy's (a great invention on Wendy's part), Teen Burgers from A&W, Brazier Burgers from Dairy Queen, Sonic, Krystal Hamburgers, Rally, Harvey's and many more. I've eaten the $50 Kobe burger stuffed with braised short ribs and foie gras. I've had burgers raw to well-done. I've had little ones and big ones, and I have had singles, doubles, triples, quads, even five-high ones.

I have made thousands of burgers and grilled even more. I have topped them with a variety of cheeses and condiments, and I have even slathered them with peanut butter and jelly.

Will I ever find the Ultimate Hamburger? I hope not, because eating burgers has been spiritually enlightening as well as belly pleasing. This burger train just needs to keep on rolling.

For this cookbook, I have assembled 112 different hamburger recipes. Some are favorites that I created over the years, such as the Surf and Turf Burger (p. 72), which I did for Regis and Kelly. Or the Ludicrous Burger, which I created a number of years ago and which first appeared in my *King of the Q Blue Plate BBQ Cookbook.*

The Ludicrous comes between two grilled cheese sandwiches, and is unofficially the most expensive hamburger in the world. Yup, the world. I was in the Dominican Republic, and I did a grilling demonstration for a charity event and sold two Extremely Ludicrous Burgers for $1500 U.S. each. The burger was assembled in this order from top to bottom: fried egg, sausage, grilled cheese sandwich, bacon, three cheeses, 8-oz (240 g) sirloin burger, onions, tomato, lettuce, grilled cheese sandwich, bacon, three cheeses, 8-oz (240 g) sirloin burger, onions, tomato, lettuce and a third grilled cheese sandwich.

This book of burger recipes is meant to be fun. Whether it's the Classic All-Beef Burger (p. 47) or The Great American Cheeseburger (p. 48), the Ying Yang Fireworks Shrimp Burger (p. 274), the Turducken Burger (p. 224, a foie-gras-stuffed chicken burger inside a duck burger inside a turkey burger) or the Buffalo Chicken Wing Burger (p. 192), it is all about making delicious, mouth-watering hamburgers that your friends and family will enjoy. There are burgers that are grilled and sizzled, planked and smoky. Chin drippers and belly pleasers. All of them are inspired by my heart and come from my passion for food and barbecue cooking. They are burgers to get the whole family excited about, and make you the Burger Master of Your Grill—and maybe entice you into creating delicious, mouth-watering hamburgers of your own.

Get sticky!

CHEF TED READER

While going over research we've done over the years on grilling, the classic burger always came first for the most often cooked meal on the grill.

Chicken and steak are next on the list with the majority being cooked on a gas or propane grill, although charcoal cooking is getting more popular year after year.

The burger's number one ranking inspired us to team up with Ted Reader and Key Porter Books to produce a book solely dedicated to the common burger and bring it to an all new level of excitement.

You'll find recipes for beef, lamb, chicken, pork, salmon, wild game and much more along with incredible ingredients like back bacon, avocado, apples, asiago cheese and black forest ham!

Grilled, glazed, smoked, baked, planked, broiled. You'll be amazed at the number of ways to cook burgers and never be bored again with this age old classic.

We're sure you'll enjoy trying all these recipes and they may just inspire you to come up with your own fabulous creation.

Enjoy and get grilling!

NAPOLEON APPLIANCE CORPORATION

Top row, left to right: Beef Tenderloin, Beef Chuck, Beef Rib Eye, Beef Eye of Round

Second row, left to right: Beef Sirloin, Veal, Lamb, Chicken

Third row, left to right: Duck, Venison, Ostrich, Kangaroo

Fourth row, left to right: Salmon, Big Shrimp, Pork, Turkey

Far left: a comparison of three grocery grinds, with regular on the top, medium in the middle, and lean on the bottom

Near left: grinding Chicken

IT'S A MATTER OF MEAT

GROUND MEAT VARIETIES

The most important part of a burger is the meat. Toppings, condiments, garnishes and buns are the least of your worries when you want to create that perfectly grilled burger. It all comes down to the meat. Here are the varieties of ground meats:

EXTRA-LEAN GROUND BEEF: Approximately 90% lean with 10% fat content. Burgers tend to be not so moist but have less shrinkage and are heart-healthy.

LEAN GROUND BEEF: Approximately 80–85% lean with 15–20% fat content. Burgers tend to be a little juicier than those made with extra-lean. A healthier choice.

MEDIUM GROUND BEEF: Approximately 75–80% lean with 20–25% fat content. A much juicer burger, with good flavor.

REGULAR GROUND BEEF: Approximately 70% lean with 30% fat content. Makes a pretty juicy and flavorful burger.

GROUND EYE OF THE ROUND: similar to extra-lean ground beef, with a ratio of 85–90% lean and 10–15% fat.

GROUND SIRLOIN: similar to lean ground beef, but has great steak flavors and quality. Runs at about 80% lean with 20% fat.

GROUND CHUCK: the best for making burgers. Similar to medium and regular ground beef, with approximately 25–30% fat and 75–70% lean. Has the best flavor and holds up well on the grill. My favorite!

GROUND VEAL: Approximately 90% lean with 10% fat content. Burgers tend to be not so moist but have less shrinkage and are heart-healthy.

GROUND LAMB: Approximately 90% lean with 10% fat content. Burgers tend to be not so moist but have less shrinkage and are heart-healthy.

GROUND CHICKEN: Approximately 90% lean with 10% fat content. Burgers tend to be not so moist but have less shrinkage and are heart-healthy.

GROUND TURKEY: Approximately 90% lean with 10% fat content. Burgers tend to be not so moist but have less shrinkage and are heart-healthy.

GROUND DUCK WITH SKIN: Approximately 70% lean with 30% fat content. Makes a pretty juicy and flavorful burger.

GROUND VENISON, BISON, MOOSE, OSTRICH: Approximately 90% lean with 10% fat content. Burgers tend to be not so moist but have less shrinkage and are heart-healthy.

GROUND PORK: Approximately 70% lean with 30% fat content which makes the burgers moist and juicy. Ground pork is an easy way to boost fat in other meats like turkey, chicken, veal, beef, lamb, and game.

Experiment with the varieties of ground meats available. Enjoy making your burgers your way.

FAT VS. LEAN

When it comes to flavor, fat is what gives your burgers the flavor that you need to make it moist and juicy. Fat is the enhancer that helps the meat. Never let it be said that lean is not good. Lean is a healthier choice, but when it comes to full flavor and an explosion of burger deliciousness, fat is what you need. Fat, however, comes with a downside. Yes, it is not heart healthy, but it also has more shrinkage than lean meat. In the end, you have a smaller burger and sometimes might ask yourself, "Where's the beef?"

All meats have fat in them, but sometimes it is not enough and sometimes you may just want to add a little extra fat to make that burger succulent.

The following fats are great ways to enhance the flavor of a variety of ground meats that sometimes end up a little dry on the grill:

Beef Suet	Butter
Beef Marrow	Olive Oil
Pork Fat	Duck Fat
Salted Pork Fat	Chicken Fat
Bacon and Bacon Fat	

By no means do you have to add extra fat to your burgers. Think of it this way: Fat is flavor; lean is clean.

You decide. Food is about flavor and eating what you enjoy. Have fun and make your burgers delicious.

1.	Marrow	**7.**	Smoked Thick-Slice Bacon
2.	Roasted Marrow Butter	**8.**	Bacon Fat
3.	Beef Fat	**9.**	Beef Suet
4.	Butter	**10.**	Duck Fat/Skin
5.	Salted Pork Fat	**11.**	Chicken Fat/Skin
6.	Sliced Bacon		

BURGER BINDERS

When I eat a burger, I want it made from 100% meat. I don't mind a variety of flavorings in my burgers, but I am opposed to a burger having some kind of binder in it. I like meat, and if and where possible, I want a burger to be a burger. When a burger has enough fat, it will hold together better than a burger that is lean. Lean or extra-lean beef, veal, chicken, turkey, game such as bison, venison, kangaroo, moose, vegetables and seafood—here is where you need to add a binder to the meat to hold the burger together as it cooks. A binder will keep the shape, reduce shrinkage and reduce the overall cost of the burger patty.

Most people use an egg *and* bread crumbs as binders, but you don't always have to use both. Egg tends to make the burger a little rubbery, so be cautious.

And there are other binders than just plain old egg and bread crumbs. A variety of items can actually add great flavor and texture to your burgers. For example, oats soaked in dark ale and then added to venison burgers not only help hold the venison together, but also increase moisture in the burger because of the added ale—making for a juicy burger. The ale also softens the oats, so that they break down and mix well with the meat. Crushed cheese nachos are another good binder, especially for a chicken fajita burger. I also love hickory sticks crushed and used in a turkey burger or a pork burger.

Rule of thumb: When making your burgers, try to make them without binders. If, after you mix the meat, you find that it is either too wet or too loose, add a binder at this time. This is a great way not to make a mess of your grill or undermine your burger prowess.

SUGGESTED BINDERS:

Bread crumbs
Bulgur wheat
Cereals (Corn Flakes, Rice Krispies, Corn Pops, Captain Crunch and Shreddies)
Cooked potatoes or sweet potatoes
Cooked rice
Corn chips in a variety of flavors (plain or BBQ)
Cornmeal
Crispy fried onion pieces
Egg (whole, or yolk or white)
Ground nuts (pecan, almond, hazelnut, peanut)
Hickory potato sticks

Oats
Panko (Japanese-style) bread crumbs
Popcorn
Potato chips in a variety of flavors (rippled or straight cut, plain, salt and vinegar, BBQ or ketchup—all work well)
Ritz Crackers, cheese-flavored
Saltine crackers, crushed
Tortilla chips in a variety of flavors
Triscuit crackers, crushed
Whole wheat crackers, crushed

Don't be afraid to experiment. Have fun and keep your burgers together. There is nothing worse than a burger that falls apart as you grill it.

GRINDING MEATS

You can usually buy a variety of ground meats in most grocery stores—extra-lean, lean, medium and regular ground beef; ground chuck, eye of the round and sirloin; ground pork, lamb and occasionally veal. You will also find ground chicken and turkey. But that's about it. For bison and kangaroo, you'll have to try specialty grocery stores and butcher shops. For venison and moose, you may well have to be a hunter to get these, although venison is farm-raised and processed.

Sometimes you just want to make a burger truly from scratch. For this, you will need a meat grinder. You'll discover a variety on the market today. The old-fashioned hand crank is heavy and requires a lot a muscle to grind the meat. Some stand mixers have a meat-grinding attachment, and these work well. For those of you who want some professionalism in your grinding, you can purchase a restaurant-quality meat grinder with a variety of different horse powers that will make grinding your meat a lot easier. You can find these at specialty restaurant supply stores or outdoor stores such as Gander Mountain and Bass Pro. These are great for quickly grinding meats well. They can power through 5 lbs (about 2 kg) of meat in a minute. Now, that's good grinding!

Most grinders come with a couple of different grinding plates—traditionally, a small plate for fine grinds, and a large plate for coarse grinds. I like to grind beef on the large plate first and then grind it a second time on the small plate. This gives you a pretty tender burger that sticks together well on the grill.

For all meats other than beef, I use the small plate.

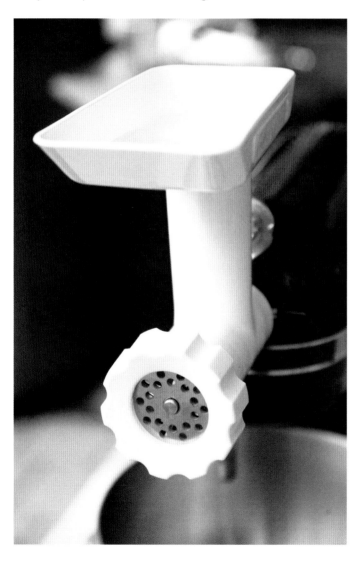

GETTING DOWN TO THE GRIND

Set up your grinder according to the manufacturer's instructions.

Keep your meat cold and in the refrigerator.

Fill a large bowl with 2 to 3 lbs (1–1.5 kg) of ice and place another bowl on top. Place both under the grinder where the meat comes out. (This will keep your ground meat cold while you are grinding. Keeping the meat cold is important so that you do not lose the valuable fats that offer that great burger flavor.)

Grind the cold meat a little at a time, pushing the meat into the feeder tube with a plunger.

When you're finished grinding, cover the meat and transfer it to the refrigerator. Let it rest there for 1 hour before making your burgers.

Note: A bowl of ice keeps your meat cold while grinding and mixing.

THE BASICS OF MAKING GREAT BURGERS

Nothing is more satisfying than making your own stack of burgers. Grillin' them up and chowing down on them afterward. Why buy frozen when you can create the best and it's easy?

Once you've bought your meat and it's ground, the key to making all your burgers great is starting out with the meat ice-cold. Not frozen, but cold enough to slightly numb your fingers when mixing. Cold meat mixes better because your hands will add warmth to the meat as you mix it, and as the meat warms up the fat separates and ends up on your hands and not in your burgers! You need what fat there is to keep your burgers moist and juicy. So put your meat in the refrigerator and get it ice-cold.

When the ground meat is cold, take it out of the refrigerator and place it in a large bowl so that you can have plenty of room to mix efficiently. I like to place my mixing bowl on top of another bowl filled with ice to ensure that the meat stays cold.

Next, season your meat with your favorite burger seasonings. I use my World Famous Bone Dust™ BBQ Seasoning or my Orgasmic Onion Burger Seasoning, but you can use what you want. Be creative and create your favorite burger seasoning depending on the type of burger you want. As I've said, have fun!

I'm often asked how you know how much seasoning to add. Here is my tip, and it works for any amount of ground meat: Sprinkle your seasoning over the meat. When you can no longer see the meat, you've added enough. But go easy on using salt—it robs meat of moisture.

After you've added seasoning, put on a pair of disposable gloves and mix your burgers.

You should mix quickly and efficiently. I use my fingers like claws and squeeze the meat through them. About a dozen hand mixes is plenty. Remember—keep the meat cold.

When you've finished mixing, portion your seasoned ground meat into uniform-sized balls, gently squeezing the meat to remove any air. This will help keep your burgers together during grilling.

Season

Mix with claw fingers

It's mixed

Portion

Squeeze and press the air out

Portioned burger balls

Working with one burger ball at a time, slap the burger onto a flat work surface, then dome each ball by slightly cupping your hand around it. Then, while patting the top of the burger ball with one hand to make it flat, use your other hand to push in the sides to meet the top. I like to make my burgers approximately 1 inch (2.5 cm) thick and 4 inches (10 cm) in diameter for a 6-oz (180 g) burger.

A number of burger presses on the market today can make forming your burgers a little easier. Some have thickness adjusters; others poke a dimple in the center of the burger to keep the burgers round; others add slash marks to give your burger tiny little troughs that hold the juices and fats in the burger and keep them out of the fire; and some make circular cuts, also for juice and fat retention.

You decide what works best for you. There are no rules—just delicious burgers to be made and eaten.

Now you should have a perfect-looking burger. Take a pallet knife or spatula and slide it underneath the burger to separate it from the work surface. Transfer the burger to a piece of patty paper or parchment paper and repeat with remaining burger balls.

Once all the burgers are formed, don't head straight to the grill. Place the formed burgers in the refrigerator for a minimum of 1 hour, allowing the meat to rest, the flavors to blend and the meat to get ice-cold again.

Slap it down

Pat to flatten

Flatten

Pat to shape

Push the sides up

Remove from work surface

Stack 'em!

BURGER SHAPES

Sometimes a round burger gets to be a bit boring. But then again, so does a square burger. For some fun, try shaping your burgers into different shapes and thicknesses. A thicker burger will be a more juicy and succulent burger. And a fun shape makes for a little burger excitement, especially with kids.

I use cookie cutters to shape most of my fun burgers. Be creative and have a good time.

I can't say this often enough: have fun with your burgers.

GRILLING YOUR BURGERS

When it comes to grilling burgers, there are some simple rules that you should follow:

- Don't grill your burgers over high heat. Medium to medium-high (350–550°F/180–280°C) is best. This temperature will still sear your burgers but keep them from burning.
- Grill burgers with grill lid open. This way you can see if there is a flare-up and you can react to it quickly.
- Always grill frozen burgers from frozen, never thawed.
- Grill fresh burgers from a very cold state. Not frozen, but never with the meat at room temperature. Burgers should be cold.
- Spray burgers lightly with a nonstick cooking spray to help prevent them from sticking.
- Use a sharp-edged spatula to flip your burgers, and only flip your burgers once.
- Don't press or cut your burgers when they're grilling. It will enable the juices to run out and will give you a drier burger.
- Leave your burgers alone. Every time you want to squish, poke, cut or mash them, have a sip of beer instead.
- If you should get flare-ups or big flames, reduce the heat, move the burgers to the top rack for a few minutes and wait for the flare-ups to stop. Do not spray water on flare-ups. Hot grease and water do not mix. Turn down the heat and wait.

- Use a meat or instant-read thermometer to ensure that meat is cooked properly:
  — Poultry should be fully cooked to 170-180°F (75-85°C).
  — Burgers should always be fully cooked to a minimum of 160°F (70°C).
  — Beef, veal, lamb, roasts and steaks can vary from 140°F to 160°F (60–70°C) and pork should be a minimum of 160°F (70°C).
- Have all your buns, condiments, toppings and all your salads ready first before you start grilling your burgers. Most burgers cook in 15 to 20 minutes. With everything else ready ahead of time, you won't be running around like a chicken with your head cut off as your burgers burn.
- Never leave your grill. Once you start grilling your burgers, stay put. Watch and sip your beer(s) and grill up some tasty burgers.

Not everyone wants to make burgers following the steps I've just outlined—they *are* a bit of work—but they truly do give you great burgers.

TIP:
No squishing.
No pressing.
No cutting.
No flames.
No excessive flipping.
Keep them moist.

No cutting!

No squishing and no flames

Flip when the juices form on the surface

Fully cooked!

TED READER'S TIPS FOR GETTING YOUR GRILL READY

Each spring once the cold harsh winter has passed, you should inspect your grill—and all its working parts—and give it a really good cleaning. Whether you use your grill during the winter months or not, give your grill some extra attention come springtime so that it is in top condition for the busy grilling months ahead.

Here is my list of things that you should do to get your grill ready for some serious grilling excitement. Take it from me, a man with 105 grills and barbecue smokers, being prepared for cooking is as important as the cooking itself.

- Pull the cover off your grill. (I hope you are using a grill cover. A grill cover will protect your grill from the elements and give the grill a longer life.)
- Unhook the grill from its fuel source (natural gas line or propane tank) and then remove all the easily removable parts from the grill (cooking grills, burner heat or sear plates, lava rocks, ceramic stones or plates, grease drip catch tray and upper grill rack).
- Remove your grill burners (some burners are attached with screws or clips, so for ease of removal, review your Owner's Manual). Inspect your burners for evidence of burn-through. If any part of the burner is burned through or even rusted through, the burner is unsafe and should be replaced. Consult your Owner's Manual. If the burners look good, clear the portholes with a pipe cleaner or small nail. I use a canister of compressed air to assist in this process, but make sure your fuel sources are disconnected and your grill is cold. Lightly brush off carbon residue from the burners.
- Inspect the venturi tubes. These are the tubes that extend down from the bottom of the burner. Spiders, moths and other insects can nest in the tubes and cause fuel blockage. This poses a safety issue, so make sure they are clear. Purchase a flexible venturi tube cleaner and insert it into the tubes, then use a brushing motion to clear the tubes. Some grills have an adjustable air shutter on the end of the venturi tubes. The shutter should be open 3/8 to 1/2 inch (1–1.5 cm). If this shutter is closed, the flame pressure at the burner head will be reduced, causing a cool yellow flame. When operational, you want to have as much of a clear blue flame as possible, because this is where the greatest heat comes from.

- Check your burner valves for smooth operation. The burner controls should turn easily. Remove and clean if necessary.
- Using a grill brush or scraper, scrape and remove all grease and carbon buildup in the main firebox of the grill.
- Clean your grill. There are a lot of cleaning solutions that you can use, but I prefer hot soapy water and good old-fashioned elbow grease. They are environmentally friendly and save you dollars. Scrub the grill down inside and out and rinse to remove all soap. Let all parts dry completely before reassembly.
- Inspect your fire starter control button. Make sure it is working properly. Sometimes it is as simple as changing a battery. Refer to your Owner's Manual, and replace the battery if necessary.
- Re-install the burners, making sure the orifices on the valves are seated correctly inside the venturi tubes. Replace all cleaned grill parts, and make sure you put in a fresh drip-catch tray.
- Make sure all burners are in the off position and the grill lid is open, and then attach your fuel source. Check that the fuel lines are not cracked or broken. If so, replace.
- If using a propane tank, inspect your tank for excessive rust, for any dents or for damage threads. Replace older tanks. I use a propane tank exchange program to ensure that the replacement tanks are relatively new and in good order.
- Ignite your grill:

  —Make sure the grill lid is open when you light the grill.
  —Make sure all the burners are in the off position.
  —Open the fuel valve on either your natural gas line or propane tank. Turn on one burner and ignite one burner only. Once the burner has ignited, turn on the remaining burners one at a time.
  —Once the entire grill is on, inspect the flame pattern. You want an even flame pattern with a clear blue flame. Not all flames will be fully blue, due either to the normal impurities in propane and natural gas or grease buildup. Remember—a blue flame is a hot flame.
- Remember—all grill parts, such as valves, temperature gauges, grills, warming racks, lava rocks, ceramic stones or plates, hoses, burners, handles and burner knobs should be inspected regularly and replaced as required.
- Hit your local BBQ supply store and purchase a couple of grill brushes. A grill brush is your most important barbecue tool. A clean grill is a healthy grill, and a clean grill is a hotter grill.
- If you have any questions about your grill, review your Owner's Manual, or contact your local BBQ supply store or the grill's manufacturer.
- Have fun, be safe and make all your food delicious!

GRILLING SAFETY TIPS

Grilling safely is the most important ingredient for delicious outdoor cooking. Use common sense. Read the manufacturer's Owner's Manual for proper assembly and maintenance of your grill. Be safe!

- Keep your grill clean. A clean grill is a healthy grill and a clean grill is a hotter grill.
- Use your barbecue grill or smoker only outdoors. Position your grill in an open area away from any enclosures, overhangs. NEVER bring your grill indoors. Grills and smokers produce carbon monoxide and the accumulation can cause fatalities.
- Be sure that all grill parts of your grill or smoker are firmly in place and that the leggings are secure and stable. Check your grill regularly for wear and tear.
- Have a fire extinguisher on hand.
- Keep children away from your grill when cooking.
- Never leave your hot grill unattended.
- Use proper long-handled grilling utensils to avoid burns and splatters.
- Use flame retardant gloves or mitts when adjusting hot parts of your grill.
- When lighting your grill, always have the grill lid open to prevent a buildup of gas.
- Never spray water on a hot grill, as you can warp and crack your burners, firebox, grills and lid.
- Clean your grill brush regularly. A grill brush with excess grease and carbon buildup is unhealthy. Replace grill brush as needed.
- Clean your grill firebox and drip-catch tray regularly. I recommend after every fifth use.
- If a grease fire should occur (you will know this by the excessive amount of black billowing smoke coming from your grill and by the large orange flames), turn off burners, turn off fuel source, close lid and allow the fire to burn out on its own. Baking soda is a good way to control a grease fire. If the fire is burning out of control, use a fire extinguisher or call 911. Don't be embarrassed and don't try to be a hero. Better to be safe than sorry.
- When you have finished cooking, turn off the fuel supply first and then the burners. Then, using a grill brush, scrub your grill clean. Leaving a dirty grill will attract insects and rodents. Never clean your grill by turning it on high and closing the lid to burn off the carbon and grit and food particles. This is a waste of fuel and puts excessive wear and tear on your grill. Think green.
- Store your propane tanks outside and in an upright position.
- Be patient. You don't have to cook everything on high heat. Remember—the longer it takes to cook, the more beer you get to drink.
- Never squish, push or flatten your burgers while they are grilling. Let them cook at their own speed. This will reduce flare-ups and give you a moister, juicier burger.
- For charcoal grilling, never add lighter-fluid coals that are hot or warm.
- For charcoal grilling, never use gasoline or other highly volatile fuels as a starter; they can explode.
- For charcoal grilling, keep your grill vents open; charcoal and wood chunks need oxygen to burn.
- Watch the direction of the wind when grilling, and always grill with the wind to your back.
- When you have finished grilling, allow hot coals to completely cool for a minimum of 48 hours before disposing of them. Dispose of coals by wrapping them in aluminum foil and placing them in a non-combustible container with no combustible materials nearby.
- For more information, check out www.tedreader.com or www.napoleongrills.com.

TIPS FOR GOOD BBQ ETIQUETTE

When it comes to attending someone else's barbecue party or hosting your own backyard barbecue bash, there are a few rules of etiquette that you should use as guidelines. Take it from me, I host a number of barbecue fests and I've learned a bit about the rights and wrongs.

WHEN ATTENDING A BBQ PARTY:

- **Don't Touch the Grill:** That is the domain of the host and/or hostess, and moving in on their BBQ turf is the biggest faux pas that you can make. As a guest, you can watch but never touch. Asking questions, though, is completely acceptable.
- **Bring Something:** A bottle of wine or some beer or a bottle of Jack; or, if you feel up to it, even a side dish you've made. But make sure there is enough to go around. Even a jar of your favorite barbecue sauce is a great gift. I suggest Ted's World Famous BBQ Sauces and Seasonings.

- **Be Respectful:** Your hosts have enough stress throwing a party. They don't need any added aggravation. Never tell the person working the grill how to do it, or that what he or she is doing is wrong. Mind your manners and only offer suggestions when asked.

WHEN HOSTING A BBQ PARTY:

- Make sure your grill is clean. A clean grill is a healthy grill, and it makes you look professional.
- If using propane as your fuel source, make sure you have a full tank and a backup tank. There is nothing worse than running out of fuel while you're in the middle of cooking. The same goes for charcoal. Make sure you have enough. Stock up.
- Invest in proper utensils. Make yourself look like a professional. Rusted, dirty gear can make you look bad, and your food taste bad, too!
- Prepare recipes that you are comfortable and familiar with. Test recipes on your family (they will forgive you), not your guests.
- Prepare a checklist for your party so you can be sure you don't forget any detail, because after a cocktail or two we tend to forget stuff.
- Create a theme for your BBQ party: a birthday, Father's Day, Canada Day, the Fourth of July or any other celebration; a barbecue theme will make it easier to plan a menu and get yourself organized.
- If, for example, you're nervous about grilling a whole bunch of burgers and getting them all perfect, ask your guests if they want to grill their own. Provide barbecue tongs and let the guests go at it. This makes your job as host or hostess easier, and your guests get to have some fun.
- Do have all foods ready at relatively the same time. For instance, if you're grilling steaks, have everything else prepared, so that the steaks are the last thing you cook.
- Have a vegetarian option. Meat is the mainstay of barbecue, but not all your guests may eat meat. So offer something else. Grilled portobello mushroom caps topped with assorted grilled vegetables and maybe cheese makes for a tasty burger.
- Don't feel obligated to invite your neighbors. Not all parties require their presence.
- Provide taxi rides for those who have a little too much fun.
- KISS: Keep It Simple, Sexy!
- Last, have fun. Enjoy your family and friends and don't worry. It's a barbecue party. Get sticky!

THE ESSENTIAL GRILLING UTENSILS FOR MAKING BURGERS EASILY

There are tons of grilling utensils on the marketplace. With such a huge variety, choosing can be difficult. You really need only four items to get the job of grilling burgers done efficiently: grill brush, spatula, basting brush and tongs. That's it!

SIR GRILL BRUSH: I call the grill brush "Sir" because it is the most important grilling utensil you should own. And not just one brush—you need a small arsenal. Sir Grill Brush should be heavy-duty, with thick, long durable bristles that can get between the grates to deliver a good cleaning. The bristles should be well secured. Starting to clean your grill and having your brush lose its bristles is disheartening. To make sure the bristles are firmly anchored, give them a tug before you buy the brush.

Sir Grill Brush should have a long shaft so that you can get both hands on it when you have a real mess of a grill to clean—a brush that is not too flexible and that is heat-resistant, so you can use it when necessary during your grilling session. The head of the brush should be large. You want a brush that covers a lot of grill area and can take a bit of abuse. Durability is important. A really good grill brush should last the entire season.

Cleaning your grill brush is paramount. You can't clean your grill if the bristles of your grill brush are clogged with grease. Food particles and carbon build up. Soak your brushes in boiling hot soapy water for 20 minutes to release as much of the grime as possible. Then use another brush to remove the final particles. Your grill brush will last a lot longer.

Note: If your grill brush starts to lose its bristles, or the bristles become completely flattened, or there is no hope of removing the grease in them, it's time to replace the brush.

Remember—the grill brush is the key to keeping your grill clean, and a clean grill is a healthy grill.

THE ALMIGHTY SPATULA: Spatulas come in all shapes and sizes. Some have teeth, some have a sharp cutting edge, some even have a bottle opener attached. Great stuff, but all you really need is a spatula with a flexible blade about as wide as a burger patty and long enough to hold one or two burgers. It should have a long handle to keep your hands out of the direct heat, but not too long that you can't control it. It should be lightweight but durable, and it should fit comfortably in your hand. There is nothing worse than trying to flip a burger with a spatula that has a shaft the size of a baseball bat.

BASTING BRUSH: Nothing completes grilled foods like the sauce, and to apply the sauce, you need a great basting brush. I like a brush that is about 10 inches (25 cm) in length and has fine bristles that soak up lots of sauce and apply it evenly. Look around. There are a lot of basting brushes available. Find the one that is right for you.

TONGS: Owning a great pair of tongs is essential to making the grilling job easier. In fact, tongs are the second most important grilling utensil to have. You want tongs that feel right. Some pairs are so big and cumbersome they make grilling difficult. Tongs should be comfortable in your hand. They should have a snap action that allows you to grip the food and either move it on the grill or remove it from the grill. I like restaurant-style chef tongs. You can find them in many restaurant supply stores and specialty kitchen shops. My favorite are 9 inches (25 cm) in length. I like their quick action, and they are heavy-duty but lightweight. They don't bend when I pick up a 3-lb (1.5 kg) steak. Most restaurant-style chef tongs come in 9- or 11-inch (20–25 cm) lengths, both of which are easy to handle. They're also available in 14- and 18-inch (35–45 cm) lengths. These are useful when you're working over a very hot grill, but they're a little more difficult to handle. Test the tongs and get what fits right.

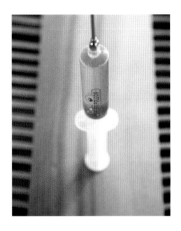

NAPOLEON GRILL ACCESSORIES THAT AID IN MAKING BURGERS

CAJUN INJECTOR: Great for injecting marinades, sauces and other liquids into the center of your burger and other grilled items.

BURGER GRILL BASKET: A grill basket that makes it easy to grill many burgers at once because you flip the burgers all together. And it's fabulous for doing more delicate burgers (vegetarian or seafood) because it keeps them from sticking to your grill.

MULTI-GRILL BASKET: A grill basket that allows you to grill burgers more easily, especially small burgers, because you only have to flip the basket, not each burger.

CHARCOAL TRAY: A cast-iron charcoal tray that fits on top of your Napoleon gas burners and under the Wave™ rod-cooking grids. Fill with lump or briquette charcoal, use the gas to ignite the charcoal and then turn off the gas. Once the coals are white-hot, you are ready to get grilling or smoking. It's the best accessory for any Napoleon Gas Grill. Now with every Napoleon you can grill with gas and/or charcoal. What a treat. One grill does it all.

GRIDDLE: A stainless-steel griddle pan that fits right on the grill. If your grill does not have a side burner, this is a great accessory for sautéing onions and mushrooms, or frying an egg, or even making pancakes, French toast or a stir-fry.

ASSEMBLING YOUR BURGERS

Meat is the most important ingredient in a burger, but to enhance your burger and make it truly outstanding, you need a couple of other ingredients:

A BUN. You don't want a bun that is bigger than the burger. A burger should hang off the edges of the bun. At the very least, the bun should be the same size as the burger.

Bun style is a personal matter. I like my buns simple and plain so the flavors of the bun don't overpower the burger. But that's me. Experiment with a variety of buns and breads. Use them fresh, or brush them with butter or olive oil and grill them up toasty. The burger is yours. Have fun with it!

CONDIMENTS AND TOPPINGS. Whether you like ketchup on your burger or peanut butter, the choice is up to you. Having it your way is the most important thing. If you like onions, load 'em on—if you don't, forget 'em. Slather on that special sauce or mayonnaise, dunk that burger in gravy and load it up with your favorite cheeses or bacon or vegetables. Creating your burger is personal. The grocery store and markets are your burger playground.

The picture here is of what I call the Tundra Burger. A fully loaded burger with a ton of toppings. You don't have to be this elaborate, but it's always good to know you have options. Assemble your burgers! Be the burger architect of your backyard barbecue. Create and enjoy.

Frilly Toothpick

Stuffed Olive

Pickle

Bun Top

Bacon

Tomato

Red Onion

Cambazola Cheese

Grilled Chicken Burger Patty

Fire-Roasted Tomato Bruschetta

Olives

Grilled Portobello Mushroom Cap

Lettuce

American Processed Cheese Slice

Grilled Turkey Burger Patty

Grilled Eggplant

Grilled Orange Pepper Rings

Edam Cheese

Grilled Crispy Pancetta

Grilled Pork Burger Patty

Grilled White Onion

Grilled Peameal Bacon or Canadian Back Bacon

Hand-Leafed Lettuce

Bun Middle

Grilled Red Pepper Rings

Buffalo Mozzarella

Grilled Lamb Burger Patty

Crispy Double-Smoked Bacon

Hot Pepper Rings

Cheddar Cheese

Grilled Veal Burger Patty

Grilled Yellow Pepper Rings

Hand-Leafed Lettuce

Grilled Smoked Ham

Grilled Sliced Red Onion

Sliced Dill Pickle

American Processed Cheese Slice

Grilled Beef Burger Patty

Sliced Tomato

Hand-Leafed Lettuce

Bun Bottom

CORN   GREEN   TOMATO

French Whole Grain Mustard

Old Style Grain Mustard

Dijonnaise

Dijon Mustard

Prepared Yellow Mustard

Hot English Style Mustard

Honey Mustard

Wasabi Mustard

Red Pepper Mustard

Top row, from left: hot sauces, bases, BBQ sauces
Second row, from left: creamy sauces, relishes
Third row, from left: mustards, ketchup, soy sambal
Above: salsas
Near left: types of mustard

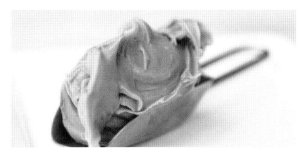

Top row, from left: fries and onion rings, bacon, buns
Second row, center: pickles
Third row, from left: onions, peanut butter, cheeses
Fourth row, from left: lettuce, mustard, roasted garlic
Near right: tomatoes

BURGER SEASONINGS

MY ORIGINAL BONE DUST™ BBQ SEASONING

½ cup	paprika	125 ml
¼ cup	chili powder	60 ml
3 Tbsp	salt	45 ml
2 Tbsp	coriander, dried	30 ml
2 Tbsp	garlic powder	30 ml
2 Tbsp	sugar	30 ml
2 Tbsp	curry powder	30 ml
2 Tbsp	hot mustard powder	30 ml
1 Tbsp	black pepper	15 ml
1 Tbsp	basil, dried	15 ml
1 Tbsp	thyme, dried	15 ml
1 Tbsp	cumin, ground	15 ml
1 Tbsp	cayenne pepper	15 ml

I created Bone Dust™ in the nineties and this recipe has been one of my favorites. It's a staple in my books.

• Mix together the paprika, chili powder, salt, coriander, garlic powder, sugar, curry powder, mustard powder, black pepper, basil, thyme, cumin and cayenne.

• Store in an airtight container in a cool, dry place away from heat and light.

MAKES ABOUT 2 1/2 CUPS

BETTER BUTTER BURGER SEASONING

4 Tbsp	Bone Dust™ BBQ Seasoning	60 ml
1 Tbsp	kosher salt	15 ml
1 Tbsp	onion, minced	15 ml
1 Tbsp	garlic, minced	15 ml
1 Tsp	mustard powder	5 ml
1 Tsp	chives, dehydrated	5 ml
1 Tsp	parsley flakes, dehydrated	5 ml
1 Tbsp	black pepper, coarsely ground	15 ml
3 Tbsp	Better Buds Natural Butter Flavor Granules	45 ml

Bone Dust™ and butter—it's like being "kicked up a notch."

• Mix together the Bone Dust™ BBQ Seasoning (see above), kosher salt, minced onion, minced garlic, mustard powder, dehydrated chives, dehydrated parsley flakes, pepper and Butter Buds Natural Butter Flavor Granules.

• Store in an airtight container in a cool, dry place away from heat and light.

NOTE: Butter Buds or butter flavor granules can be found in the spice section of many grocery stores.

TIP: When you can't see the meat, it's perfectly seasoned.

MAKES ABOUT 1 CUP

TANDOORI BURGER SEASONING

2 Tsp	salt	10 ml
¼ cup	paprika	60 ml
2 Tbsp	cumin, ground	30 ml
1 Tbsp	smoked paprika	15 ml
1 Tbsp	cayenne pepper	15 ml
1 Tbsp	coriander, ground	15 ml
1 Tbsp	cardamom, ground	15 ml
1 Tbsp	cinnamon	15 ml
1 Tbsp	black pepper	15 ml
1 Tbsp	brown sugar	15 ml
1 Tsp	clove, ground	5 ml

Mix this spice with a little yogurt and use it as a marinade and baste for chicken, shrimp, lamb, and of course, burgers.

• Combine salt, paprika, cumin, cayenne, smoked paprika, coriander, cardamom, cinnamon, pepper, brown sugar, and ground clove. Mix well.

• Store in an airtight container in a cool, dry place away from heat and light.

MAKES ABOUT 1/2 CUP

JAMMIN' JERK BURGER SEASONING

2 Tbsp	onion, granulated	30 ml
2 Tbsp	allspice, ground	30 ml
1 Tbsp	brown sugar	15 ml
1 Tbsp	black pepper, ground	15 ml
1 Tbsp	garlic salt	15 ml
2 Tbsp	cayenne pepper	30 ml
1 Tbsp	habanero pepper, ground	15 ml
1 Tbsp	kosher salt	15 ml
½ Tsp	nutmeg	3 ml
¼ Tsp	cinnamon	1.5 ml
1 Tsp	mustard powder	5 ml
2 Tbsp	dried cilantro	30 ml
1 Tbsp	dehydrated chives	15 ml

Boston Bay, Jamaica is the home of jerk. My recipe is based on that great jerk seasoning for chicken, pork, and seafood.

• Combine onion, allspice, brown sugar, pepper, garlic salt, cayenne, habanero, salt, nutmeg, cinnamon, mustard powder, dried cilantro, and chives. Mix well.

• Store in an airtight container in a cool, dry place away from heat and light.

NOTE: Ground habanero or scotch-bonnet chili powder can be found either on the internet or in specialty food shops and hot spice/sauce stores.

MAKES ABOUT 1/2 CUP

HOT AND SPICY BONE DUST™ BBQ SEASONING

½ cup	paprika	125 ml
¼ cup	Mexican chili powder	60 ml
3 Tbsp	salt	45 ml
3 Tbsp	brown sugar	45 ml
2 Tbsp	garlic powder	30 ml
2 Tbsp	hot mustard powder	30 ml
2 Tbsp	cayenne pepper	30 ml
2 Tbsp	chipotle powder, dried	30 ml
1 Tbsp	black pepper	15 ml
1 Tbsp	basil, dried	15 ml
1 Tbsp	thyme, dried	15 ml
1 Tbsp	cumin, ground	15 ml
1 Tbsp	coriander, dried	15 ml
1 Tbsp	curry powder	15 ml
1 Tbsp	smoked paprika	15 ml

This is not killer–hot but nice–hot.

• Combine the paprika, chili powder, salt, garlic powder, brown sugar, mustard powder, cayenne, chipotle powder, black pepper, basil, thyme, cumin, coriander, curry, and smoked paprika.

• Store in an airtight container in a cool, dry place away from heat and light.

MAKES ABOUT 2 CUPS

SWEET AND SMOKY BBQ BURGER SEASONING

1 cup	brown sugar	250 ml
2 Tbsp	kosher salt	30 ml
3 Tbsp	black pepper, coarsely ground	45 ml
2 Tbsp	white pepper, coarsely ground	30 ml
2 Tbsp	mustard seeds	30 ml
2 Tbsp	cracked coriander seeds	30 ml
2 Tbsp	garlic, granulated	30 ml
2 Tbsp	onion, granulated	30 ml
2 Tbsp	smoked paprika	30 ml
1 Tbsp	red chilies, crushed	15 ml
1 Tbsp	cayenne pepper	15 ml
1 Tbsp	celery salt	15 ml

The smoked paprika is the key to this smoky seasoning.

• Combine the brown sugar, salt, black pepper, white pepper, mustard seeds, coriander seeds, garlic, onion, smoked paprika, crushed chilies and cayenne pepper, smoked paprika and celery salt.

• Store in an airtight container in a cool, dry place away from heat and light.

MAKES APPROXIMATELY 3 CUPS

ORGASMIC ONION BURGER SEASONING

¼ cup	powder beef base	60 ml
¼ cup	onion flakes, dehydrated	60 ml
½ cup	crispy-fried onion pieces	125 ml
3 Tbsp	granulated onion, dehydrated	45 ml
2 Tbsp	granulated garlic, dehydrated	30 ml
2 Tbsp	cream of wheat powder	30 ml
1 Tbsp	kosher salt	15 ml
1 Tbsp	sugar	15 ml
1 Tbsp	butchers ground black pepper	15 ml
1 tsp	mustard powder	5 ml
1 tsp	coriander, ground	5 ml
½ tsp	cayenne pepper	3 ml

This is what makes your burger shake, rattle, and roll!

• In a bowl, combine powdered beef base, onion flakes, crispy-fried onion pieces, granulated onion and garlic, cream of wheat powder, kosher salt, sugar, black pepper, mustard powder, coriander and cayenne pepper.

• Store in an airtight container in a cool, dry place away from heat and light.

NOTE: You can find crispy-fried onion pieces in specialty food shops and ethnic grocery stores.

MAKES APPROXIMATELY 3 CUPS

BEEF BURGERS

THE CLASSIC ALL-BEEF BURGER

2 lb	ice-cold regular ground beef chuck	907 g
1 Tbsp	kosher salt	15 mL
1½ tsp	black pepper, freshly ground	7.5 mL
	Nonstick cooking spray	
8	plain hamburger buns	8
¼ cup	butter, melted	60 mL
	Crisp hand-leafed iceberg lettuce	
	Red ripe beefsteak tomatoes, sliced	
	Red onion, sliced	
	Pickles	

My recipe for the classic all-beef burger is quite simple, and sometimes simple is the better way when it comes to burgers.

• Place the ice-cold regular ground beef in a large bowl. Season with kosher salt and freshly ground black pepper. Mix until well combined.

• Form into eight 4-oz (120 g) patties as uniform in size as possible. Cover and refrigerate for 1 hour to allow the burgers to rest.

• Preheat grill to medium-high, 450–550°F (230–280°C).

• Spray burgers lightly on both sides with nonstick cooking spray.

• Grill burgers for 4 to 5 minutes per side, for medium-well done burgers that are still moist and juicy.

• Brush burger buns with melted butter and grill, cut-side down, until crisp and golden brown.

ASSEMBLE YOUR BURGERS! Bun bottom, burger, lettuce, tomato, red onion, bun top. Garnish with your favorite burger toppings and serve with a pickle.

TIP: Don't squish your burger! (At least not before eating!)

MAKES 8 BURGERS

THE GREAT AMERICAN CHEESEBURGER

2 lb	ice-cold regular ground beef chuck	907 g
3 Tbsp	Bone Dust™ BBQ Seasoning (p. 39)	45 mL
8	American processed cheese slices	8
8	plain hamburger buns	8
¼ cup	butter, melted	60 mL
	Crisp green leaf lettuce	
2	red ripe beefsteak tomatoes, sliced	2
1	red onion, thinly sliced	1
4	pickles, sliced	4
	Nonstick cooking spray	

For this burger recipe, I mix the ground beef with my signature Bone Dust™ BBQ Seasoning. Make up a batch of Bone Dust™ and use it not only as a burger seasoning mix but also for rubbing your ribs, chicken, chops and steaks. And it makes a great seasoning for crispy fries.

• Place the ice-cold regular ground beef in a large bowl. Season with Bone Dust™ BBQ Seasoning. Mix until well combined.

• Form into eight 4-oz (120 g) patties as uniform in size as possible. Cover and refrigerate for 1 hour to allow the burgers to rest.

• Preheat grill to medium-high, 450–550°F (230–280°C).

• Spray burgers lightly on both sides with nonstick cooking spray.

• Grill burgers for 4 to 5 minutes per side, for medium-well doneness and for burgers that are still moist and juicy.

• Top each burger with a slice of American processed cheese. Close lid and allow cheese to melt.

• Brush burger buns with melted butter and grill, cut-side down, until crisp and golden brown.

ASSEMBLE YOUR BURGERS! Bun bottom, leaf lettuce, tomato, red onion, sliced pickle, cheeseburger, bun top. Garnish with your favorite burger toppings and serve with a pickle.

NOTE: Switch up the type of cheese every once in a while for a delicious, simple twist to your burgers. Try Blue, Swiss, Provolone, Brie, and white cheddar.

MAKES 8 CHEESEBURGERS

TIP: If you want your burgers bigger than 4 oz (90 g) go ahead and make them the size you want. No rules! Just your way!

THE BANQUET BURGER À LA FRAN'S

1 lb	thick sliced strip bacon	454 g
2 lb	ice-cold regular ground beef chuck	907 g
2 Tbsp	Bone Dust™ BBQ Seasoning (p. 39)	30 mL
½ cup	white onion, finely diced	125 mL
2	cloves garlic, minced	2
1 Tbsp	Worcestershire sauce	15 mL
8	American processed cheese slices	8
8	plain hamburger buns	8
¼ cup	butter, melted	60 mL
	Crisp green leaf lettuce	
2	red ripe beefsteak tomatoes, sliced	2
1	red onion, sliced	1
	Nonstick cooking spray	

Stories abound over who first topped a cheeseburger with bacon. Reputedly, it was the chef at the original Fran's restaurant in Toronto. I remember stumbling into Fran's late one night after a good fest with some buddies, planning to finish off the evening with a big juicy Banquet Burger. To make the recipe that follows truly a Ted Reader Banquet Burger, I've added diced bacon to the meat mixture to give that extra flavor of bacon.

• Fry the bacon in small batches over medium heat until just crisp and the fat has been rendered from the bacon. Drain on paper toweling and set aside. Reserve the bacon fat.

• Take half of the cooked bacon and coarsely chop. Set aside.

• Place the ice-cold regular ground beef in a large bowl. Add chopped bacon and 2 Tbsp (30 mL) of bacon fat. Add Bone Dust™, white onion, garlic and Worcestershire sauce.

• Form into six 6-oz (180 g) patties as uniform in size as possible. Cover and refrigerate for 1 hour to allow the burgers to rest.

• Preheat grill to medium-high, 450–550°F (230–280°C).

• Spray burgers on both sides lightly with nonstick cooking spray.

• Grill burgers for 5 to 6 minutes per side for medium-well doneness, basting burgers lightly with reserved bacon fat.

• Warm remaining cooked sliced bacon. Top each burger with a slice of American processed cheese. Place 2 slices of bacon on top of the cheese. Close lid and allow cheese to melt.

• Brush burger buns with melted butter and grill, cut side down, until crisp and golden brown.

ASSEMBLE YOUR BURGERS! Bun bottom, leaf lettuce, tomato, red onion, bacon cheeseburger, bun top. Garnish with your favorite burger toppings and serve with a pickle.

NOTE: Bacon really is the miracle meat!

MAKES 6 BURGERS

THE BETTER BUTTER BURGER

THE BURGER

3 lb	regular ground beef or ground chuck	1.5 kg
4 Tbsp	butter, softened	60 mL
1	onion, finely chopped	1
3	cloves garlic, minced	3
1 Tbsp	fresh parsley, chopped	15 mL
1 Tbsp	Worcestershire sauce	15 mL
1 Tbsp	Dijon mustard	15 mL
Pinch	cayenne pepper	Pinch
	Salt and freshly ground black pepper, to taste	
6 or 12	burger buns	6 or 12
½ cup	butter (for brushing buns), melted	125 mL

Sometimes you just want a burger to be juicy. Adding butter will give you the juiciest burger.

One of my favorite burgers is one that's fried in butter. This recipe comes from my love of butter.

Butter is a great way to add a little more succulence to leaner meats like veal, lamb, game, chicken, and turkey.

THE BURGER: Preheat grill to medium-high, 450–550°F (230–280°C).

• In a large bowl, combine the beef, butter, onion, garlic, parsley, Worcestershire sauce and Dijon mustard. Season to taste with cayenne pepper, salt and black pepper.

• Form into twelve 4-oz (120 g) patties as uniform in size as possible. Grill burgers for 4 to 5 minutes per side for medium-well doneness.

• Brush burger buns with melted butter and grill, cut-side down, until crisp and golden brown.

ASSEMBLE YOUR BURGER! Bun, burger, garnish with your favorite burger toppings, bun.

MAKES 12 BURGERS OR 6 DOUBLE-STACKED BURGERS

NOTE: Everything is better with butter!

THE IN-N-OUT BURGER WITH SPECIAL SAUCE

THE SPECIAL SAUCE

You can create Special Sauce a couple of different ways. The first version is the recipe that follows.

1 cup	mayonnaise	250 mL
1	green onion, finely chopped	1
1 Tbsp	green relish	15 mL
1 Tbsp	ketchup	15 mL
Dash	hot sauce	Dash
Pinch	salt	Pinch

THE BURGER

2 lb	ice-cold regular ground beef chuck	907 g
3 tsp	kosher salt	15 mL
1½ tsp	black pepper, freshly ground	7.5 mL
8	American processed cheese slices	8
8	plain hamburger buns	8
¼ cup	butter, melted	60 mL
	Crisp hand-leafed iceberg lettuce	
2	red-ripe beefsteak tomatoes, sliced	2
1	white onion, sliced	1
	Nonstick cooking spray	

The In-N-Out burger, you know exactly what I am talking about when I say it's a great hamburger. No one should go to the West Coast of the United States without stopping by an In-N-Out for the original drive-thru California hamburger. In-N-Out does one thing and does it well. The menu is simple: burgers, fries and shakes. That's it. The burgers are griddled; the toppings are fresh sliced onions (raw or griddled), sliced, ripe tomatoes, crisp, hand-leafed iceberg lettuce, a warm bun and secret Special Sauce. Fries are cut to order, and the shakes are thick and rich. If you're daring, ask for the not-on-the-menu Animal Burger. Chefs Gordon Ramsay, Anthony Bourdain and Thomas Keller all love In-N-Out burgers.

THE SPECIAL SAUCE: In a bowl, combine the mayonnaise, green onion, green relish, ketchup, hot sauce and salt. Stir well, transfer to a small dish, cover and refrigerate until needed. The second version of Special Sauce is store-bought Thousand Island dressing. Simple, eh!

THE BURGER: Place the ice-cold regular ground beef in a large bowl. Season with kosher salt and freshly ground black pepper. Mix until well combined.

• Form into eight 4-oz (120 g) patties as uniform in size as possible. Cover and refrigerate for 1 hour to allow the burgers to rest.

• Preheat grill to medium-high, 450–550°F (230–280°C).

• Spray burgers lightly on both sides with nonstick cooking spray.

• Grill for 4 to 5 minutes per side for medium-well doneness but burgers that are still moist and juicy. Please—no squishing your burgers. In-N-Out burgers are always juicy.

• Top each burger with a slice of American processed cheese. Close lid and allow cheese to melt.

• Brush burger buns with melted butter and grill, cut-side down, until crisp and golden brown. Spread the bottom or top bun or both liberally with the Special Sauce.

ASSEMBLE YOUR BURGERS! Bun bottom, Special Sauce, hand-leafed iceberg lettuce, tomato, white onion, cheeseburger, bun top. Garnish with your favorite burger toppings and serve with a pickle.

MAKES 8 BURGERS

MICKEY D'S BIG MAC

THE BURGER

1½ lb	ice-cold regular ground beef chuck	675 g
2 tsp	kosher salt	10 mL
1 tsp	black pepper, freshly ground	5 mL
½ cup	Special Sauce (p. 55)	125 mL
2 cups	iceberg lettuce, shredded	500 mL
8	American processed cheese slices	8
2	pickles, sliced into rounds	2
1	white onion, finely diced	1
8	sesame seed buns, sliced into three layers	8
¼ cup	melted butter	60 mL
	Nonstick cooking spray	

Here is my version of Mickey D's Big Mac Hamburger. We all know the jingle—two all-beef patties, Special Sauce, lettuce, cheese, pickles and onions on a sesame seed bun. The key to making my burger a true success is the bun. Mickey D's buns are specially baked and sliced, so having their buns will make things easier for you and will look great. Go to your local Mickey D's and ask if you can purchase a few Big Mac buns. They might be a little pricey, but the result is worth it!

THE BURGER: Place the ice-cold regular ground beef in a large bowl. Season with kosher salt and freshly ground black pepper. Mix until well combined.

• Form into eight 3-oz (100 g) patties as uniform in size as possible. Cover and refrigerate for 1 hour to allow the burgers to rest.

• Preheat grill to medium-high, 450–550°F (230–280°C).

• Spray burgers lightly on both sides with nonstick cooking spray.

• Grill for 4 to 5 minutes per side for burgers that are done medium-well but are still moist and juicy.

• Top each burger with a slice of American processed cheese. Close lid and allow cheese to melt.

• Brush burger buns with melted butter and grill, cut-side down, until crisp and golden brown. Remove buns from grill and spread the bottom and the middle buns with the Special Sauce.

ASSEMBLE YOUR BURGERS! Bun bottom, Special Sauce, shredded lettuce, sliced pickles, diced onion, cheeseburger, bun middle, Special Sauce, onions, pickle and cheeseburger, sesame seed bun top. Serve immediately.

TIP: Buns can be purchased at Mickey D's.

MAKES 4 BURGERS

SWISS MUSHROOM MELT

THE BURGER

2 lb	ice-cold ground sirloin	907 g
1 Tbsp	room-temperature butter	15 mL
6	cloves garlic, minced	6
½ cup	onion, finely diced	125 mL
1 Tbsp	Dijon mustard	15 mL
1 tsp	Worcestershire sauce	5 mL
1	bottle of your favorite dark ale beer	1
1 tsp	liquid beef-stock concentrate	5 mL
½ cup	whole wheat crackers (about 8–10 crackers), crushed	125 mL
	Kosher salt and freshly ground black pepper, to taste	

MUSHROOMS AND ONIONS

	Napoleon Griddle Topper	
2 Tbsp	butter	30 mL
1	large yellow-skinned onion, sliced	1
1	bottle of your favorite dark ale beer	1
2 cups	white mushrooms, sliced	500 mL
2 cups	cremini mushrooms, sliced	500 mL
4	cloves garlic, minced	4
1 Tbsp	fresh thyme, chopped	15 mL
12	Swiss cheese slices	12
6	hamburger buns, your choice	6
¼ cup	melted butter	60 mL
	Nonstick cooking spray	

Beer-infused burgers with sautéed mushrooms and onions. Load on the Swiss!

THE BURGER: In a large bowl, combine ground sirloin, butter, garlic, onion, Dijon mustard, Worcestershire sauce, ¼ cup (60 mL) of dark ale, beef-stock concentrate and cracker crumbs. Season to taste with salt and freshly ground black pepper.

• Form into six 6-oz (180 g) burgers approximately 1½ inches (3.5 cm) thick. Cover and refrigerate for 1 hour to allow the burgers to rest.

MUSHROOMS AND ONIONS: Preheat grill to medium-high, 450–550°F (230–280°C).

• Place your Napoleon Griddle Topper on the grill over one burner. (Note: If you do not have a Griddle Topper, then use a fry pan.) Add butter and allow it to melt.

• Add onions to the griddle and sauté, stirring frequently, for 10 to 15 minutes, until golden brown and tender. Drizzle onions with a little dark ale. Push the onions to the front of the griddle and add the mushrooms to the back of the griddle. Drizzle mushrooms with a little beer and sauté mushrooms for 8 to 10 minutes, until tender. Mix with onions, add garlic and continue to cook onions and mushrooms for 1 to 2 minutes longer. Add thyme and reduce heat to low to keep warm. Season to taste with salt and freshly ground black pepper.

• Spray burgers lightly on both sides with nonstick cooking spray.

• Grill burgers for 5 to 6 minutes per side, drizzling with a little extra dark ale, until burgers are medium-well-done but still moist and juicy.

• Top each burger with a heaping spoonful of dark ale, sautéed mushrooms and onions, then top with two slices of Swiss cheese. Close lid and allow cheese to melt.

• Brush burger buns with melted butter and grill, cut-side down, until crisp and golden brown.

ASSEMBLE YOUR BURGERS! Bun bottom, burger, mushroom-onion mix, Swiss cheese and bun top. Garnish with your favorite burger garnishes. Serve immediately with whole grain mustard.

MAKES 6 BURGERS

STEPHEN BALCERZAK'S WHITE CLOUD ISLAND BURGER

HORSERADISH MAYO

½ cup	mayonnaise	125 mL
1 Tbsp	extra-hot prepared horseradish	15 mL
Pinch	salt	Pinch

FOUR-ONION SLAW

1	small white onion, thinly sliced	1
1	small red onion, thinly sliced	1
1	small sweet Vidalia onion, thinly sliced	1
2	green onions, chopped	2
1 Tbsp	fresh parsley, chopped	15 mL
3 Tbsp	white vinegar	45 mL
2 Tbsp	olive oil	30 mL
2 tsp	yellow prepared mustard	10 mL
2 tsp	honey	10 mL
	Salt and freshly ground black pepper, to taste	

Every so often I run into people who tell me about a recipe they've created, and by the time they've finished I'm starving. That's what happened during my chance meeting with Stephen Balcerzak. Stephen is an avid sailor and spends much of his summer sailing around Lake Huron with family and friends. His favorite burger recipe is named after a favorite island of his called White Cloud Island. What intrigued me most was that the burger was loaded with onions and topped with the ever-stinky Limburger cheese. Stephen's tip was to use Limburger cheese from Oak Grove Cheese House in New Hamburg, Ontario. We did. The burger was still stinky, but it's a burger that truly rocks the burger world.

HORSERADISH MAYO: In a small bowl, combine mayonnaise and horseradish. Season to taste with a pinch of salt. Stir, cover and refrigerate until needed.

FOUR-ONION SLAW: In a bowl, combine the onions, parsley, vinegar, olive oil, mustard and honey. Season to taste with salt and freshly ground black pepper. Set aside, refrigerated.

NOTE: I really love this burger. Onions, garlic, and stinky cheese….Try it!

THE BURGER

1 lb	ice-cold regular ground beef	454 g
1 lb	ice-cold regular ground pork	454 g
1	large red onion, finely diced (about 1½–2 cups/375–500 mL)	1
8	cloves garlic, minced	
3 tsp	salt	15 mL
1 tsp	black pepper, freshly ground	5 mL
	Nonstick cooking spray	
8	thick slices of Limburger cheese	8
4	fresh onion buns	4
¼ cup	butter, melted	60 mL
	Lettuce	

THE BURGER: In a large bowl, combine ground beef and pork, red onion and garlic. Season to taste with salt and freshly ground black pepper.

• Form into four 8-oz (225 g) burgers about 1½ to 2 inches (3.5–5 cm) thick. Cover and refrigerate for 1 hour to allow the burgers to rest. Steve recommends overnight so that the onion and garlic flavors truly come out.

• Preheat grill to medium-high, 450–550°F (230–280°C).

• Spray burgers lightly on both sides with nonstick cooking spray.

• Grill burgers for 8 to 10 minutes per side until they are cooked to medium-well doneness but are still moist and juicy.

• Top each burger with two slices of Limburger cheese. Close lid and allow cheese to melt.

• Brush onion buns with melted butter and grill, cut side down, until crisp and golden brown.

ASSEMBLE YOUR BURGERS! Bun bottom, Horseradish Mayo, lettuce, burger, Four-Onion Slaw and bun top. Garnish with your favorite burger garnishes. Serve immediately.

MAKES 4 BURGERS

PORTOBELLO MUSHROOM BURGER

BALSAMIC GLAZING SAUCE

½ cup	balsamic vinegar	125 mL
¼ cup	honey	60 mL
4	cloves roasted garlic, minced	4
½ tsp	black pepper, coarsely ground	2.5 mL
2 tsp	cold butter	10 mL

THE BURGER

12	portobello mushroom caps	12
NOTE:	For this recipe, purchase portobello mushroom caps that are all about the same size in width and thickness. I like to use ones that are about 3 inches (4 cm) in diameter and ½ to 1 inch (1.5–2.5 cm) thick.	
	Kosher salt to taste	
	Boiling water	
3 Tbsp	olive oil	45 mL
	Black pepper to taste	
1½ lb	ice-cold regular ground beef	675 g
½ cup	red onion, diced	125 mL
2	green onions, finely chopped	2
1 Tbsp	rosemary, chopped fresh	15 mL
4	cloves garlic, minced	4
2 tsp	kosher salt	10 mL
1 tsp	freshly ground black pepper	5 mL
¼ cup	panko (Japanese-style) bread crumbs	60 mL
4	thick slices crusty Italian bread	4
	Olive oil	
2	cloves garlic	2
1	bunch arugula, cleaned	1
2	vine-ripened tomatoes	2
4	slices buffalo mozzarella cheese	4
	Nonstick cooking spray	

This recipe is richly delicious. The portobello mushrooms eat like a steak!

BALSAMIC GLAZING SAUCE: In a deep saucepan, bring the balsamic vinegar to a boil over high heat, reduce heat to medium-low and reduce the vinegar by half its volume. This will intensify the flavor of the vinegar and make it sweeter.

• Remove from heat, stir in honey and season with garlic and black pepper.

• Stir in the cold butter until it has been fully incorporated. Set aside.

MAKES APPROXIMATELY 3/4 CUP (175 ML)

THE BURGER: Remove the stems from the portobello mushroom caps and reserve to use for another recipe.

• Brush portobello mushroom caps to remove excess grit and dirt.

• Place caps in a large bowl. Season mushroom caps on both sides with kosher salt and let stand for 10 minutes.

• Pour boiling water over caps, turning to coat, and let mushrooms soak for 20 minutes. This will allow the mushrooms to absorb more moisture, so that when they are grilled, they won't dry out. Drain mushrooms and place on paper toweling, gill-side down.

• Preheat grill to medium-high, 450–550°F (230–280°C).

• Take 4 of the mushroom caps only and season with a little olive oil and salt and freshly ground black pepper. Grill mushroom caps for 10 to 15 minutes, until lightly charred and tender. Remove from heat and fully cool. Pat grilled mushroom caps dry to remove excess moisture.

• Cut each mushroom cap in half and thinly slice. Place in a large bowl. Add ground beef, red and green onions, rosemary, garlic, salt, black pepper and panko bread crumbs. Mix gently to combine; cover and refrigerate for 1 hour to set.

• Form into four 6-oz (180 g) round burgers approximately ½ inch (1.5 cm) thick and the same diameter as the reserved soaked portobello mushroom caps.

• Place one portobello mushroom cap on either side of each formed burger, pressing firmly so that the mushrooms stick to the meat. The burger should look like a big mushroom sandwich. Place burgers on a tray or plate, cover and put in the refrigerator for 1 hour, allowing the burgers to rest.

• Leave grill heat at medium-high, 450–550°F (230–280°C).

• Spray burgers lightly on both sides with nonstick cooking spray.

• Grill burgers for 8 to 10 minutes per side, basting frequently with Balsamic Glazing Sauce during the last half of cooking, until burgers are done medium-well but are still moist and juicy.

• While the burgers are grilling, lightly toast crusty Italian bread slices. Remove from heat and brush with olive oil. Take a clove of garlic and rub each toasted bread slice to extract the garlic flavor.

ASSEMBLE YOUR BURGERS! Toasted garlic bread, arugula, vine-ripened tomato, buffalo mozzarella and Portobello Mushroom Burger. Drizzle with Balsamic Glazing Sauce.

TIP: You may want to use and knife and fork for this burger.

MAKES 4 BURGERS

Mmm.... Cheesy!

ULTIMATE CHEESEBURGER MELT

FOUR-CHEESE BLEND

2 cups	white cheddar, shredded	500 mL
2 cups	yellow cheddar, shredded	500 mL
2 cups	mozzarella, shredded	500 mL
2 cups	smoked provolone, shredded	500 mL

THE BURGER

	Napoleon Griddle Topper	
2 lb	ice-cold regular ground beef	907 g
2 cups	Four-Cheese Blend, shredded	500 mL
3 Tbsp	Bone Dust™ BBQ Seasoning (p. 39)	45 mL
	Nonstick cooking spray	
4	sesame seed hamburger buns	4
¼ cup	butter, melted	60 mL

Sometimes too much cheese is a good thing. This is it. Four varieties of cheese loaded on thick juicy burgers and melted into a gooey mess. You'll need lots of napkins when you eat these burgers!

As the photo shows, I've put four patties on one bun. You don't have to—one is plenty. I used four just to show you how crazy you can make the cheeseburger.

FOUR-CHEESE BLEND: In a bowl, combine the four types of shredded cheese. Cover and refrigerate until needed.

THE BURGER: In large bowl, combine ground beef, shredded Four-Cheese Blend and Bone Dust™.

• Form into eight 4-oz (120 g) burgers approximately 1 inch (2.5 cm) thick. Cover and place burgers in the freezer for 1 to 2 hours.

• Preheat grill to medium-high, 450–550°F (230–280°C).

• Place Napoleon Griddle Topper over one burner and set to medium temperature.

• Remove burgers from the freezer and spray lightly on both sides with nonstick cooking spray.

• Grill burgers over direct heat for 5 to 6 minutes per side until they are cooked to medium-well doneness but are still moist and juicy.

• Place four burgers on the Griddle Topper. Cover each burger with a handful of reserved Four-Cheese Blend. Close lid and allow the cheese to melt. Repeat with remaining four burgers.

• Brush buns with melted butter and grill, cut-side down, until crisp and golden brown.

ASSEMBLE YOUR BURGERS! Bun bottom, cheesy-melted burger, another cheesy-melted burger and bun top. Garnish with your favorite burger garnishes.

MAKES 8 BURGERS

BRÛLÉE CHEESEBURGER

BRÛLÉE CHEESE DIPPER

1 cup	mayonnaise	250 mL
1 cup	Swiss cheese, shredded	250 mL
1 cup	brie cheese, finely diced	250 mL
1 cup	onion, diced	250 mL
2	cloves garlic, minced	2
Pinch	salt	Pinch

MUSHROOMS AND ONIONS

	Napoleon Griddle Topper	
2 Tbsp	butter	30 mL
1 cups	oyster mushrooms, torn	250 mL
1 cups	cremini mushrooms, sliced	250 mL
4	large shallots, sliced	4
2	cloves garlic, minced	2
1 Tbsp	fresh thyme, chopped	15 mL
	Salt and freshly ground black pepper	
6	hamburger buns, your choice	6
¼ cup	butter, melted	60 mL

THE BURGER

1½ lb	ground prime rib of beef	675 g
2 Tbsp	Dijon mustard	30 mL
4	cloves garlic, minced	4
6 Tbsp	Orgasmic Onion Burger Seasoning (p. 44)	100 mL
2 tsp	fresh thyme, chopped	10 mL
1 oz	cognac	30 mL
	Nonstick cooking spray	
1	fresh baguette, cut in half lengthways	1
¼ cup	butter, melted	60 mL
1	bunch arugula, cleaned	1

My good friends Ed and Laurie inspired this recipe. Laurie makes this delicious cheese dip, and at any party of her and Ed's that I've been to, it is devoured in minutes. I got to thinking that it would be a great topping for a burger. Voilà! Divide meat mixture into 4 equal portions and shape into 6-inch (15 cm) long rectangular burgers, approximately 1 to 1½ inches (2.5–3.5 cm) thick. Cover and refrigerate for 1 hour.

BRÛLÉE CHEESE DIPPER: In a bowl, combine mayonnaise, Swiss cheese, Brie, onion, garlic and salt. Mix well and set aside, refrigerated.

MUSHROOMS AND ONIONS: Preheat grill to medium-high, 450–550°F (230–280°C).

• Place your Napoleon Griddle Topper on the grill over one burner. (Note: If you do not have a Griddle Topper, then use a fry pan.) Add butter and allow to melt.

• Add mushrooms and sauté for 8 to 10 minutes, stirring occasionally, until tender; add shallots and garlic and continue to cook for a few minutes more.

• Add thyme, season to taste with salt and freshly ground black pepper, and reduce heat to low to keep warm.

THE BURGER: In a bowl, combine ground beef, Dijon mustard, garlic, Orgasmic Onion Burger Seasoning, thyme and cognac.

• Preheat grill to medium high, 400–500°F (200–250°C).

• Spray burgers lightly on both sides with nonstick cooking spray.

• Grill burgers for 5 to 6 minutes per side, until cooked to medium-well doneness but the burgers are still moist and juicy. Top each burger with heaping spoonful of sautéed oyster mushrooms and shallots. Spoon Brûlée Cheese Dipper overtop the oyster-mushroom mixture. Close lid and allow the cheese to melt and get hot and bubbly.

• Brush cut side of baguette with melted butter and grill, cut-side down, until crisp and golden brown.

ASSEMBLE YOUR BURGERS! Baguette bottom, arugula, burger, oyster-mushroom mix, Brûlée Cheese Dipper and baguette top. Serve immediately with Dijon mustard.

MAKES 4 BURGERS

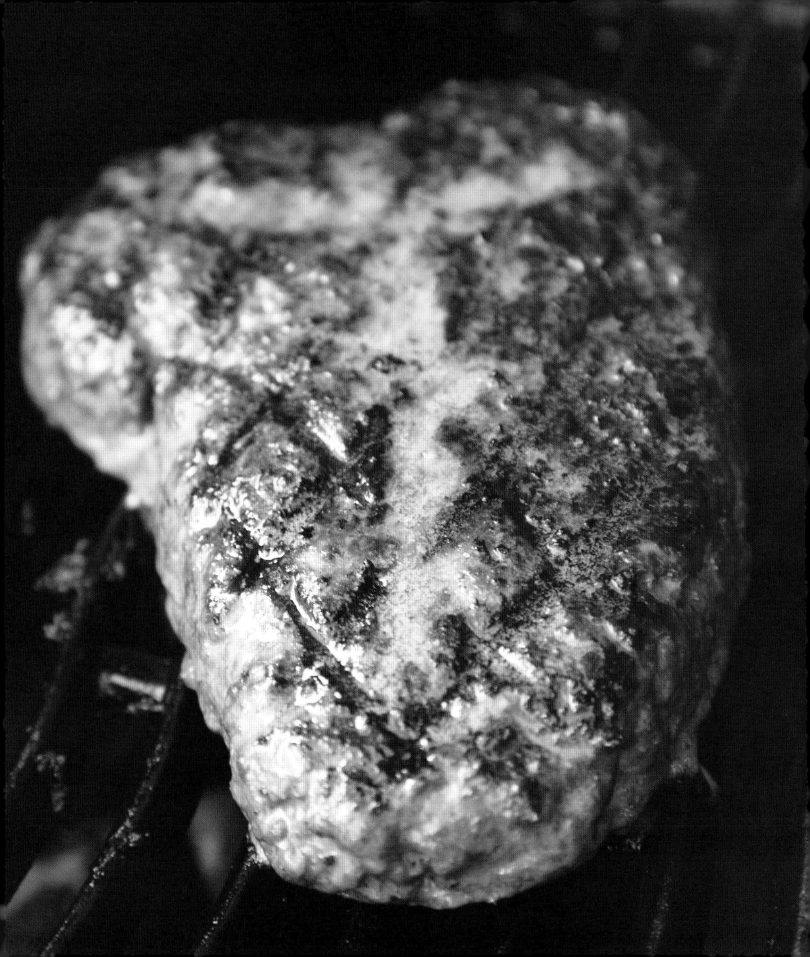

ONE-POUND PORTERHOUSE BURGER
WITH MARROW BUTTER

MARROW BUTTER

1	regular hickory plank, soaked in water	1
	aluminum foil	
2 lb	medium to large beef or veal marrow bones (about 6 to 8 bones, each cut 2–3 inches/ 5–7.5 cm long)	907 g
3 Tbsp	sea salt, coarsely ground or fleur de sel	45 mL
3 Tbsp	fresh black pepper, coarsely ground	45 mL
2 Tbsp	softened butter	30 mL

THE BURGER

2 lb	ice-cold ground sirloin steak	907 g
6 Tbsp	Orgasmic Onion Burger Seasoning (p. 44)	100 mL
2 Tbsp	room-temperature Marrow Butter	30 mL

MAKES 2 BURGERS FOR SUPER-HUNGRY FOLKS OR 8 OTHERWISE

When I worked for President's Choice back in the '90s, I developed the One-Pounder, a one-pound-2-inch-thick burger in the shape of a T-bone steak. The burger was crazy-big. Here's a version that is rich and delicious.

MARROW BUTTER: Preheat grill to medium-high (450–550°F/230–280°C).
• Pat marrow bones dry with paper towel. In a bowl, combine sea salt and pepper. Season both ends of the marrow bones liberally with a sea salt-pepper mixture.

• Cut a 4-inch by 4-inch (10 cm by 10 cm) square of aluminum foil for each bone. Place largest end of marrow bone down on a square of foil and crimp the foil around the base of the bone to make a little tray to catch any drippings. Repeat with remaining marrow bones.

• Evenly space marrow bones on hickory plank. Place plank on center of grill and close lid. Plank-grill seasoned marrow bones for 20 to 30 minutes, until the bones are golden brown and the marrow has started to render its fat. (Note: If you overcook the bones, you will end up with nothing because all the marrow will have melted away. You want to render only about 25 percent of the fat so that you get lots of hot, rich marrow.)

• Remove marrow bones from grill. Using a small spoon or knife, scoop the hot marrow into a bowl. Set aside to cool.

• In a food processor, combine the cooled marrow with 2 Tbsp (30 mL) of softened butter. Add a pinch of salt, a little black pepper and blend until smooth. Transfer into a small dish, cover and refrigerate until needed.

THE BURGER: In a bowl, combine the ground sirloin with the Orgasmic Onion Burger Seasoning and marrow butter.

• Divide mixture into 2 equal portions and form into a 1½- to 2-inch (3.5–5 cm) thick burger in the shape of a T-bone steak. Cover, refrigerate and allow to rest for at least 2 hours.

• Preheat grill to high, 550°F (280°C).

• Sear one-pound burgers over high heat for 2 to 3 minutes per side. Reduce heat to low, close lid and grill-roast burgers indirectly, basting occasionally with reserved Marrow Butter, for 15 to 20 minutes, until burgers are fully cooked but still moist and juicy.

• To serve, top each burger with a dollop of Marrow Butter and present with a knife and fork. Or you can serve it on a super-big bun.

SURF AND TURF BURGER

½ cup	cream cheese, softened	125 mL
½ cup	Brie cheese	125 mL
1 cup	lobster meat, fresh or frozen (if using frozen, drain)	250 mL
2 tsp	fresh dill, chopped	10 mL
1 tsp	lemon juice	5 mL
	Salt and pepper, to taste	
1½ lb	fresh ground sirloin	675 g
1	small onion, finely diced	
2	cloves garlic, minced	2
1 Tbsp	Dijon mustard	15 mL
1–2 Tbsp	Bone Dust™ BBQ Seasoning (p. 39)	15–30 mL
1–2 tsp	Worcestershire sauce	5–10 mL
¾ cup	clarified butter	175 mL
1 Tbsp	fresh herbs, chopped	15 mL
1–2 tsp	Worcestershire sauce	5–10 mL
¼ cup	ketchup	60 mL
6	lobster claws	6
6	leaves hand-leafed iceberg lettuce	6
1	small onion, thinly sliced	1
2	ripe tomatoes, thinly sliced	2
6 Tsp	mayonnaise (optional)	30 mL

I made this for Regis and Kelly a few years ago. It was yummy. I even think I heard Kelly moan!

• In a food processor, blend cream cheese until smooth. Add Brie cheese, lobster meat, dill and lemon juice, and season to taste with salt and pepper. Pulse until mixed.

• Form lobster-and-cheese mixture into small patties about 2 inches (5 cm) in diameter and ½ inch (1.5 cm) thick. Place on a wax-paper-lined plate and refrigerate while you prepare the burgers.

• In a bowl, combine the ground sirloin, onion, garlic and mustard. Season to taste with Bone Dust™ BBQ Seasoning and Worcestershire sauce. Mix until well combined.

• Form into twelve 3-oz (100 g), 3- to 4-inch (7.5–10 cm) in diameter patties, pressing each patty firmly to ensure a burger that sticks together. Place burgers on a wax-paper-lined tray and refrigerate for 30 minutes.

• Remove lobster patties from refrigerator. Place one sirloin burger on a flat surface. Top with one lobster patty. Top with another sirloin burger. Crimp edges of sirloin burgers to form a tight seal around the lobster patties. Repeat with remaining lobster patties and sirloin burgers, and freeze for 30 minutes to get everything very cold and to allow the meat to rest before cooking.

• In a small saucepan, over low heat, combine clarified butter, herbs, Worcestershire sauce and ketchup. Stir until mixed. Keep warm.

• Preheat grill to medium-high, 450–550°F (230–280°C).

• Grill burgers for 4 to 6 minutes on one side. Turn over, baste with butter sauce and continue to cook for 3 to 5 more minutes, until the beef is just cooked and the lobster-cheese center is warm and creamy.

• While the burgers are cooking, brush the lobster claws with the butter-herb mixture and grill for 1 to 2 minutes, turning once, until lightly charred and heated through. Brush burgers with butter-herb mixture, turn over and brush with more butter-herb mixture.

• Top with grilled lobster claws.

ASSEMBLE YOUR BURGERS! Spread the bottom half of the bun with mayonnaise (optional), place leaf lettuce on top, place burger on top of that and finish with thinly sliced fresh onion and tomato.

MAKES 6 BURGERS

STEAK TARTAR BURGER

THE BURGER

1 lb	beef tenderloin, fully trimmed	454 g
1	large shallot, finely diced	1
½	jalapeño pepper, seeded and finely chopped	½
2	quail egg yolks	2
2 Tbsp	flat-leaf parsley, chopped	30 mL
1 Tbsp	capers, chopped	15 mL
1 Tbsp	Dijon mustard	15 mL
1 Tbsp	ketchup	15 mL
1 Tbsp	olive oil	15 mL
2 tsp	Worcestershire sauce	10 mL
	Salt and freshly ground black pepper, to taste	
Dash	hot sauce, if you like meat spicier (optional)	Dash
	A squeeze of lemon juice to increase the acidity (optional)	

OK, it's not really a burger...but it should be!

When preparing this recipe, make sure your beef is very cold—you don't want to serve warm steak tartar. Plus, cold meat is easier to chop. I prefer to use a chef's knife rather than a food processor to chop the beef, but a meat grinder will work just as well.

THE BURGER: Using a sharp chef's knife, finely chop the beef tenderloin or use a meat grinder. Place in a large bowl.

• Add the shallot, jalapeño pepper, egg yolks, parsley, capers, mustard, ketchup, olive oil, Worcestershire sauce, salt and pepper. Mix well with a wooden spoon. Adjust seasoning with hot sauce or lemon juice, if desired.

• Divide the steak tartar among four plates. Serve with toasted thin slices of baguette and fries, if desired, or form into a burger patty and serve on a bun.

MAKES 4 BURGERS

LUDICROUS BURGER

FIRE-ROASTED TOMATO KETCHUP

Napoleon Grill Topper

1	small sweet onion, peeled and cut into ½-inch (1.5 cm) rounds	1
1	red bell pepper, cut in half lengthways and seeded	1
1 pint	grape tomatoes	500 mL
1–2	long hot red finger chili peppers	1–2
2 Tbsp	olive oil	30 mL
1 tsp + 2 tsp	Bone Dust™ BBQ Seasoning (p. 39)	5 mL +10 mL
1	14-oz (398 mL) can crushed tomatoes	1
¼ cup	brown sugar	60 mL
¼ cup	light corn syrup	60 mL
½ cup	cider vinegar	125 mL
¼ cup	water	60 mL
3	cloves garlic, minced	3
½ tsp	salt	2.5 mL
1–2 drops	liquid hickory smoke	1–2 drops

GRILLED BACON AND CHEESE

Napoleon Multi-Grill Basket

½ cup	butter, melted	125 mL
16	slices Texas Toast or thick-sliced white sandwich bread	16
16	slices processed cheese, thick slices or double up	16
1½ cups	cooked double-smoked bacon, diced	375 mL

It all started with serving a burger between two grilled cheese sandwiches. It may be crazy and it will be thick, but it's delicious.

FIRE-ROASTED TOMATO KETCHUP: Preheat grill to medium-high, 450–550°F (230–280°C).

• Place Grill Topper on grill to preheat.

• In a large bowl, toss together the onion, bell pepper, grape tomatoes, long hot red finger chili pepper(s) and olive oil, and season with 1 tsp (5 mL) of Bone Dust™ BBQ Seasoning.

• Place seasoned vegetables on Grill Topper and grill with the lid open for 8 to 10 minutes, turning occasionally, until the onions, peppers and tomatoes are lightly charred and tender.

• Remove from grill, coarsely chop the onions and pepper and place in a medium saucepan. Add crushed tomatoes, brown sugar, corn syrup, cider vinegar, water, garlic, salt and remaining 2 tsp (10 mL) of Bone Dust™ BBQ Seasoning. Add a drop or two of liquid hickory smoke.

• Over medium-high heat, while stirring bring mixture to a boil, reduce heat to low. All to simmer for 15 to 20 minutes, stirring frequently. Using a hand-held blender, blend until smooth.

• Remove from heat and transfer mixture to container. Allow to cool, cover and refrigerate for up to 2 weeks. Use with your favorite grilled burgers.

MAKES ABOUT 3 CUPS (750 ML)

• **NOTE:** When using liquid smoke, a little will go a long way, so be careful. Start with a drop or two, If you want to use more, then add a drop at a time. Remember—you can always add, but you can never take away.

GRILLED BACON AND CHEESE: Preheat grill to medium, 350°F (175°C).

• Generously butter one side of each slice of bread. Place 4 slices butter-side down. Lay 1 slice of processed cheese on each piece of bread, sprinkle with 2 Tbsp (45 mL) of diced bacon, then another slice of cheese. Top with the remaining bread slices, butter-side up.

• Secure the sandwiches snugly in the Multi-Grill Basket. Grill for 4 to 5 minutes a side, turning frequently to prevent burning. Grill until the sandwiches are golden brown, crisp and cheese has melted.

MAKES 4 SANDWICHES

THE BURGER

2 lb	ice-cold ground beef chuck	907 g
4 Tbsp	Bone Dust™ BBQ Seasoning (p. 39)	60 mL
1	small red onion, minced	1
2 Tbsp	powdered cheese (like what you get in a box of mac and cheese)	30 mL
1 Tbsp	Dijon mustard	15 mL
4	slices thick-sliced processed cheese, unwrapped and frozen	4
	Nonstick cooking spray	

THE BURGER: In a large bowl, combine the ice-cold ground beef chuck, Bone Dust™, red onion, powdered cheese and Dijon mustard. Mix gently but thoroughly.

• Form into eight 4-oz (120 g) square burgers about ½ inch (1.5 cm) thick and 4 inches (10 cm) square.

• Lay 1 burger on a flat work surface. Place a slice of frozen processed cheese on top of the burger. There should be approximately a ½-inch border of meat showing around the cheese. Place a second burger on top of the cheese; firmly press, and form the burger so that the cheese is hidden and the burgers are now one.

• Repeat with remaining burgers and cheese. Place burgers on a tray or plate, cover and put in the freezer for 30 minutes. This will allow the meat to rest and get very cold.

• Preheat grill to medium-high, 450–550°F (230–280°C).

• Spray burgers on both sides lightly with nonstick cooking spray.

• Grill burgers for 5 to 6 minutes per side, until cooked to medium-well doneness but burgers are still moist and juicy. While the burgers are cooking, prepare the grilled cheese sandwiches.

• Remove burgers from grill.

ASSEMBLE YOUR BURGERS! Grilled bacon and cheese sandwich, burger, grilled bacon and cheese sandwich. Serve with Fire-Roasted Tomato Ketchup.

NOTE: This makes me soooo hungry! Come on, you know you want to make and eat this!

MAKES 4 BURGERS

PLANKED BEERLICIOUS™ BASEBALL BURGER

THE BURGER

2	cedar planks, 10 to 12 inches long by 6 to 8 inches wide by ½ inch thick (25–30 cm by 15–20 cm by 1.5 cm), soaked in water for a minimum of 1 hour	2
2 lb	ice-cold, regular ground beef	907 g
¼ cup + ¼ cup	your favorite dark ale beer	60 mL + 60 mL
¼ cup + 1 Tbsp	Bone Dust™ BBQ Seasoning (p. 39)	60 mL + 15 mL
½ cup	Ted's World Famous BBQ Beerlicious™ BBQ Sauce or your favorite smoky BBQ sauce	125 mL
6	slices American processed cheese	6

Planking burgers creates the juiciest burgers. I like to shape them into baseballs and plank them as big round burgers rather than thin burgers, which dry out quickly. These burgers may take a little longer to cook, but just think—the longer they take to cook, the more beer you get!

Some people have asked how you're supposed to eat such big burgers. My answer is either squish them, or use a knife and fork; or if you have a flip-top head, then there should be no issue. No worries is what I say. Trust me, these will be the juiciest burgers you ever cook, and your friends will call you "King!"

THE BURGER: Place the ground beef in a large bowl. Drizzle ¼ cup (60 mL) of beer over the ground beef. Sprinkle the Bone Dust™ BBQ Seasoning evenly over the meat. Mix gently but thoroughly.

• Form meat mixture into 6 large baseball-shaped burgers. (Note: Do not flatten the burgers; leave them shaped like baseballs. This will help keep your burgers moist and juicy.) Place burgers on a tray or plate, cover and refrigerate for 1 hour. This will allow the meat to rest.

• In a bowl, combine the remaining ¼ cup (60 mL) of beer with the BBQ sauce and set aside.

• Preheat grill to medium-high, 450–550°F (230–280°C).

• Evenly space 3 burgers on each plank. Place on grill and close lid. Plank-bake for 25 to 30 minutes, basting with reserved Beer-BBQ Sauce during the last 15 minutes of planking, until the burgers are fully cooked but still moist and juicy.

• Top each burger with a slice of processed cheese, turn grill off and close lid, allowing the cheese to melt over the meat.

• Remove burgers from grill.

ASSEMBLE YOUR BURGERS! Serve with a knife and fork, or serve on your favorite buns with all your favorite burger condiments. I like mine on soft buns with thinly sliced red onions, crisp lettuce and a dollop of mayo.

MAKES 6 BURGERS

THE JACKINATOR BURGER

JACKINATOR GLAZING SAUCE

¼ cup	Jack Daniel's Tennessee Whiskey	60 mL
¼ cup	Ted's World Famous BBQ Crazy Canuck Sticky Chicken and Rib Sauce or your favorite sweet BBQ sauce	60 mL
3 Tbsp	bacon fat	45 mL
3 Tbsp	Map-o-Spread, spreadable maple syrup or maple syrup	45 mL

THE BURGER

2	hickory planks, 10 to 12 inches long by 6 to 8 inches wide by ½ inch thick (25–30 cm by 15–20 cm by .5 cm), soaked in water for a minimum of 1 hour	2
	Napoleon Injector	
1 lb	ice-cold regular ground beef	454 g
1 lb	ice-cold regular ground pork	454 g
¼ cup + ½ cup	Jack Daniel's Tennessee Whiskey	60 mL + 125 mL
¼ cup + 1 Tbsp	Bone Dust™ BBQ Seasoning (p. 39)	60 mL + 15 mL
6	balls bocconcini, frozen	6

Boy these burgers are good. It's all in the Jack. You may need a flip-top head to eat them!

JACKINATOR GLAZING SAUCE: In a small pot, combine Jack Daniel's Tennessee Whiskey, BBQ sauce, bacon fat and Map-o-Spread or maple syrup. Heat over low heat, stirring occasionally, until the bacon fat has melted and the sauce is incorporated. Set aside, keeping warm.

THE BURGER: Place the ground beef and pork in a large bowl. Drizzle the ¼ cup (60 mL) of Jack Daniel's over the meat. Sprinkle the Bone Dust™ BBQ Seasoning evenly over the meat. Mix gently but thoroughly. Divide the meat mixture into 6 equal parts and form into 6 balls.

• Poke a hole into the center of each burger and stuff a frozen bocconcini into the hole. Form meat into 6 large firmly packed baseball-shaped burgers. (Note: Do not flatten the burgers; leave them shaped like baseballs. This will help keep your burgers moist and juicy.) Place burgers on a tray or plate, cover and refrigerate for 1 hour. This will allow the meat to rest.

• Preheat grill to medium-high, 450–550°F (230–280°C).

• Evenly space 3 burgers on each plank. Place on grill and close lid. Plank-bake for 25 to 30 minutes, basting with reserved Jackinator Glazing Sauce during the last 15 minutes of planking, until the burgers are fully cooked but still moist and juicy.

• Take your injector and fill the syringe with the ½ cup (125 mL) of remaining Jack Daniel's. Inject a little Jack Daniel's into the center of each burger.

• Remove burgers from grill.

ASSEMBLE YOUR BURGERS! Serve with a knife and fork, or serve on your favorite buns with all your favorite burger condiments.

NOTE: You may need to squish the burgers a little to get them in your mouth.

MAKES 6 BURGERS

I love my JD!

SUPER THICK AND CHEEZY BURGER

2	maple planks, 10 to 12 inches long by 6 to 8 inches wide by ½ inch thick (25–30 cm by 15–20 cm by 1.5 cm), soaked in water for a minimum of 1 hour	2
4	mozzarella cheese strings, cut into ½-inch (1.5 cm) chunks	4
4	yellow cheddar cheese strings cut into ½-inch (1.5 cm) chunks	4
2 lb	regular ground beef, ice-cold from the refrigerator	907 g
1 cup	crispy, fried onions	250 mL
¼ cup + 1 Tbsp	Bone Dust™ BBQ Seasoning (p. 39)	60 mL + 15 mL
6	hamburger buns	6

Back in 1995–96 when I worked as a product developer at President's Choice, one of the best products that I developed was a thick beef burger with pieces of cheddar and mozzarella in it. When you grilled the burger, the cheese melted slowly, so that by the time the meat was cooked the cheese was just starting to melt. Here is my 2010 updated Super Thick and Cheezy Burger.

• Place both mozzarella and cheddar cheese string chunks into a bowl and place in the freezer for at least 1 hour. Freeze the cheese, baby!

• In a large bowl, combine ground beef, crispy, fried onions, mozzarella and cheddar-cheese strings. Sprinkle the Bone Dust™ BBQ Seasoning evenly over the meat-and-cheese mixture. Mix gently but thoroughly.

• Form into 6 large baseball-shaped burgers, pressing firmly to keep the burgers intact. (Note: Do not flatten the burgers; leave them shaped like baseballs. This will help keep your burgers moist and juicy.) Place burgers on a tray or plate, cover and place in the freezer for 30 minutes. This will allow the meat to rest.

• Preheat grill to medium-high, 450–550°F (230–280°C).

• Evenly space 3 burgers on each plank. Place on grill and close lid. Plank-bake for 25 to 30 minutes until the burgers are fully cooked, the cheese is oozing but still moist and juicy.

• Remove burgers from grill.

ASSEMBLE YOUR BURGERS! Serve with a knife and fork, or serve on your favorite buns with all your favorite burger condiments.

NOTE: You may need to squish the burgers a little to get them in your mouth.

MAKES 6 BURGERS

SLOPPY JOE BURGER

THE BURGER

¼ cup	vegetable oil	60 mL
1	small sweet onion minced	1
¼ cup	Hot and Spicy Bone Dust™ BBQ Seasoning (p. 43)	60 mL
1½ lb	regular ground beef	675 g
½	bottle beer	
½ cup + ¼ cup	Ted's World Famous BBQ Beerlicious™ BBQ Sauce or your favorite spicy chipotle-style BBQ sauce	125 mL + 60 mL
6	burger buns	6
	Butter	

Technically, this may not be a real burger, since it's not formed and it's made from ground beef and pork. But it is thick and rich, and it makes for a good cold winter's day meal. It's a must-do.

THE BURGER: In a large heavy-bottomed pot, heat the oil over high heat for 2 to 3 minutes or until you start to see a wisp of smoke rising from the oil.

• Add the onion and cook, stirring continuously, for 1 to 2 minutes. Add in the Hot and Spicy Bone Dust™ BBQ Seasoning and continue to stir while cooking the onion and spices for 2 minutes more.

• Add in the beef and, while stirring, cook the meat for 5 to 6 minutes, until the meat is grayish. Drain excess liquid and fat from the pan.

• While over high heat, add the beer to the pan to deglaze. Stir. Add in BBQ Sauce and continue to cook, stirring occasionally, for 5 minutes.

• Reduce heat to low and allow the meat mixture to simmer for 15 more minutes. Remove from heat and allow the meat mixture to rest for 10 minutes.

• Brush buns with butter and grill until golden brown and crisp.

• Using a large ice-cream scoop or a spoon, scoop meat mixture onto the toasted buns. Serve immediately.

MAKES 6 BURGERS

CHILI CHEESEBURGER

CHILI BURGER TOPPING

2 cups	Sloppy Joe meat (p. 85)	500 mL

THE BURGER

6	jalapeño peppers	6
1	small white onion, cut in quarters	1
1½ lb	ice-cold regular ground beef	675 g
½ lb	ice-cold regular ground pork	125 mL
1 cup	spicy nacho cheese chips, crushed	250 mL
1 Tbsp	fresh cilantro, chopped	15 mL
2 Tbsp	Bone Dust™ BBQ Seasoning (p. 39)	30 mL
2–3 Tbsp	El Jimador Reposado Tequila	30–45 mL
6	burger buns	6
2 cups	pepper jack cheese, shredded	500 mL
	Nonstick cooking spray	

CHILI BURGER TOPPING: Warm Sloppy Joe meat in a heavy-bottomed pan over low heat, stirring occasionally, until heated through. Set aside and keep warm.

THE BURGER: Preheat grill to high, 550°F (280°C).

• Grill the jalapeño peppers for 5 to 10 minutes, until the skin is charred and the peppers are tender. Remove from grill and allow the peppers to cool.

• Grill the onion quarters for 10 to 15 minutes, turning occasionally, until lightly charred and a little tender. Remove from grill and allow to cool.

• Cut the jalapeños in half and remove seeds. Finely chop the charred peppers. Set aside.

• Chop the char-grilled onion into a fine dice. Set aside.

• In a large bowl, combine the chopped jalapeños and onions, ice-cold ground beef and pork, nacho cheese chips, cilantro and Bone Dust™ BBQ Seasoning. Drizzle mixture with 2 to 3 Tbsp (30–45 mL) of tequila. Mix gently but thoroughly.

• Form into six 6-oz (180 g) burgers approximately 1½ inches (3.5 cm) thick. Place burgers on a tray or plate, cover and put in the freezer for 30 minutes. This will allow the meat to rest.

• Reduce heat on grill to medium-high, 450–550°F (230–280°C).

• Spray burgers lightly on both sides with nonstick cooking spray.

• Grill burgers for 5 to 6 minutes per side, until cooked to medium-well doneness but burgers are still moist and juicy.

• Top each burger with a spoonful of Chili Burger Topping, top with shredded pepper jack cheese if you so desire; close grill lid and continue to cook for 3 more minutes, until the cheese is melted.

• Remove burgers from grill.

ASSEMBLE YOUR BURGERS! Serve on your favorite buns with all your favorite burger condiments.

MAKES 6 BURGERS

El Jimador is a registered trademark ©2010
Please enjoy Mexico's number 1 tequila responsibly.

HOT DIGGITY DOG BURGER

1 lb	ice-cold regular ground beef	454 g
½ lb	ice-cold regular ground pork	225 g
¼ cup	sweet onion, finely diced	60 mL
2 Tbsp	Bone Dust™ BBQ Seasoning (p. 39)	30 mL
1 Tbsp	hot English-style prepared mustard	15 mL
1 Tbsp	Worcestershire sauce	15 mL
3	cloves garlic, minced	3
	Salt and ground black pepper, to taste	
6	hot dogs	6
	Ted's World Famous BBQ Crazy Canuck Sauce or your favorite gourmet-style BBQ sauce	
6	hot dog buns	6
	Plastic wrap	
	Nonstick cooking spray	

• In a large bowl, combine ground beef, ground pork, sweet onion, Bone Dust™ Seasoning, hot English-style prepared mustard, Worcestershire sauce and garlic. Season to taste with salt and pepper.

• Using your hands, mix well to incorporate. Cover and refrigerate for 1 hour to allow meat to rest and set.

• Remove meat mixture from refrigerator. On a clean cutting board or flat surface, lay down a piece of plastic wrap. Spread ⅙ of the refrigerated meat mixture in a smooth layer on top of the plastic wrap to a thickness of about ½ inch (1.5 cm) and about 1 inch (2.5 cm) longer than the hot dog. The meat mixture should form a small rectangle.

• Remove cheese string from wrapping and place in center of meat mixture. Using the plastic wrap as a guide, roll the meat mixture around the hot dog into a roll about 2 inches (5 cm) in diameter and press the edges of the meat together around the hot dog. You should now have a large hot dog-shaped burger. To seal the ends of the hot dog burger, gently twist one end of the plastic wrap until it tightens on the end of the meat mixture, pressing the meat together to seal in the cheese.

• Repeat with other end, securing plastic wrap at each end to seal. Repeat with remaining meat mixture and cheese strings to form 6 Hot Diggity Dog Burgers. Cover and refrigerate Hot Diggity Dog Burgers for 30 minutes to allow the meat to rest and set.

• Preheat grill to medium, 350°F (175°C).

• Remove burgers from refrigerator and remove plastic wrappings. Spray evenly with nonstick cooking spray. Place burger dogs on grill and cook for 15 to 20 minutes until fully cooked, turning occasionally and basting with BBQ sauce during the last 2 to 3 minutes of grilling.

• Place hot dog buns, cut-side down, on grill and grill until golden brown, about 1 to 2 minutes.

ASSEMBLE YOUR BURGERS! Remove Hot Diggity Dog Burgers from grill and place one into each toasted hot dog bun. Serve immediately with extra BBQ sauce and garnish with your favorite condiments.

MAKES 6 BURGERS

KING OF THE Q BURGER

THE BURGER

1	large iron Bundt pan (crown shaped if you have or regular round and fluted Bundt will do)	1
5 lb	icy cold ground beef chuck	2270 g
½ cup	Bone Dust™ BBQ Seasoning (p. 39)	125 g
2 cups	crispy, fried onion pieces	500 mL
1 cup	hickory stick potato snack, crushed	250 mL
2 Tbsp	liquid beef concentrate	30 mL
2 Tbsp	Worcestershire sauce	30 mL
1 large	sweet Vidalia onion, diced	1
8	cloves garlic, minced	8
¼ bottle	your favorite dark ale beer	90 mL
¼ cup	ketchup	60 mL
1 Tbsp	Dijon mustard	15 mL
½ bunch	fresh parsley, chopped	¼ bunch
8 mini wheels	baby bel gouda cheese	6 mini wheels
½ cup	Ted's World Famous BBQ Crazy Canuck Sauce or your favorite bbq sauce	
	Nonstick cooking spray	
6	hamburger buns	5
	Leaf lettuce	
	Red onion, sliced	
	Tomato, sliced	
	Cucumber, sliced	

This burger is a tribute to my life as King of the Q. It is a super big burger cooked not just on its own, but in a crown shaped Bundt pan. Now this burger will feed a crowd. It's 5 lbs. This is a fun and funky burger that can be sliced and served. It also makes a great birthday burger for the kids. Stick some candles in it and have some fun. Cheers!

THE BURGER: In a large bowl combine ground beef chuck, Bone Dust™ BBQ Seasoning, crispy, fried onions, hickory sticks, beef concentrate, Worcestershire sauce, onion, garlic, dark ale, ketchup, mustard and parsley. Mix well.

• Spray the Bundt pan liberally with the nonstick cooking spray. Pack half of the mixed ground beef into the Bundt pan pressing the meat firmly into the pan so to remove all pockets of air. Push the wheels of baby gouda into the bottom half of the meat mixture, evenly spaced. Pack the remaining meat on top of the cheese and press firmly to pack. Cover and refrigerate for 1 hour.

• Preheat grill to medium heat, 350–450°F (175–230°C).

• Place burger in Bundt pan onto the grill meat-side down and sear the burger surface for 2–4 minutes. Using oven mitts turn the pan over so the meat side is facing up. Baste with Crazy Canuck BBQ Sauce or your favorite sauce. Cover with aluminum foil and close lid.

• Grill/Bake for 60 to 75 minutes, basting occasionally with extra BBQ Sauce and checking occasionally to insure that the burger is not burning, until an internal temperature of 170 degrees minimum has been reached. Note: You may need to reduce the heat directly under the pan as to keep it from burning.

• Remove from the grill and allow to rest.

• Drain away excess fat and juices from around the burger in the pan. Carefully tilt the pan to drain. Remember this is very hot.

• Place a large plate over top of the burger. Carefully turn over and let the burger slip out of the pan and onto the plate.

ASSEMBLE YOUR BURGER! Serve immediately with your favorite burger garnishes and condiments.

MAKES 6 BURGERS

BLACK CHERRY BURGER
WITH VERY CHERRY SAUCE

VERY CHERRY SAUCE

¼ cup	cherries, dried	60 mL
½ cup	Finlandia Vodka	125 mL
1 cup	cherry-pie filling	250 mL
½ cup	brown sugar	125 mL
½ cup	Cherry Coke or Coke	125 mL
1 Tbsp	soy sauce	15 mL

THE BURGER

2 lb	ice-cold ground eye of the round	907 g
½ cup	cherries, dried	125 mL
3 Tbsp	Orgasmic Onion Burger Seasoning (p. 44)	45 mL
1 Tbsp	fresh thyme, chopped	15 mL
2 Tbsp	whole grain mustard	30 mL
6	burger buns	6
	Leaf lettuce	
	Red onions, sliced	
	Nonstick cooking spray	

It's very cherry.

VERY CHERRY SAUCE: Coarsely chop the dried cherries. Cover with Finlandia Vodka and marinate cherries for 2 to 4 hours, until they are moist and plump.

• Place in a medium saucepan. Add cherry-pie filling, brown sugar, Cherry Coke and soy sauce. Bring to a boil over medium heat, stirring frequently to keep from scorching.

• Remove from heat and allow to cool. Cover and refrigerate until needed.

MAKES APPROXIMATELY 3 CUPS (750 ML)

THE BURGER: In a large bowl, combine the ice-cold ground eye of the round, dried cherries, Orgasmic Onion Burger Seasoning, thyme and mustard. Mix gently but thoroughly.

• Form into six 6-oz (180 g) round burgers approximately ½ inch (1.5 cm) thick. Place burgers on a tray or plate, cover and place in the refrigerator for 1 hour, allowing the burgers to rest.

• Preheat grill to medium-high, 450–550°F (230–280°C).

• Spray burgers lightly on both sides with nonstick cooking spray.

• Grill burgers for 5 to 6 minutes per side, basting frequently during the last half of cooking, until burgers are done medium-well but are still moist and juicy. Remove burgers from grill.

ASSEMBLE YOUR BURGERS! Bun, lettuce, onions, burger, extra Very Cherry Sauce and, if you so desire, garnish with crumbled Stilton cheese.

MAKES 6 BURGERS

VIETNAMESE BURGER LETTUCE WRAPS

SWEET AND SOUR SLAW

2 cups	bean sprouts	500 mL
2	medium carrots, julienned or grated	2
2 cups	daikon radish, julienned	500 mL
1	bunch Thai basil, picked	1
4	green onions, thinly sliced	4
6	fresh shiitake mushrooms, thinly sliced	6
½ tsp	sambal chili	2.5 mL
¼ cup	rice wine vinegar	60 mL
2 Tbsp	mirin	30 mL
2 Tbsp	lime juice, fresh-squeezed	30 mL
	Salt	

HOISIN BASTE

½ cup	hoisin sauce	125 mL
½ cup	soy sauce	125 mL
1 Tbsp	sambal chili sauce	15 mL

THE BURGER

1½ lb	ice-cold regular ground beef	675 g
1	red onion, minced	1
2	cloves garlic, minced	2
1 tsp	sambal chili sauce	5 mL
1 Tbsp	soy sauce	15 mL
1 tsp	rice vinegar	5 mL
2 Tbsp	cilantro	30 mL
2	green onions, finely chopped	2
	Nonstick cooking spray	
1	head green leaf lettuce, washed of all dirt and grit	1

Wrap up slices of spicy burgers in leaves of crisp green leaf of iceberg lettuce.

SWEET AND SOUR SLAW: In one bowl, combine bean sprouts, carrots, daikon radish, picked basil, green onions and shiitake mushrooms. Cover and refrigerate until needed.

• In another bowl, combine sambal chili, rice wine vinegar, mirin and lime juice. Season with a pinch of salt. Cover and refrigerate until needed.

HOISIN BASTE: In a bowl, combine hoisin sauce, soy sauce and sambal chili sauce. Mix well and set aside for basting burgers.

THE BURGER: In a bowl, gently combine ice-cold regular ground beef, red onion, garlic, sambal chili sauce, soy sauce, rice vinegar, cilantro and green onions. Cover and refrigerate for 1 hour to set.

• Form into four 6-oz (180 g) round burgers approximately ½ inch (1.5 cm) thick. Place burgers on a tray or plate, cover and put in the refrigerator for 1 hour, allowing the burgers to rest.

• Preheat grill to medium-high, 450–550°F (230–280°C).

• Spray burgers lightly on both sides with nonstick cooking spray.

• Grill burgers for 5 to 6 minutes per side, basting frequently during the last half of cooking, until cooked to medium-well doneness but burgers are still moist and juicy.

• Remove burgers from grill.

ASSEMBLE YOUR BURGERS! Leaf lettuce, burger, Sweet and Sour Slaw, extra basting sauce drizzle and top with Thai basil.

MAKES 4 BURGERS

ORGASMIC ONION BURGER

This truly is a burger to make you shake, rattle and roll.

PORT WINE GRAVY

1 Tbsp + 3 Tbsp	cold butter	15 mL + 45 mL
2	medium shallots	2
2	cloves garlic, minced	2
1 tsp	fresh thyme, chopped	5 mL
1	bay leaf	1
2 cups	port wine	500 mL
1 cup	beef or veal demi-glace (reduced beef stock)	250 mL
	Salt and pepper, to taste	

THE BURGER

1½ lb	ice-cold ground chuck	675 g
½ cup	Orgasmic Onion Burger Seasoning (p. 44)	125 mL
	Nonstick cooking spray	
4	onion buns	4
2 lb	frozen store-bought battered or breaded onion rings	907 g
½ cup	goat cheese, crumbled	125 mL
	Butter, melted	

PORT WINE GRAVY: To prepare the sauce, melt 1 Tbsp (15 mL) of butter in a medium saucepan. Sauté the shallots and garlic for 1 minute, until tender and transparent. Add the thyme, bay leaf and port. Bring to a boil and reduce liquid by half the amount. Remove from stove and strain sauce into another pot. Return to boil and add demi-glace. Reduce heat to low and simmer for 10 to 15 minutes, until the sauce has intensified and is thick. Remove from heat and season to taste with salt and pepper. Whisk in the cold butter until it is fully incorporated. Keep sauce warm.

THE BURGER: In a bowl, combine ice-cold ground beef chuck and Orgasmic Onion Burger Seasoning. Mix gently to combine. Cover and refrigerate for 1 hour to allow meat to set.

• Form into four 6-oz (180 g) round burgers approximately ½ inch (1.5 cm) thick. Place burgers on a tray or plate, cover and put in the refrigerator for 1 hour, allowing the burgers to rest.

• Preheat grill to medium-high, 450–550°F (230–280°C).

• Spray burgers lightly on both sides with nonstick cooking spray.

• Grill burgers for 5 to 6 minutes per side, basting frequently during the last half of cooking, until cooked to medium-well doneness, but burgers are still moist and juicy.

• While the burgers are cooking, fry the frozen onion rings according to package instructions until crisp and golden brown.

• Butter onion buns and toast on grill until golden brown and heated through.

• Remove burgers from grill.

ASSEMBLE YOUR BURGERS! Bun bottom, burger, stack of crispy, fried onion rings, crumbled goat cheese, Port Wine Gravy and bun top.

MAKES 4 BURGERS

CAESAR SALAD THREE-MEAT BURGER

ROASTED GARLIC CAESAR AIOLI

2	large head garlic, peeled, about 24 cloves	2
1 ½ cups	olive oil	375 mL
6	egg yolks	6
6	anchovies, minced	6
¼ cup	Dijon mustard	60 mL
1	lemon, juiced (about ¼ cup/60 mL)	1
2 Tbsp	red wine vinegar	30 mL
1 Tbsp	Worcestershire sauce	15 mL
¼ tsp	hot sauce	1 mL
½ cup	Parmesan cheese, grated	125 mL
	Salt and pepper, to taste	

THE BURGER

1 lb	ice-cold regular ground beef	454 g
1 lb	ice-cold ground veal	454 g
1 lb	ice-cold ground pork	454 g
6	cloves garlic, minced	6
1	small onion, finely diced	1
2	green onions, finely chopped	2
1	small egg	1
1 Tbsp	fresh parsley, chopped	15 mL
2 tsp	Worcestershire sauce	10 mL
	Salt and pepper	
	Nonstick cooking spray	
6	squares focaccia bread	6
	Olive oil	
2	cloves garlic	2
2	heads of hearts of romaine, cleaned and left whole	2
12	slices bacon, cooked crisp	12

Caesar salad on a burger. It's all the rage!

ROASTED GARLIC CAESAR AIOLI: Preheat oven to 325°F (170°C).

• Place garlic cloves in an ovenproof dish. Cover with olive oil and roast for 30 to 40 minutes, or until the garlic is golden brown and tender. Remove from oven and allow to cool.

• Remove the cloves from the oil, reserving the oil, and in a medium-sized bowl, mash roasted garlic until smooth.

• Add egg yolks. Stir in the anchovies and mustard. While stirring continuously, add the lemon juice, red wine vinegar, Worcestershire sauce and hot sauce. Continue stirring and add the reserved roasted garlic oil in a slow steady stream so that the aioli emulsifies and the mixture is thick.

• Stir in the Parmesan cheese and season to taste with salt and pepper. Transfer to a sealed container and refrigerate until needed.

MAKES ABOUT 2 1/2 CUPS (625 ML)

THE BURGER: In a large bowl, mix the beef, veal, pork, garlic, onion, green onion, egg, parsley and Worcestershire sauce. Season to taste with salt and black pepper.

• Form into six 8-oz (250 g) patties approximately 1 inch (2.5 cm) thick. Place burgers on a tray or plate, cover and put in the refrigerator for 1 hour, allowing the burgers to rest.

• Preheat grill to medium-high, 400–500°F (200–250°C).

• Spray burgers lightly on both sides with non-stick cooking spray.

• Grill burgers for 8 to 10 minutes per side, until cooked to medium-well doneness. Burgers should still be moist and juicy.

• While the burgers are grilling, lightly toast focaccia squares. Remove from heat and brush with olive oil. Take a clove of garlic and rub each toasted focaccia square to extract the garlic flavor.

• In a large bowl, toss romaine lightly with Roasted Garlic Caesar Aioli.

ASSEMBLE YOUR BURGERS! Toasted focaccia, Roasted Garlic Caesar Aioli, burger. Top with a few leaves of dressed romaine and 2 slices of crispy bacon. Drizzle with more Roasted Garlic Caesar Aioli and garnish with shavings of Parmesan.

MAKES 6 BURGERS

STEAK OSCAR BURGER

SAUCE BÉARNAISE

¼ cup	cider vinegar	60 mL
2	sprigs fresh tarragon	2
1	small shallot, diced	1
2 Tbsp	water	30 mL
4	black peppercorns	4
4	egg yolks	4
2 Tbsp	dry white wine	30 mL
1 Tbsp	dry sherry	15 mL
1 cup + 2 Tbsp	clarified butter	250 mL + 30 mL
1 Tbsp	fresh tarragon, chopped	15 mL
1 Tbsp	Dijon mustard	15 mL
1 tsp	lemon juice	5 mL
Dash	hot sauce	Dash
Dash	Worcestershire sauce	Dash
	Salt and pepper, to taste	

THE BURGER

	Toothpicks	
6	slices thick-cut bacon	6
1½ lb	beef tenderloin steaks or sirloin steaks	675 g
2 tsp	kosher salt	10 mL
3	cloves garlic, minced	3
2 tsp	soft butter	10 mL
1 tsp	cracked black pepper	5 mL
2 tsp	Dijon mustard	10 mL
1 lb	tender baby asparagus, cleaned and trimmed	454 g
2 tsp	olive oil	10 mL
	Salt	
1½ cups	lump crabmeat	375 mL
3 cups	Creamy Mashed Potatoes (p. 105)	750 mL

Knife and fork required.

SAUCE BÉARNAISE: In a small saucepan, bring the cider vinegar, tarragon sprigs, shallot, water and peppercorns to a boil. Reduce heat and simmer for 3 to 4 minutes, or until the liquid has reduced by half. Remove from heat and strain. Discard solids and let the liquid cool.

• In a medium bowl, whisk the egg yolks, white wine, sherry and cooled vinegar mixture. Place over a pot of simmering water and whisk constantly until the mixture is thick enough to form a ribbon when drizzled from the whisk. Be careful not to turn this into scrambled eggs. Remove from heat.

• Whisking constantly, slowly add the clarified butter a little at a time until all the butter has been absorbed. Season with chopped tarragon, mustard, lemon juice, hot sauce, Worcestershire sauce, salt and pepper. Remove from heat and keep warm over the hot water.

THE BURGER: Fry the bacon for 2 to 3 minutes per side or until slightly done. (You don't want to fry the bacon crisp, or you won't be able to wrap it around the filets.) Remove from pan and pat dry with paper towels to remove excess fat. Set aside.

• In a bowl, combine ice-cold ground beef tenderloin or sirloin. Add salt, garlic, butter, pepper and Dijon mustard. Gently mix and form into six 4-oz (120 g) 2-inch (5 cm) thick burger patties. Shape the burgers so that they resemble a thick filet steak, approximately the same thickness as the width of the bacon.

• Wrap each filet burger with a slice of bacon. Use a half slice extra if the bacon does not quite make it all the way around. Seal with a toothpick, cover and refrigerate to rest for at least 1 hour.

• Preheat grill to medium-high, 450–550°F (250–280°C).

• Grill beef for 4 to 5 minutes per side for medium-rare doneness and until the bacon is crispy. Top each filet burger with a ¼ cup (60 mL) of lump crabmeat.

• While the steaks are cooking, season the asparagus with salt and olive oil. Grill for 3 to 4 minutes, turning once, until lightly charred, bright green, yet tender. Set aside, keeping warm. Remove toothpicks from burgers.

ASSEMBLE YOUR BURGERS! Spoon ½ cup (125 mL) of hot Mashed Potatoes onto a plate, top with grilled filet burger with crabmeat, top with 2 or 3 spears of grilled asparagus and spoon Sauce Béarnaise overtop or serve on your favorite bun. Serve immediately.

MAKES 6 BURGERS

BLUE CHEESE-STUFFED BURGER

SUN-DRIED TOMATO BLUE CHEESE TOPPING

¼ cup	sun-dried tomatoes, thinly sliced	60 mL
½ cup	red onion, thinly sliced	125 mL
2	green onions, thinly sliced	2
4	cloves garlic, roasted	4
¼ cup	blue cheese, crumbled	60 mL

THE BURGER

1½ lb	ice-cold ground beef chuck	675 g
4 Tbsp	Bone Dust™ BBQ Seasoning (p. 39)	60 mL
1	small white onion, minced	1
4	cloves garlic, roasted	4
4	thick slices blue cheese, frozen	4
4	ciabatta rolls	4
	Nonstick cooking spray	

Try a variety of different styles of blue cheese. I love Roquefort, Gorgonzola and Cambozola.

SUN-DRIED TOMATO BLUE CHEESE TOPPING: In a bowl, combine sun-dried tomatoes, red onion, green onion, roasted garlic and blue cheese. Season with freshly ground black pepper and set aside.

THE BURGER: In a large bowl, combine the ice-cold ground beef chuck, Bone Dust™, onion and roasted garlic. Season to taste with freshly ground black pepper. Mix gently but thoroughly.

• Form into eight 3-oz (100 g) round burgers approximately ½ inch (1.5 cm) thick and 4 inches (10 cm) in diameter.

• Lay one burger on a flat work surface. Place a slice of frozen blue cheese on top of the burger. There should be about a ½-inch (1.5 cm) border of meat showing around the cheese. Place a second burger on top of the cheese; firmly press and form the burger so that the cheese is hidden within and the burgers are now one. Repeat with remaining burgers and cheese.

• Place burgers on a tray or plate, cover and put in the freezer for 30 minutes. This will allow the meat to rest and get very cold.

• Preheat grill to medium-high, 450–550°F (230–280°C).

• Spray burgers lightly on both sides with nonstick cooking spray.

• Grill burgers for 5 to 6 minutes per side, until cooked to medium-well doneness but burgers are still moist and juicy.

• Toast the rolls. Remove burgers from grill.

ASSEMBLE YOUR BURGERS! Bottom of roll, Blue Cheese-Stuffed Burger, Sun-Dried Tomato Blue Cheese Topping and top of roll. Serve immediately.

MAKES 4 BURGERS

PLANKED MEAT LOAF BURGER
WITH CREAMY MASHED POTATOES

Use a knife and fork for these yummy burgers.

CREAMY MASHED POTATOES

8	large Yukon Gold potatoes, peeled and quartered	8
½ cup	table (18%) cream	125 mL
2 Tbsp	butter, softened	30 mL
¼ cup	fresh parsley and/or fresh chives, chopped	60 mL
	Salt and freshly ground black pepper, to taste	

MUSHROOM WINE GRAVY

2 Tbsp	olive oil	30 mL
2 cups	½ inch (1.5 cm) thick slices white or cremini mushrooms	500 mL
1	small onion, finely diced	1
2	cloves garlic, minced	2
¼ cup	Lindemans Bin 45 Cabernet Sauvignon	60 mL
¼ cup	beef gravy (homemade or out of tin if you like)	60 mL
2 Tbsp	Ted's World Famous BBQ Crazy Canuck Chicken and Rib Sauce	30 mL

THE BURGER

2	regular cedar planks, untreated and soaked for 1 hour in water	2
1 ¼ lb	ice-cold regular ground beef	500 g
2 Tbsp	panko (Japanese-style) bread crumbs	30 mL
3	cloves garlic, minced	3
½ cup	red onion, finely diced	125 mL
1 Tbsp	fresh parsley, chopped	15 mL
1 large	egg	1
1 Tbsp	Dijon Mustard	15 mL
Big Splash	Worcestershire sauce	Big Splash
	Kosher salt and freshly ground black pepper, to taste	

CREAMY MASHED POTATOES: The day before serving, cook potatoes until tender in a large pot of salted boiling water (about 15 to 20 minutes). Drain well and set aside for 10 to 15 minutes to dry out.

• Meanwhile, combine the butter and cream in the pot and warm slightly. Return the potatoes and mash together with the butter and cream mixture, seasoning with salt and pepper and the chopped herbs. Take care not to over-mash. There should be lumps.

• Set aside to cool to room temperature, cover and refrigerate overnight.

MUSHROOM WINE GRAVY: Place a large sauté pan over medium-high heat, add the olive oil and let it get hot, about 1 minute. Add the mushrooms and sauté, stirring often, for 4 to 5 minutes, until lightly browned and tender. Add the onion and continue to sauté, stirring often, for 1 minute until the onion is tender. Add garlic, stir and deglaze with red wine. Add gravy and barbecue sauce and bring mixture to a low boil; reduce heat to low and allow gravy to simmer for 5 minutes. Remove from heat and keep warm.

THE BURGER: In a large bowl, combine ground beef, bread crumbs, garlic, red onion, parsley, egg and mustard. Season to taste with a big splash of Worcestershire sauce, kosher salt and freshly ground black pepper, and gently mix until everything is incorporated.

• Portion burger mixture into 4 equal-sized balls, pressing the meat gently together so it adheres. Form each ball into a 2-inch (5 cm) round and 4-inch (10 cm) tall cylindrical shape. Place on burger patty paper, cover and refrigerate for a minimum of 1 hour, to allow the meat to rest.

• Preheat grill to high, 550°F (280°C).

• Sear meat-loaf burgers on one side only for 1 to 2 minutes to lightly char.

• Lower grill temperature to medium, 400°F (200°C).

• Evenly space the meat-loaf burgers, seared-side up, on the planks, two per plank.

• Mold the mashed potatoes around the seared burgers into a ring approximately 2 inches (5 cm) thick and formed to the top of the meat-loaf burger, leaving the seared burger exposed.

• Place planked mashed-potato-wrapped meat-loaf burgers on the grill and close lid.

• Plank-roast burgers and potatoes for 20 minutes for medium-rare doneness and potatoes that are golden brown and crisp.

• Remove from grill and serve immediately with Mushroom Wine Gravy.

MAKES 4 BURGERS

TEXAS LONGHORN BRISKET BURGER

BREAD-AND-BUTTER PICKLES

12	medium cucumbers	12
6	medium sweet onions, peeled and sliced	6
¼ cup	kosher salt	60 mL
1 cup	sugar	250 mL
1 tsp	turmeric	5 mL
1 tsp	dill seed	5 mL
2 cups	white vinegar	500 mL
1 tsp	mustard seeds	5 mL
1 tsp	celery seeds	5 mL
1 tsp	red chili flakes, crushed	5 mL
8	canning jars (2-cup/500 mL) with lids	8

GRILL SMOKED BRISKET

	Napoleon Charcoal Tray	
1	beef brisket (8 lb/3.75 kg)	1
3 Tbsp	Orgasmic Onion Burger Seasoning (p. 44)	45 mL
1	bottle of your favorite dark ale beer	1
1 cup	Ted's World Famous BBQ Beerlicious™ BBQ Sauce or your favorite smoky spicy BBQ sauce	250 mL
	Kosher salt and cracked black pepper, to taste	

These big juicy burgers are made with slowly smoked beef brisket. Serve them Texas-style on garlic toast with onions, prepared mustard and bread-and-butter pickles.

BREAD-AND-BUTTER PICKLES: Slice the cucumbers into ¼-inch (1 cm) thick rounds and place in a large bowl. Add sliced onions and sprinkle with kosher salt. Mix and cover with ice-cold water. Place in refrigerator for 2½ hours.

• In a medium saucepan, combine sugar, turmeric, dill seed, white vinegar, mustard seeds, celery seeds and chili flakes. Stir and bring to a boil.

• Drain cucumber-and-onion mixture. Pour boiled vinegar mixture over cucumbers and onions. Let stand for a couple of minutes and then pack into clean sterilized jars. Seal and store in a cool dark place for up to 8 months.

MAKES APPROXIMATELY 8 JARS

GRILL SMOKED BRISKET: Set up your gas grill to accommodate the Napoleon Charcoal Tray accessory, placing the charcoal tray over the left or the right burner. Place a mound of 12 to 15 charcoal briquettes in the center of the charcoal tray. Ignite gas burner under the charcoal tray and let it burn until the charcoal ignites. Turn off the gas. Let the coals burn to white-hot.

• Meanwhile, as the coals are getting hot, rub the brisket all over with the Orgasmic Onion Burger Seasoning. Place the seasoned brisket on the other side of the grill, far away from the charcoal.

• Add wood chips and close lid. You will want to maintain a smoking temperature of 180–225°F (80–110°C). Replenish the coals as need be.

• Smoke beef brisket for 10 to 12 hours. Wrap in 4 sheets of aluminum foil and smoke for 2-3 hours longer, until tender but still moist. You should be able to easily shred the meat with two forks.

• Shred the meat. Season with dark ale, BBQ sauce, kosher salt and black pepper. Mix well and set aside.

NOTE: If you don't want to make your own pickles, use store-bought. Hey, that's easy!

THE BURGER

1 lb	ice-cold ground chuck	454 g
1 lb	chilled smoked-beef brisket, shredded	454 g
2 Tbsp	Orgasmic Onion Burger Seasoning (p. 44)	30 mL
1	small onion, finely diced	1
¼ cup	your favorite dark ale beer	60 mL
½ cup	Ted's World Famous BBQ Beerlicious™ BBQ Sauce or your favorite smoky spicy BBQ sauce	125 mL
	Nonstick cooking spray	

THE GARNISH

¼ cup	butter, softened	60 mL
4	cloves garlic, roasted	4
1 Tbsp	Parmesan cheese	15 mL
8	slices Texas Toast	8
2 cups	shredded smoked-beef brisket, warmed	500 mL
	white onion, thinly sliced	
	Prepared yellow mustard	
8	slices Bread-and-Butter Pickles	8

THE BURGER: In a large bowl, combine ground chuck, shredded, chilled smoked-beef brisket, Orgasmic Onion Burger Seasoning, onion and dark ale. Gently mix.

• Portion burger mixture into 4 equal-sized balls. Pressing the meat gently together so it adheres, form each ball into a 1 to 1½ inches (2.5–3.5 cm) thick, uniformly shaped round burger patty. Place on burger patty paper, cover and refrigerate for a minimum of 1 hour, to allow the meat to rest.

• In a bowl, combine butter, roasted garlic, Parmesan cheese and mix well. Set aside.

• Preheat grill to medium-high, 450–550°F (230–280°C).

• Spray burgers with nonstick cooking spray.

• With the grill lid open, grill the burgers for 5 to 6 minutes per side, basting frequently with BBQ sauce, until burgers are fully cooked but still moist and juicy.

• Brush Texas Toast with roasted garlic Parmesan butter. Grill toast until golden brown and crisp.

ASSEMBLE YOUR BURGERS! Texas Toast, burger, warmed shredded beef brisket, onion, mustard, Bread-and-Butter Pickles and Texas Toast. Repeat with remaining burgers.

MAKES 4 BURGERS

POUTINE BURGER

POUTINE GRAVY

2 Tbsp	butter	30 mL
1	small onion, finely diced	1
2	cloves garlic, minced	2
¼ cup	Jack Daniel's Tennessee Whiskey	60 mL
3 Tbsp	all-purpose flour	45 mL
1 cup	beef stock	250 mL
½ cup	Ted's World Famous BBQ Crazy Canuck Sticky Chicken and Rib BBQ Sauce	125 mL
	Salt and pepper, to taste	

THE BURGER

2 lb	ice-regular ground beef	907 g
2 Tbsp	Bone Dust™ BBQ Seasoning (p. 39)	30 mL
¼ cup	Ted's World Famous BBQ Crazy Canuck Sticky Chicken and Rib BBQ Sauce or your favorite BBQ sauce	60 mL

GRILLED POTATO WEDGES

	Napoleon Multi-Grill Basket	
3	large baking potatoes, cut into 1-inch (2.5 cm) thick wedges	3
	Salt	
3 Tbsp	olive oil	45 mL
	sea salt	
	Bone Dust™ BBQ Seasoning (p. 39), to taste	

THE GARNISH

1 cup	yellow or white cheese curds	250 g

This burger is not for the faint of heart. Share it with close friends and family. It's as decadent as a burger should get— moist and juicy, on top of grilled potato wedges, with white cheddar cheese curds and poutine gravy.

POUTINE GRAVY: Place a large sauté pan over medium-high heat; add the butter. Add the onion and sauté, stirring often, for 1 minute, until the onion is tender. Add garlic, stir and deglaze with Jack Daniel's. Add the flour and stir continuously until the flour mixture is thick. While stirring, add the beef stock a little at a time, stirring until mixture is smooth. Add the BBQ sauce and bring mixture to a low boil, reduce heat to low and allow gravy to simmer for 5 minutes. Using a hand-held blender, purée until smooth and strain to remove any lumps or particles. Remove from heat and keep warm.

THE BURGER: In a large bowl, combine ground beef, Bone Dust™ and BBQ sauce. Gently mix well. Form into twelve 3-oz (90 g) burgers. Cover and refrigerate, allowing burgers to rest.

GRILLED POTATO WEDGES: Place potatoes in a large pot and cover with cold water. Bring potatoes to a rolling boil, add salt and reduce heat to simmer. Simmer for 10 to 15 minutes, until the potatoes are just tender. Drain and allow to cool.

• Toss potato wedges with olive oil and sea salt. Set aside.

• Preheat grill to medium-high, 450–550°F (230–280°C).

• Place potatoes into a Napoleon Multi-Grill Basket and grill potatoes for 4 to 5 minutes per side, until golden brown and lightly crisp. When the potato wedges are almost done, grill the burgers for 3 to 4 minutes per side, until fully cooked but still moist and juicy.

• Remove potatoes from Grill Basket and season with Bone Dust™ BBQ Seasoning.

ASSEMBLE YOUR BURGERS! Place potatoes on a large serving platter. Top with grilled burgers. Sprinkle with cheese curds. Drizzle with Poutine Gravy. Serve immediately.

MAKES 12 BURGERS

Jack Daniel's is a registered trademark ©2010
Your friends at Jack remind you to drink responsibly.

PRIME RIB BURGER
WITH HORSERADISH COMPOUND BUTTER

HORSERADISH COMPOUND BUTTER

½ cup	butter, softened	125 mL
3 Tbsp	freshly grated horseradish or prepared horseradish	45 mL
2 Tbsp	fresh parsley, chopped	30 mL
½ tsp	black pepper, coarsely ground	2.5 mL
	Salt, to taste	

THE BURGER

	Meat grinder	
2 lb	boneless prime rib of beef	907 g
1	medium onion, minced	1
6	cloves garlic, minced	6
2 tsp	salt	10 mL
1½ tsp	black pepper, coarse ground	7.5 mL
2 tsp	hot mustard powder	10 mL
2 Tbsp	Better Butter Burger Seasoning (p. 39)	30 mL
6	burger buns	6
½ cup	butter, melted	125 mL

The most succulent cut of beef is the rib steak. Full-flavored, this juicy steak makes an amazing burger. Some people say that grinding such a beautiful steak is a waste. Well, yes, but sometimes you just want a dripping burger that makes you drool. For this recipe, I grind my own prime rib steaks, but you can ask your butcher to do it. Cut the prime rib of beef into 1- to 2-inch (2.5–5 cm) chunks. Lay chunks evenly on a parchment-paper-lined cookie sheet and place in freezer. Freeze meat for 10 to 15 minutes, until the meat is very cold.

HORSERADISH COMPOUND BUTTER: In a bowl, combine butter, horseradish, parsley and black pepper. Season to taste with salt. Set aside.

THE BURGER: With a hand or electrical meat grinder, grind meat using the larger grind plate. Change grind plate to smaller-sized one and grind meat for a second time.

• Add onion and garlic to grinder and pass through. Add salt, pepper, mustard and Better Butter Burger Seasoning to meat mixture.

• Form into 8 equal-sized 6-oz (180 g) patties. (A flatter burger will cook more evenly and faster than a ball-like burger.)

• Preheat grill to medium-high, 450–550°F (230–280°C).

• Grill burgers for 4 to 5 minutes per side for medium-well doneness.

• Brush buns with melted butter and grill, cut-side down, until crisp and golden brown.

ASSEMBLE YOUR BURGERS! Serve on grill-toasted buttered buns and garnish with Horseradish Compound Butter.

MAKES 8 BURGERS

KEBBE TORPEDO BURGER
WITH HUMMUS AND TABBOULEH SALAD

TABBOULEH

½ cup	bulgur wheat	125 mL
2	bunches fresh parsley, washed, drained and finely chopped	2
¼ cup	fresh mint, chopped	60 mL
1	medium sweet onion, finely diced	1
6	plum tomatoes, finely chopped	6
1 Tbsp	kosher salt	15 mL
½ tsp	black pepper, freshly ground	2.5 mL
⅓ cup	lemon juice, fresh	80 mL
⅓ cup	olive oil	80 mL

HUMMUS

2 cups	chickpeas or garbanzo beans, drained but reserving liquid (16 oz can/470 mL)	500 mL
NOTE:	For ease, I use canned chickpeas, but if you prefer, you can soak your chickpeas overnight in water, then drain, rinse and bring to a boil in salted water, and cook for 1½ to 2 hours until tender. Canned is the way to go for this recipe.	
4	cloves garlic, minced	4
1½ Tbsp	tahini	22.5 mL
2 Tbsp	lemon juice	30 mL
3 Tbsp	olive oil	45 mL
	Salt and pepper, to taste	

THE BURGER

¾ cup	bulgur wheat	175 mL
1	small onion, finely grated	1
3	cloves garlic, minced	3
1 tsp	allspice, ground	5 mL
½ tsp	cumin, ground	2.5 mL
½ tsp	coriander, ground	2.5 mL
¼ tsp	paprika	1 mL
¼ cup	flat-leaf parsley, finely chopped	60 mL
1 lb	regular ground beef	454 g
½ lb	regular ground lamb	225 g
	Salt and pepper, to taste	
4	pocket pitas	4
3 Tbsp	olive oil	45 mL

TABBOULEH: Place bulgur in a large bowl and add just enough boiling water to cover. Let stand for 30 minutes, until bulgur is tender. Drain well and place in a large bowl.

• Add chopped parsley, mint, onion, tomatoes, salt, pepper, lemon juice and olive oil. Mix well and set aside, refrigerated.

HUMMUS: Place chickpeas in a food processor.

• Add ¼ cup (60 mL) of chickpea juice from the can. Add garlic, tahini, lemon juice and olive oil. Season with salt and pepper.

• Purée until smooth.

• Adjust seasoning. Transfer to a small bowl, cover and refrigerate until needed.

THE BURGER: In a large bowl, soak the bulgur in enough boiling water to cover it. Soak for 30 minutes, stirring once in a while. Drain any remaining water from the bulgur and dry.

• Place the drained bulgur in a bowl and add the onion, garlic, spices and parsley. Mix well and let stand for 15 minutes. Add the ground beef and lamb, mix well and shape into 12 torpedo-shaped logs. Place on a plate, cover and refrigerate, allowing the meat to rest for 1 hour.

• Preheat grill to medium high, 550°F (280°C).

• Grill Kebbe Burgers for 3 to 4 minutes per side, until medium-well done but still moist and juicy. Brush pitas with olive oil and season to taste with salt and freshly ground black pepper.

• Grill pitas to lightly toast.

ASSEMBLE YOUR BURGERS! Spread Hummus over pita top with a few spoonfuls of Tabbouleh. Top with 2 Kebbe Burgers. Drizzle with hot sauce, if desired, and serve immediately.

MAKES 6 BURGERS

HAMBURGER SOUP

½ cup	butter	125 mL
1	large yellow onion, diced	1
4	cloves garlic, minced	4
2	stalks celery, diced	2
2	medium carrots, diced	2
2	potatoes, peeled and diced	2
½ cup	all-purpose flour	125 mL
10 cups	beef stock or broth	2.5 L
2 lb	ice-cold regular ground beef	907 g
1 tsp	cumin, ground	5 mL
1 tsp	chili powder, ground	5 mL
1 tsp	salt	5 mL
1 tsp	black pepper, ground	5 mL
1 Tbsp	oregano, dry rubbed	15 mL
¼ cup	vegetable oil	60 mL
1 Tbsp	Worcestershire sauce	15 mL
1 tsp	hot sauce	5 mL
	Salt and pepper	

THE GARNISH

2 cups	cheddar cheese, grated	500 mL
½ cup	bacon bits	125 mL
½ cup	sour cream	125 mL
2	green onions, finely chopped	2

A hot soup burger in a bun bowl. It's winterlicious!

• In a large soup pot, melt the butter over medium-high heat. Add the onion, garlic, celery, carrots and potatoes and sauté for 4 to 5 minutes, stirring, until the onions are transparent.

• Stir in the flour and continue to cook, stirring constantly for 2 minutes. Add the beef stock in stages, stirring, until fully incorporated. Bring to a boil, reduce heat and simmer for 30 minutes, stirring frequently to prevent sticking.

• Meanwhile, prepare the ground beef. Mix the cumin, chili, salt, pepper and oregano with the ground beef.

• Heat the oil in a large fry pan and sauté the ground beef until fully cooked. Drain.

• Add ground beef to simmering soup and season with Worcestershire sauce, hot sauce and salt and pepper. Simmer for another 15 minutes.

• Serve in warmed soup crocks garnished with a generous sprinkling of cheddar cheese, bacon bits, sour cream and green onions. Serve with lightly buttered and toasted hamburger buns.

NOTE: Hollow out large pre-sliced burger buns or Kaiser-style rolls to make a bread bowl.

MAKES 8 TO 10 SERVINGS

MEATZZZA ALL-BURGER PIZZA

2	perforated stainless-steel pizza pans	2
2	sheets nonstick aluminum foil	2

THE BURGER

1½ lb	ice-cold regular ground beef	675 g
1	onion, chopped	1
3	cloves garlic, minced	3
3 Tbsp	Better Butter Burger Seasoning (p. 39)	45 mL
¼ cup	bread crumbs	60 mL
¼ cup	gourmet-style BBQ sauce	60 mL
	Salt and pepper, to taste	

THE GARNISH

¼ cup	Ted's World Famous BBQ Crazy Canuck Sticky Chicken and Rib Sauce	60 mL
2½–3 cups	mozzarella cheese, grated	625–750 mL
¼ cup	pearl bocconcini	60 mL
1	small red onion, sliced	1
½ pint	red and yellow grape tomatoes, halved	250 mL
¼ cup	green olives, sliced	60 mL
4	slices bacon cut into 1-inch (2.5 cm) pieces	4
¼ cup	Parmesan cheese	60 mL

I first made Meatzzza while shooting my *King of the Q* television show in the Dominican Republic. I was at Ocean World swimming with dolphins, walruses, and rubbing noses with a white tiger. This is a great burger. You get pizza and a burger all in one!

• Preheat grill to medium-high heat, 450°F (230°C).

• In a large bowl, combine ground beef, onion, garlic, Better Butter Burger Seasoning, bread crumbs, BBQ sauce, salt and pepper. Mix well and refrigerate for 30 minutes to allow meat mixture to firm and set up.

• Lay non-stick foil, nonstick side up, on pizza pan, and seal foil over pan. Lay meat in an even layer on foil-lined pan, pressing meat out to edges and removing as much air as possible. Create a rim of meat around edges to form a crust, which will later hold your toppings in.

• Place another sheet of nonstick foil on second perforated pan, nonstick side up, and place pan upside down on meat layer. (You will need this pan to flip the crust-less BBQ pizza later.)

• Grill meat crust for 6 to 8 minutes until nearly cooked through. Reduce grill temperature to low, flip pizza pans over and return to grill. (The bottom pan should now be on top.) Grill for 5 to 8 minutes to sear.

• Flip meat crust, pan-side down, remove top pan and, using a brush, spread a generous layer of BBQ sauce onto meat.

• Spread cheese evenly over meat crust and top with pearl bocconcini, red onion, tomatoes, olives and bacon. Add mushrooms or any of your favorite burger toppings to create your own Meatzzza. Sprinkle with Parmesan and grill-bake pizza for 10 to 12 minutes, until meat is fully cooked but still moist and juicy and cheese is ooey-gooey and delicious.

• Slice Meatzzza into 8.

MAKES 4 TO 8 SERVINGS

THE SCHWARZENEGGER BURGER

THE BURGER

2	maple or cedar grilling planks, approximately 12 x 6x½ inches thick, soaked in water for a minimum of 1 hour	2
1 lb	icy cold ground sirloin	454 g
½ lb	icy cold ground pork	250 g
6 Tbsp	Orgasmic Onion Burger Seasoning (p. 44)	90 g
2	green onions, finely chopped	2
2	egg whites	2
1 Tsp	fresh thyme, chopped	5 g
4	bocconcini cheese, frozen (1 oz balls)	120 g
4 strips	bacon, thick-sliced	4
2	jumbo hot dogs, approximately 4 oz (120 g) each	2

My tribute to Arnold Schwarzenegger, truly a burger that will pump you up.

THE BURGER: In a bowl, combine ground sirloin, ground pork, Orgasmic Onion Seasoning, green onions, egg whites and thyme. Mix well.

• Divide mixture into 4 equal sized (approximately 6 oz/180 g) balls. Push one frozen ball of bocconcini cheese into the center of each burger, folding the meat around it. Smooth the burger into a nice uniformly shaped large baseball.

• Next wrap a slice of bacon around each burger. Wrap it around the polar ends not the equator.

• Next take one hot dog and push it into one burger approximately 1–2 inches deep. Now take a second burger and push the other end of the hot dog into the burger. You are making a burger that will resemble a barbell. Repeat with remaining 2 burgers and one hot dog.

• Place one barbell burger centered on a soaked plank. Repeat with remaining burger and plank. Cover and refrigerate for 1 hour allowing the burger to rest.

• Preheat grill to medium-high, 450–550°F (230–280°C).

• Place burgers on planks on the grill and close lid. Plank bake for 25–30 minutes, checking periodically to insure the plank is not on fire, until the burgers are fully cooked (160°F).

• Remove from grill and serve.

ASSEMBLE YOUR BURGER! Serve with your favorite burger garnishes and condiments.

MAKES 2 BURGER BARBELLS

SERVES 2-4

A burger to make your friends say, "I'll be back!"

THE BILLION-DOLLAR BURGER

THE BURGER

	Napoleon Griddle Pan	
2 cups	smoked shredded beef brisket (p. 106)	500 mL
½	lobe ice-cold foie gras	½
1 Tbsp	apple butter	15 mL
½ cup	bread crumbs	125 g
Splash	Gentleman Jack Rare Tennessee Whisky	Splash
1 Tbsp	fresh thyme, chopped	15 mL
	Fleur de sel (fancy French sea salt)	
	Freshly ground black pepper to taste	
1½ lb	ice-cold Kobe beef (chuck or rib-eye or tenderloin)	750 g
2 Tbsp + 2 Tbsp	truffle oil	60 mL
1 cup	morels	250 mL
4	brioche buns	4
	butter	
	Hundred-year-old balsamic vinegar (it's sweet, fragrant and syrupy)	
½ lobe	ice-cold foie gras	½ lobe
1	small wheel (5 oz/150 g) Providence Oka or Oka or St. Pauline or a soft creamy cheese with a washed yellow-orange rind	1
4	leaves, green leaf lettuce, washed of grit and dirt and patted dry	4
1	white or black truffle, shaved	1
4	espresso spoons of Sevruga or Osetra or Beluga caviar	4
	Sprigs of thyme	
	Fleur de sel	

It's all so expensive, but so delicious!

A few years back, chefs started creating some pretty amazing —although ridiculously priced—burgers. In 2001, Daniel Boulud created a $27 (U.S.) burger that was stuffed with braised short ribs and foie gras. The burger itself was made from ground sirloin. My version is a little different, but it is still a very expensive burger. A little decadence is worth the money!

I use Kobe beef imported from Japan. The Japanese cattle are massaged daily and fed a special diet that includes lots of sake and beer. (These animals truly have only one bad day.) You can find a variety of Kobe beef from the United States, Canada and Australia. Kobe beef is high in fat and should be cooked to medium-rare at most. Search out a butcher who sells ground Kobe beef and have some fun.

NOTE: If Kobe is not in your budget, then try this burger with either ground prime rib or beef tenderloin.

THE BURGER: Place the shredded smoked beef brisket in a large bowl. Set aside.

• Break apart the lobe of foie gras and remove any veins. Keep the largest part of the lobe for slicing and pan searing. Use about half a lobe for the brisket mixture.

• Break the foie gras into 1- to 2-inch (2.5–5 cm) chunks and add to the beef brisket. Add apple butter, bread crumbs, drizzle with Gentleman Jack and add chopped fresh thyme. Season with fleur de sel (fancy French sea salt) and freshly ground black pepper. Quickly mix, making sure not to mush up the foie gras too much. Keep the chunks as large as possible.

• Cover and refrigerate for 30 minutes.

• Remove from refrigerator; scoop into 2-oz (60 g) little balls and form into a ½-inch (10 mm) thick disc. Return to the refrigerator and keep cold.

• Next, grind the Kobe beef. Grind it once and quickly, to keep the meat cold.

• Divide the ground Kobe beef into 8 equal portions. Form each portion into a 1-inch (2.5 cm) thick patty that weighs about 3 oz (90 g). Work quickly so as to not extract too much of that delicious Kobe fat—the gold of flavor.

• Place a foie gras–brisket patty on top and in the center of the burger patty. Top with a second patty, crimp and form the burger to a thickness of approximately 2 inches (5 cm). Place on a parchment-paper-lined plate, cover and refrigerate until needed.

• Preheat grill to medium-high, 450–550°F (230–280°C).

• Place Napoleon Griddle Pan on grill, with the heat underneath the pan on medium-low.

• Brush burgers with truffle oil. Grill burgers quickly for 6 to 8 minutes per side, for medium doneness and a hot inside filling. Don't you dare squish the burgers! Keep the lid open while the burgers cook. Turn the heat down if you have flare-ups.

• Drizzle griddle pan with truffle oil and sauté morels for 2 to 3 minutes, turning until tender. Remove from griddle. Set aside and keep them warm.

• Brush buns with butter. Place buns, buttered side down, on the griddle pan and fry until golden brown.

• Remove and keep warm on the upper grill rack.

• Baste burgers with really old (100 years), expensive balsamic vinegar.

• Remove from grill and allow to rest for 2 to 3 minutes.

• Cut the reserved foie gras lobe into ½-inch (1.5 cm) thick slices. Quickly pan-sear on the griddle pan for 20 to 30 seconds per side. Remove from grill and place a slice on top of each burger.

ASSEMBLE YOUR BURGERS! Griddled bun bottom, creamy Providence Oka cheese, leaf lettuce, Kobe burger, shaved white or black truffle, caviar and sprig of thyme.

• Serve with sautéed shallots and morels and drizzle with 100-year-old balsamic vinegar.

MAKES 4 VERY EXPENSIVE BUT DELICIOUS BURGERS

It's a lot of work, but so worth it!

PORK BURGERS

HOT CROSS BURGER

THE BURGER

1¼ lb	ice-cold ground pork	500 g
4 oz	black forest ham, chopped	120 g
1 Tbsp	honey mustard	15 mL
¼ cup	Bone Dust™ BBQ Seasoning (p. 39)	60 mL
¼ cup	panko (Japanese-style) bread crumbs	60 mL
1	small onion, finely diced, approximately ½ cup (125 mL)	1
2	cloves garlic, minced	2
2 Tbsp	fresh parsley, chopped	30 mL
8 slices	bacon, thick-sliced	
	Nonstick cooking spray	
½ cup	Ted's World Famous BBQ Pineapple Rum Sauce or pineapple preserves	125 mL

THE GARNISH

4	pineapple rings, fresh slices	4
	Nonstick cooking spray	
4 tsp	honey mustard	20 mL
1 cup	Muenster cheese, shredded	250 mL
4	onion or hot cross buns	4

Try these burgers served on hot cross buns. An Easter BBQ treat.

• In a large bowl, combine ground pork, ham, honey mustard, Bone Dust™ BBQ Seasoning, bread crumbs, onion, garlic and parsley. Gently mix.

• Portion burger mixture into 4 equal-sized balls. Pressing the meat gently together so it adheres, press each ball into a 1- to 1½-inch (2.5–3.5 cm) thick, uniformly shaped round burger patty.

• Criss-cross 2 slices of bacon around each patty. Place on burger patty paper, cover and refrigerate for a minimum of 1 hour, to allow the meat to rest.

• Preheat grill to medium-high, 450–550°F (230–280°C). Spray burgers with non-stick cooking spray.

• With the grill lid open, grill the burgers for 5 to 6 minutes per side, basting frequently with Pineapple Rum Sauce, until fully cooked but still moist and juicy.

• At the same time as the burgers are cooking, prepare the pineapple rings. Spray pineapple rings with nonstick cooking spray and grill for 2 to 3 minutes per side, until lightly charred and tender. Set aside and keep warm.

• Brush each burger with a little honey mustard. Top each burger with a slice of grilled pineapple and ¼ cup (60 mL) of shredded Muenster cheese. Close grill lid and heat for 1 minute to melt cheese.

• Toast buns.

• Remove burgers from grill.

ASSEMBLE YOUR BURGERS! Bun bottom, burger with grilled pineapple and cheese, bun top. (Additional garnishes of lettuce, tomato, ketchup, mustard or other burger condiments are completely optional.) Repeat with remaining burgers. Serve your burgers with a knife and fork.

NOTE: To keep your burgers juicy, do not press or poke or squish them during grilling. The squishing should only come when you try to stuff a burger into your mouth.

NOTE: I used the Napoleon Travel Q Portable Propane BBQ to grill these burgers. A great grill to take anywhere!

MAKES 4 BURGERS

JERK PORK BURGER
WITH MANGO ORANGE SALSA

MANGO ORANGE SALSA

1	ripe mango, peeled and diced ¼ inch (1 cm)	1
1	orange, peeled, segmented and diced; save the juice	1
½	red onion, diced ¼ inch (1 cm)	½
1	small red bell pepper, diced ¼ inch (1 cm)	1
1	green onion, chopped	1
1	lime, juiced	1
1 Tbsp	fresh cilantro, chopped	15 mL
1	jalapeño pepper, seeded and finely diced	1
1 Tbsp	olive oil	15 mL
	Salt and freshly ground black pepper, to taste	

JERK BBQ SAUCE

1 Tbsp	Jammin'Jerk Seasoning (p. 40)	15 mL
½ cup	gourmet-style barbecue sauce	125 mL
1	lime, juiced	1
1 Tbsp	honey	15 mL

THE BURGER

1¼ lb	ice-cold ground pork	500 g
3 Tbsp	Jammin' Jerk Seasoning (p. 40)	45 mL
2	green onions, finely chopped	2
1	small white onion, finely diced, about ½ cup (125 mL)	1
¼ cup	panko (Japanese-style) bread crumbs	60 mL
	Salt and freshly ground black pepper to taste	
	Nonstick cooking spray	

THE GARNISH

	Green leaf lettuce or coleslaw	
4	hamburger buns	4

MANGO ORANGE SALSA: In a bowl, combine diced mango, orange segments, red onion, red pepper, green onion, lime juice, reserved orange juice, cilantro, jalapeño and olive oil. Season to taste with salt and freshly ground black pepper. Transfer to a container and refrigerate.

MAKES APPROXIMATELY 2 CUPS (500 ML)

JERK BBQ SAUCE: In a bowl, whisk together jerk seasoning, barbecue sauce, lime juice and honey. Set aside.

THE BURGER: In a large bowl, combine ground pork, jerk paste, green onions, white onion and bread crumbs. Season to taste with salt and freshly ground black pepper. Gently mix.

• Portion burger mixture into 4 equal-sized balls. Pressing the meat gently together so it adheres, form each ball into a 1- to 1½-inch (2.5–3.5 cm) thick, uniformly shaped oval burger patty.

• Place on burger patty paper, cover and refrigerate for a minimum of 1 hour, to allow the meat to rest.

• Preheat grill to medium-high, 450–550°F (230–280°C).

• Spray burgers with nonstick cooking spray.

• With the grill lid open, grill the burgers for 5 to 6 minutes per side, basting frequently with reserved Jerk BBQ Sauce, until fully cooked but still moist and juicy. (Note: To keep your burgers juicy, do not press, poke or squish them while grilling. The squishing should only come when you try to stuff a burger into your mouth.)

• Toast buns.

• Remove burgers from grill.

ASSEMBLE YOUR BURGERS! Bun bottom, extra Jerk BBQ Sauce, Mango Orange Salsa, bun top. (Additional garnishes of lettuce, tomato, onions, ketchup, mustard or other burger condiments are completely optional.) Repeat with remaining burgers. Serve your burgers with a knife and fork.

MAKES 4 BURGERS

CAROLINA PULLED-PORK BURGER
WITH MUSTARD SLAW

CAROLINA PULLED-PORK

	Napoleon Charcoal Tray	
	Charcaol briquettes	
	Smoking chips (hickory, mesquite, or apple)	
1	4 lb (1.8 kg) piece of boneless pork picnic shoulder	1
3 Tbsp	Bone Dust™ BBQ Seasoning (p. 39)	45 mL
	Crushed red chili flakes, kosher salt and cracked black pepper, to taste	
¼ cup	apple juice	60 mL
¼ cup	cider vinegar	60 mL

MUSTARD COLESLAW

4 cups	white cabbage, shredded	1 L
1	small white onion, thinly sliced	1
2	green onions, chopped	1
2 Tbsp	prepared yellow mustard	30 mL
¼ cup	cider vinegar	60 mL
2 Tbsp	vegetable oil	30 mL
	Kosher salt and freshly ground black pepper, to taste	

THE BURGER

2 lb	ice-cold ground pork	907 g
1 lb	pulled pork, shredded	454 g
2 Tbsp	Bone Dust™ BBQ Seasoning (p. 39)	30 mL
1	small onion, finely diced	1
¼ cup	your favorite ale beer	60 mL
	Nonstick cooking spray	
½ cup	Ted's World Famous BBQ Crazy Canuck Sticky Chicken and Rib Sauce or your favorite BBQ sauce	125 mL

THE GARNISH

2 cups	pulled-pork, shredded	500 mL
	Mustard Coleslaw	
4	hamburger buns	4

CAROLINA PULLED-PORK: Place a mound of 12 to 15 charcoal briquettes in the center of the charcoal tray. Ignite gas burner under the charcoal tray and let it burn until the charcoal ignites. Turn off the gas. Let the coals burn to white-hot.

• Meanwhile, as the coals are getting hot, rub the boneless pork shoulder all over with the Bone Dust™ BBQ Seasoning.

• Place the pork shoulder on the other side of the grill far away from the charcoal. Add wood chips and close lid. You want to maintain a smoking temperature of 180–225°F (80–110°C).

• Replenishing coals as you need, smoke pork shoulder for 10 to 12 hours, until tender but still moist. (You should be able to easily shred the meat with two forks.)

• Shred the meat. Season with crushed red chili flakes, kosher salt, black pepper, apple juice and cider vinegar. Mix well and set aside.

MUSTARD COLESLAW: In a bowl, combine cabbage, white onion, green onions, mustard, cider vinegar and oil. Season to taste with salt and freshly ground black pepper and set aside.

THE BURGER: Set up your gas grill to accommodate the Napoleon Charcoal Tray accessory, placing the charcoal tray over the left or the right burner.

• In a large bowl, combine ground pork, shredded pulled-pork, Bone Dust™, onion and beer. Gently mix.

• Portion burger mixture into 6 equal-sized balls. Pressing the meat gently together so it adheres, form each ball into a 1- to 1½-inch (2.5–3.5 cm) thick, uniformly square-shaped burger patty. Place on burger patty paper, cover and refrigerate for a minimum of 1 hour, to allow the meat to rest.

• Preheat grill to medium-high, 450–550°F (230–280°C). Spray burgers with nonstick cooking spray.

• With the grill lid open, grill the burgers for 5 to 6 minutes per side, basting frequently with BBQ sauce, until fully cooked but still moist and juicy.

• Toast buns.

ASSEMBLE YOUR BURGERS! Bun bottom, burger, warmed pulled-pork and Mustard Coleslaw, bun top. Repeat with remaining burgers. Serve your burgers with your favorite ice-cold beer.

MAKES 6 BURGERS

LUAU BURGER

2 lb	ice-cold regular ground pork	907 g
1 cup	ham, diced	250 mL
1	small onion, finely chopped	1
4	cloves garlic, minced	4
¼ cup	Dijon mustard	60 mL
1 tsp	dried parsley, ground	5 mL
2 Tbsp	fresh parsley, chopped	30 mL
Pinch	cayenne pepper	Pinch
2 tsp	black pepper, ground	10 mL
2 tsp	red chilies, crushed	10 mL
	Salt	

THE GARNISH

8 oz	smoked ham, thinly sliced	250 g
6 or 12	burger buns	6 or 12
½ cup	butter, melted	125 mL
	Leaf lettuce	
4	slices fresh pineapple, cut into ¼-inch (.5 cm) thick rings	4
4	slices tomato	4
4	slices red onion	4

• Preheat grill to medium-high, 450–550°F (230–280°C).

• In a large bowl, mix the ground pork, diced ham, onion, garlic, Dijon mustard and dried parsley. Season to taste with chopped parsley, cayenne pepper, black pepper, red chilies and salt.

• Form into four 6-oz (180 g) patties as uniform in size as possible. (A flatter burger will cook more evenly and faster than a ball-like burger.)

• Grill burgers for 4 to 5 minutes per side, until fully cooked.

• Warm sliced ham on the grill.

• Brush burger buns with melted butter and grill, cut-side down, until crisp and golden brown.

ASSEMBLE YOUR BURGERS! Bun bottom, lettuce, burger, grilled pineapple, tomato and red onion, grill-warmed ham and bun top. Garnish with your favorite condiment and serve.

MAKES 4 BURGERS

NOTE: May is National Hamburger Month. In my world, every day is a good burger day!

HUNGARIAN SCHNITZEL BURGER

GREMOLATA

1	lemon	1
½	bunch fresh parsley, chopped	½
2 Tbsp	panko (Japanese-style) bread crumbs	30 mL
6	cloves garlic, minced	6
1–2 Tbsp	olive oil	15–30 mL
	Kosher salt and freshly ground black pepper, to taste	

SMOKED PAPRIKA MAYO

½ cup	mayonnaise	125 mL
1 tsp	lemon juice	5 mL
1 tsp	paprika, smoked	5 mL
Pinch	cayenne pepper	Pinch
	Kosher salt and freshly ground black pepper, to taste	

THE BURGER

2 lb	ice-cold ground pork	907 g
1 Tbsp	paprika, smoked	15 mL
1	small onion, minced	1
3	cloves garlic, minced	3
3 Tbsp	panko (Japanese-style) bread crumbs	45 mL
	Kosher salt and freshly ground black pepper, to taste	
	Nonstick cooking spray	

GREMOLATA: Using a rasp or a zester, remove the zest from the lemon and place in a bowl. Cut lemon in half, squeeze the juice and add to the zest. Add chopped parsley, bread crumbs, garlic and olive oil. Season to taste with kosher salt and freshly ground black pepper. Set aside.

MAKES ABOUT ¾ OF A CUP (175 ML)

SMOKED PAPRIKA MAYO: In a bowl, combine mayonnaise, lemon juice, smoked paprika and cayenne pepper. Season to taste with kosher salt and freshly ground black pepper. Set aside.

MAKES APPROXIMATELY ¾ CUP (175 ML)

THE BURGER: In a bowl, combine ground pork, smoked paprika, onion, garlic and bread crumbs. Season to taste with kosher salt and freshly ground black pepper.

• Divide mixture into 4 equal-sized balls. Flatten the balls into a large, extremely thin burger—approximately ½-inch (1.5 cm) thick at maximum.

• Place on burger patty paper, cover and refrigerate for a minimum of 1 hour, to allow the meat to rest.

• Preheat grill to medium-high, 450–550°F (230–280°C).

• Spray burgers with nonstick cooking spray.

• With the grill lid open, grill the burgers for 3 to 5 minutes per side, until fully cooked but still moist and juicy.

ASSEMBLE YOUR BURGERS! Top each Schnitzel Burger patty with a spoonful of Gremolata and serve with Smoked Paprika Mayo. Serve on warmed buns with, if you like, with pickled beets and thinly sliced cucumbers.

MAKES 4 BURGERS

SPAM BURGER

	Meat grinder	
2	tins SPAM (12 oz/348 g each), refrigerated	2
1 lb	ice-cold ground pork	454 g
¼ cup	panko (Japanese-style) bread crumbs	60 mL
½ cup	crispy fried onion pieces	125 mL
2 Tbsp	Bone Dust™ BBQ Seasoning (p. 39)	30 mL
	Nonstick cooking spray	
4	hamburger buns	4

THE GARNISH

	Shredded iceberg lettuce	
1	red tomato, sliced	
4	slices, processed cheese	4
	Prepared yellow mustard	

I am a SPAM fan. It is the quintessential canned-meat product and makes for a great burger. The folks at SPAM created a burger recipe that sometimes appears on their packaging. It is a favorite of many SPAM aficionados. For this recipe, you will need two tins of SPAM, and you'll have to grind the meat in one of them.

• Using a meat grinder or food processor, grind one tin of SPAM meat. Place in a bowl and combine with ice-cold ground pork, bread crumbs, crispy fried onion pieces and Bone Dust™ BBQ Seasoning.

• Divide mixture into 4 equal-sized balls and form into equal-sized 1-inch (1.5 cm) thick patties. Place on burger patty paper, cover and refrigerate for a minimum of 1 hour, to allow the meat to rest.

• Open the second tin of SPAM and slice meat into 8 uniform slices. Set aside.

• Preheat grill to medium-high, 450–550°F (230–280°C).

• Spray burgers and sliced SPAM with nonstick cooking spray.

• With the grill lid open, grill the burgers for 5 to 6 minutes per side, until fully cooked but still moist and juicy, and grill the sliced SPAM for 2 to 3 minutes per side. Top with processed cheese and allow cheese to melt.

• Toast buns.

ASSEMBLE YOUR BURGERS! Bun bottom, lettuce, tomato, SPAM Burger, mustard, grilled sliced SPAM, bun top.

MAKES 4 BURGERS

CRAZY CANUCK BURGER

CHEDDAR PLANKED BISCUITS

1	2-foot (60 cm) maple, oak or cedar plank, soaked in water for a minimum of 1 hour	1
1¾ cup	all-purpose flour	425 mL
1 Tbsp	baking powder	15 mL
1 Tbsp	sugar	15 mL
¼ tsp	salt	1 mL
½ cup	butter	125 mL
¾ cup	buttermilk	175 mL
1 cup	aged white cheddar, shredded	250 mL
1 Tbsp	fresh sage, chopped	15 mL
½ tsp	cracked black pepper	2.5 mL

JACK DANIEL'S BBQ SAUCE

¼ cup	Jack Daniel's Tennessee Whiskey	60 mL
¼ cup	honey	60 mL
½ cup	Ted's World Famous BBQ Crazy Canuck Sticky Chicken and Rib Sauce or your favorite BBQ sauce	125 mL
1 tsp	Bone Dust™ BBQ Seasoning (p. 39)	5 mL

THE BURGER

1 lb	ground raw pork belly	454 g
1½ lb	ground pork	675 g
¼ cup	hickory stick snacks, crushed	60 mL
2 Tbsp	Bone Dust™ BBQ Seasoning (p. 39)	30 mL
¼ cup	onion, minced	60 mL
	Nonstick cooking spray	

THE GARNISH

6	slices back bacon	6
12	slices strip bacon	12
	Lettuce	
6	slices white cheddar cheese	6
	Pickles	

TIP: To keep your burgers moist, drizzle them with a little beer while on the grill. Remember, no squishing!

Jack Daniel's is a registered trademark ©2010 Your friends at Jack remind you to drink responsibly.

I am a 100% Crazy Canuck and this is one deliciously crazy burger.

CHEDDAR PLANKED BISCUITS: In a large bowl, stir together the flour, baking powder, sugar and salt.

• Using a pastry blender, cut in the butter until the mixture resembles coarse crumbs.

• Make a well in the center. Add the buttermilk, cheddar cheese, sage and black pepper all at once. Using a wooden spoon, stir just until moistened.

• Turn out dough onto a lightly floured surface. Knead dough by folding and gently pressing for 4 to 6 strokes, or just until the dough holds together.

• Gently pat or press the dough out into a 1-inch (1.5 cm) thick, 6-inch (15 cm) wide square. Using a 3-inch (7.5 cm) pastry ring, cut the dough into 6 rounds. Evenly space the raw biscuits on the plank.

• Preheat grill to medium heat, 400°F (200°C).

• Plank-bake the biscuits for 15 to 20 minutes, until golden brown, hot and flaky.

• Set aside.

MAKES 6 BISCUITS

JACK DANIEL'S BBQ SAUCE: In a bowl, combine Jack Daniel's, honey, BBQ sauce and Bone Dust™. Mix well and set aside.

THE BURGER: In a bowl, combine ground pork belly, ground pork, hickory sticks, Bone Dust™, BBQ seasoning, and onion.

• Divide mixture into 6 equal-sized balls and form into equal-sized 1-inch (2.5 cm) thick patties.

• Place on burger patty paper, cover and refrigerate for a minimum of 1 hour, to allow the meat to rest.

• Preheat grill to medium-high, 450–550°F (230–280°C).

• Spray burgers with nonstick cooking spray.

• With the grill lid open, grill the burgers for 5 to 6 minutes per side, basting with Jack Daniel's BBQ Sauce until fully cooked but still moist and juicy.

• While the burgers are cooking, grill the back bacon. Top with cheddar cheese and allow cheese to melt.

• Slice biscuits in half and warm on the grill.

ASSEMBLE YOUR BURGERS! Biscuit bottom, lettuce, back bacon, sliced bacon, burger with cheese and biscuit top.

MAKES 6 BURGERS

OKTOBERFEST BEER-MARINATED BRATWURST BURGER

THE BURGER

8	fresh bratwurst sausages	8
½ cup	onion, finely diced	125 mL
¾ cup	pretzels, crushed	175 mL
¼ cup	crispy, fried onions	60 mL
1 Tbsp	whole grain mustard	15 mL
	Kosher salt and freshly ground black pepper to taste	
3	your favorite beer	3
	Nonstick cooking spray	
4	Bretzel buns	4

THE GARNISH

4	slices Emmenthal cheese	4
	Leaf lettuce	
	Red onions	
	Whole grain mustard or spicy German-style mustard	
1 cup	sauerkraut	250 mL

Beer and bratwurst go together like peanut butter and jelly. For this recipe, I use fresh bratwurst sausages and remove the sausage meat from the casing. It is a simple and easy way to take a sausage and make it a burger. Once the burgers are shaped, I marinate them in cold refreshing beer so that the burgers soak up loads of beer flavor. They're Beerlicious!

• Remove the casings from the fresh sausages; place the meat in a bowl and discard casings. Add diced onion, crushed pretzels, crispy onion pieces and whole grain mustard. Season with kosher salt and black pepper. Mix well.

• Divide mixture into 4 equal-sized balls and form into equal-sized 1½-inch (3.5 cm) thick patties.

• Place on burger patty paper, cover and refrigerate for a minimum of 1 hour, to allow the meat to rest.

• Place burgers in a large, deep dish, evenly spaced and lying flat. Carefully pour two bottles of beer over the burgers until they are completely immersed. Cover with plastic wrap and refrigerate; allow burgers to marinate for 1 hour.

• Preheat grill to medium-high, 450–550°F (230–280°C).

• Carefully remove the burgers from the beer marinade and discard the leftover beer.

• Spray burgers with nonstick cooking spray.

• With the grill lid open, grill the burgers for 5 to 6 minutes per side, drizzling with a little beer directly from the bottle, until burgers are fully cooked but still moist and juicy.

• Top with Emmenthal cheese and allow cheese to melt.

• Toast buns.

ASSEMBLE YOUR BURGERS! Bun bottom, lettuce, onions, burger, mustard, sauerkraut and bun top.

• Serve with pickles and ice-cold beer.

MAKES 4 BURGERS

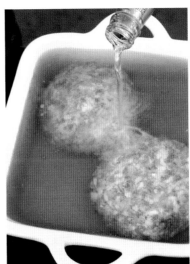

SOUVLAKI BURGER

TZATZIKI SAUCE

½ cup	shredded cucumber, squeezed of excess moisture	125 mL
2	cloves garlic, minced	2
1 Tbsp	lemon juice	15 mL
¼ cup	cream cheese, whipped	60 mL
½ cup	yogurt	125 mL
	Sea salt and freshly ground black pepper, to taste	

GREEK SALAD RELISH

8	grape tomatoes, quartered	8
1	small red onion, thinly sliced	1
1	small yellow pepper, finely diced	1
1	small seedless cucumber, halved and thinly sliced	1
¼ cup	kalamata olives, pitted and chopped	60 mL
½ cup	feta cheese, crumbled	125 mL
1	green onion, finely chopped	1
2 tsp	fresh oregano, chopped	10 mL
2 Tbsp	olive oil	30 mL
2 Tbsp	lemon juice	30 mL
	Kosher salt and freshly ground black pepper, to taste	

THE BURGER

2 lb	ice-cold ground pork	907 g
½ cup	bread crumbs	125 mL
1	egg	1
1	small sweet onion, finely diced	1
8	cloves garlic, minced	8
1 Tbsp	fresh oregano, chopped	15 mL
Big Splash	ouzo	Big Splash
	Nonstick cooking spray	
4	Greek-style pitas	4
	Leaf lettuce	

TZATZIKI SAUCE: In a bowl, mix cucumber, garlic, lemon juice, cream cheese and yogurt. Then season to taste with sea salt and freshly ground black pepper. Cover and refrigerate for at least 1 hour.

MAKE APPROXIMATELY 1½ CUPS (375 ML)

GREEK SALAD RELISH: In a bowl, combine tomatoes, red onion, yellow pepper, cucumber, olives, feta, green onion, oregano, olive oil and lemon juice. Season to taste with kosher salt and freshly ground black pepper and mix well. Cover and refrigerate until needed.

THE BURGER: In a bowl, combine ground pork, bread crumbs, egg, onion, garlic and oregano. Add a big splash of ouzo and mix well.

• Divide mixture into 4 equal-sized balls and form into equal-sized 1½-inch (3.5 cm) thick patties. Place on burger patty paper, cover and refrigerate for a minimum of 1 hour, to allow the meat to rest.

• Preheat grill to medium-high, 450–550°F (230–280°C).

• Spray burgers with nonstick cooking spray.

• With the grill lid open, grill the burgers for 5 to 6 minutes per side, until fully cooked but still moist and juicy.

• Warm pitas.

ASSEMBLE YOUR BURGERS! Spread Tzatziki Sauce on the pitas, top with lettuce, burger and Greek Salad Relish.

MAKES 4 BURGERS

BRUSCHETTA BURGER

TOMATO BRUSCHETTA

6	plum tomatoes, diced	6
1	small onion, finely diced	1
2	cloves garlic, minced	2
2	green onions, finely chopped	2
¼ tsp	cracked black pepper	1 mL
2 Tbsp	Parmesan cheese, grated	30 mL
1 Tbsp	white balsamic vinegar	15 mL
2 Tbsp	olive oil	30 mL
	Salt, to taste	
½ bunch	chopped fresh basil	½ bunch

THE BURGER

1½ lb	ice-cold ground pork	675 g
4	slices prosciutto, sliced into small strips	4
4	cloves garlic, roasted	4
1 Tbsp	fresh oregano, chopped	15 mL
3 Tbsp	Parmesan cheese, grated	45 mL
1 Tbsp	olive oil	15 mL
1 tsp	red chilies, crushed	5 mL
1 tsp	kosher salt	5 mL
½ tsp	black pepper, coarsely ground	2.5 mL
4	Italian-style rolls	4
4	slices provolone cheese	4
1	bunch arugula	1
4	slices prosciutto	4
	Arugula	
	Provolone cheese	

While traveling through Italy I had a burger that was similar to this. Where, I couldn't tell ya. There was far too much wine and beer involved! Serve it on crisp, Italian bread and load it with lots of garlic. Ciao baby!

TOMATO BRUSCHETTA: In a bowl, combine plum tomatoes, onion, garlic, green onions, black pepper, Parmesan, vinegar and olive oil. Season to taste with salt, then cover and refrigerate until needed.

• Just before garnishing your burgers with the Tomato Bruschetta, add the chopped fresh basil. Adjust seasoning.

MAKES APPROXIMATELY 2 CUPS (500 ML)

THE BURGER: In a bowl, combine ice-cold ground pork, prosciutto, roasted garlic, oregano, Parmesan cheese, olive oil, chilies, kosher salt and black pepper.

• Form into four 6-oz (180 mL) uniformly shaped burger patties. Place on a plate and refrigerate for 1 hour, allowing the meat to rest.

• Preheat grill to medium-high, 450–550°F (230–280°C).

• Brush burgers lightly with olive oil.

• Grill burgers for 5 to 6 minutes per side for medium-well doneness but burgers that are still moist and juicy.

• Toast rolls.

• Top each burger with a slice of provolone cheese, close lid and allow cheese to melt for 1 minute.

• Remove from grill.

ASSEMBLE YOUR BURGERS! Top of roll, arugula, burger, Tomato Bruschetta and a rolled slice of prosciutto and add roll top.

MAKES 4 BURGERS

CAMPFIRE PORK AND BEAN BURGER

HONEY MUSTARD DRESSING

2 Tbsp	prepared mustard	30 mL
2 Tbsp	honey	30 mL
2 Tbsp	cider vinegar	30 mL
2	cloves garlic, minced	2
1 Tbsp	parsley, chopped	15 mL
1 Tbsp	lemon juice	15 mL
2 Tbsp	warm bacon fat	30 mL
	Salt and freshly ground black pepper, to taste	

MULTI-BEAN AND BACON SALAD

6 cups	water	1.5 L
2 tsp	salt	10 mL
1½ cups	green beans	375 mL
1½ cups	yellow wax beans	375 mL
½ cup	white navy beans, cooked	125 mL
1	small red onion, thinly sliced	1
8	slices sliced bacon, cooked	8
1 Tbsp	fresh parsley, chopped	15 mL

THE BURGER

1½ lb	ice-cold ground pork	675 g
½ cup	double-smoked bacon, diced	125 mL
1	small onion, diced	1
1 Tbsp	brown sugar	15 mL
1 Tbsp	Dijon mustard	15 mL
1 Tbsp	ketchup	15 mL
1 cup	baked beans, straight from the tin	250 mL
1 tsp	Worcestershire sauce	5 mL
1 Tbsp	Bone Dust™ BBQ Seasoning (p. 39)	15 mL
	Nonstick cooking spray	

This burger looks too fancy for a campout, but it's delicious. Load on the beans! I love this burger!

HONEY MUSTARD DRESSING: In a bowl, combine mustard, honey, cider vinegar, garlic, parsley and lemon juice. Heat the bacon fat in microwave for 30 seconds on medium-high, until warm and liquid.

• While stirring the honey mustard mixture, add the bacon fat in a steady stream so that it emulsifies in the dressing. Season to taste with salt and pepper and set aside.

MULTI-BEAN AND BACON SALAD: Bring 6 cups (1.5 L) of water to a rolling boil. Add salt, then add the green and yellow beans and blanch for 30 seconds, until the beans are bright in color and crisp tender. Drain and cool under cold running water, then drain again.

• In a bowl, combine blanched green and yellow beans, white navy beans, red onion, bacon and parsley. Add reserved Honey Mustard Dressing, season to taste with salt and freshly ground black pepper and set aside.

THE BURGER: In a bowl, combine ice-cold ground pork, bacon, onion, brown sugar, mustard, ketchup, baked beans, Worcestershire sauce and Bone Dust™ BBQ Seasoning.

• Form into six 6-oz (175 g) uniformly shaped burger patties. Place on a plate and refrigerate for 1 hour, allowing the meat to rest.

• Preheat grill to medium-high, 450–550°F (230–280°C).

• Spray burgers lightly with nonstick cooking spray.

• Grill burgers for 5 to 6 minutes per side for medium-well doneness but burgers that are still moist and juicy.

• Remove from grill.

ASSEMBLE YOUR BURGERS! Multi-Bean and Bacon Salad with Honey Mustard Dressing, Campfire Pork and Bean Burgers.

MAKES 6 BURGERS

HOLY CHOW SWEET AND SOUR BURGER

SWEET AND SOUR GLAZING SAUCE

½ cup	plum sauce	125 mL
¼ cup	Thai sweet chili sauce	60 mL
2 Tbsp	rice wine vinegar	30 mL
2	cloves garlic, minced	2
1 tsp	ginger, minced	5 mL

THE BURGER

1½ lb	ice-cold ground pork	675 g
2 tsp	ginger, minced	10 mL
4	cloves garlic, minced	4
2	green onions, chopped	2
¼ cup	Thai sweet chili sauce	60 mL
2 Tbsp	rice vinegar	30 mL
2 Tbsp	plum sauce	30 mL
½ cup	panko (Japanese-style) bread crumbs	125 mL
½ tsp	cayenne pepper	2.5 mL
1 tsp	ground black pepper	5 mL
2 tsp	salt	10 mL

WOK GRILL FRY

	Napoleon Griddle Pan	
8	shiitake mushrooms, thinly sliced	8
1	small white onion, thinly sliced	1
1	small red bell pepper, thinly sliced	1
1	head broccolini, cut into 1-inch (2.5 cm) lengths	1
2	green onions, thinly sliced	2
1 cup	bean sprouts	250 mL
4	cloves garlic, minced	4
1 tsp	fresh ginger, chopped	5 mL
3 Tbsp + 3 Tbsp	vegetable oil	45 mL + 45 mL
¼ tsp	sesame oil	1 mL
1 tsp	sambal chili sauce	5 mL
1 Tbsp	soy sauce	15 mL
1 Tbsp	rice wine vinegar	15 mL
1 Tbsp	mirin	15 mL
	Nonstick cooking spray	

SWEET AND SOUR GLAZING SAUCE: In a bowl, whisk together the plum sauce, Thai sweet chili sauce, rice vinegar, garlic and ginger. Set aside.

THE BURGER: In a bowl, combine ice-cold ground pork, minced ginger, garlic, green onions, Thai sweet chili sauce, rice vinegar, plum sauce, panko bread crumbs, cayenne pepper, black pepper and salt. Mix well but gently.

• Form into twelve 2-oz (60 g) mini burger patties.

• Place on a plate and refrigerate for 1 hour, allowing the meat to rest.

WOK GRILL FRY: In a bowl, combine mushrooms and white onion. Set aside. In another bowl, combine red bell pepper, broccolini and green onions. Set aside. In a third bowl, combine bean sprouts, garlic and ginger and set aside. And in a fourth bowl, combine 3 Tbsp (45 mL) of vegetable oil with the sesame oil, sambal chili sauce, soy sauce, rice wine vinegar and mirin.

• Place a seasoned Napoleon Griddle Pan on your grill.

• Preheat grill to medium-high, 450–550°F (230–280°C).

• Spray burgers lightly with nonstick cooking spray.

• Grill burgers for 5 to 6 minutes per side, basting liberally with reserved Sweet and Sour Glazing Sauce, for medium-well doneness but burgers that are still moist and juicy.

• While the burgers are grilling, season griddle pan with 1 to 2 Tbsp (15–30 mL) of oil and heat for 1 minute.

• Add mushrooms and white onion mix and sauté for 2 to 3 minutes, stirring frequently to keep from burning, until tender and lightly browned.

• Add a little more oil and pepper–broccolini–green onion mix; stir quickly, until broccolini is bright green.

• Add bean sprouts–garlic–ginger mix and stir it all up. Add the sesame oil–sambal chili–soy sauce–rice wine vinegar–mirin mix and stir. Season to taste with a little salt and pepper, turn burner under griddle pan off and keep warm.

• Remove from grill.

ASSEMBLE YOUR BURGERS! Wok Grill Fry, Burgers and extra sauce. Serve with steamed rice, if desired.

MAKES 12 MINI BURGERS

HARMONY BURGER

Napoleon Griddle Pan

1 lb	ice-cold finely ground pork	454 g
1 lb	ice-cold coarsely ground pork	454 g
½ cup	white bread crumbs, finely ground	125 mL
2	large egg whites	2
1 Tbsp	salt	15 mL
2 tsp	white pepper, ground	10 mL
1 Tbsp	mustard powder	15 mL
½ tsp	cayenne pepper	2.5 mL
1 Tbsp	Bone Dust™ BBQ Seasoning (p. 39)	15 mL
4	cloves garlic	4
1	small onion	1
1 Tbsp + 3 Tbsp	vegetable shortening or butter or oil	15 mL + 45 mL
6	Hamburger buns	6
2	large onions, sliced	2

The Harmony Lunch Counter in Waterloo, Ontario has the most amazing pork burgers. If you're in the neighborhood, it's a must try!

• Put the finely and coarsely ground pork, bread crumbs, egg whites, salt, white pepper, mustard powder, cayenne pepper and Bone Dust™ BBQ Seasoning into the bowl of a stand mixer.

• In a food processor, blend the garlic and onions until smooth. Strain to remove excess moisture.

• Add onion and garlic-pulp to the pork mixture.

• Beat ground pork mixture on low speed for 1 to 2 minutes, until smooth.

• Beat on medium-high for 10 seconds.

• Transfer to a bowl. Cover and refrigerate for 1 hour.

• Scoop the pork using a 3- to 4-oz (100–120 g) ice-cream scoop and pressing the meat to pack firm. Unmold from scoop and set aside. Continue until all the meat has been scooped.

• Set up your grill with the Napoleon Griddle Pan accessory.

• Sauté onions in 1 Tbsp (15 mL) vegetable shortening for 15 to 20 minutes, stirring until onions are tender and golden brown. Remove from griddle and set aside, keeping warm.

• Melt ½ tsp (2.5 mL) of the shortening, per burger, on the griddle pan over medium-high heat.

• Place 1 harmony scoop, flat-side down, into the fry pan and flatten, by pressing with a spatula, to the thickness of ½ inch (1.5 cm). Repeat with 2 to 3 more burgers.

• Fry burgers for 2 to 3 minutes per side, until fully cooked.

• Toast buns.

ASSEMBLE YOUR BURGERS! Bun bottom, mustard, burger, onions, bun top.

MAKES 6 BURGERS

Yeah, these are addictive!

VEAL BURGERS

INFRARED BLACKENED VEAL BURGER   155
   WITH VOODOO RELISH

VEAL BURGER   156
   WITH KING OYSTER MUSHROOM CREAM SAUCE

GREEN CHILI BASIL PESTO VEAL BURGER   159
   WITH PANCETTA & TALEGGIO CHEESE

BBQ VEAL BURGER   160
   WITH POKER CHIP SALAD

INFRARED BLACKENED VEAL BURGER
WITH VOODOO RELISH

VOODOO RELISH

2	large red bell peppers, cut in half and seeded	2
4	jalapeño peppers	4
	Olive oil	
1	medium sweet onion, sliced into rounds	1
1 Tbsp	red chili peppers, crushed	15 mL
3	cloves garlic, minced	3
½ cup	sugar	125 mL
¼ cup	water	60 mL
	Salt	
1 Tbsp	hot sauce	15 mL

THE BURGER

2 lb	ice-cold ground veal	907 g
2 Tbsp + 4 Tbsp	Hot and Spicy Bone Dust™ BBQ Seasoning (p. 43)	30 mL + 60 mL
½ cup	onion, diced	125 mL
3	cloves garlic, minced	3
3 Tbsp	Voodoo Relish	45 mL
½ cup	panko (Japanese-style) bread crumbs	125 mL
4 Tbsp	butter, melted	60 mL
6	onion buns	6

A tribute to all the folks in New Orleans.

VOODOO RELISH: Preheat grill to medium-high, 450–550°F (230–280°C).

• Brush peppers and onions lightly with olive oil. Grill peppers and onions for 10 to 15 minutes, turning occasionally, until lightly charred and tender. Remove from grill and allow peppers and onions to cool.

• Dice grilled red peppers, onion and jalapeño peppers and place in a medium-sized saucepan. Add crushed red chilies, garlic, sugar and water. Bring mixture to a slow boil, stirring to keep from scorching. Add salt and hot sauce and continue to cook for 10 minutes, until peppers and onions are tender and the relish is thick.

• Remove from heat and cool. Cover and refrigerate until needed.

MAKES APPROXIMATELY 4 CUPS (1 L)

THE BURGER: In a bowl, combine ice-cold ground veal, Hot and Spicy Bone Dust™, onion, garlic, Voodoo Relish and bread crumbs.

• Form into six 6-oz (180 g) burgers, approximately 1½ inches (3.5 cm) thick and 4 inches (10 cm) in diameter. Place on a plate and refrigerate for 1 hour.

• Brush the burgers with melted butter and sprinkle liberally on both sides with Hot and Spicy Bone Dust™ BBQ Seasoning. Return to the refrigerator to set for 30 minutes.

• Preheat the Sizzle Zone™ on Napoleon Grill to 1800°F (900°C). That's hot, baby!

• Grill burgers over infrared for 4 to 5 minutes per side, to cook quickly, blacken the outside, yet keep burgers moist and juicy.

• Toast buns.

ASSEMBLE YOUR BURGERS! Bun bottom, Blackened Veal Burger, Voodoo Relish, bun top. Garnish with your other burger favorites.

MAKES 6 BURGERS

NOTE: Napoleon Infrared Grills get up to 1800°F in 25 seconds flat. Now that's grilling excitement!

VEAL BURGER
WITH KING OYSTER MUSHROOM CREAM SAUCE

KING OYSTER MUSHROOM CREAM SAUCE

8	king oyster mushrooms	8
¼ cup	olive oil	60 mL
¼ cup	rice wine vinegar	60 mL
2 Tbsp	butter	30 mL
6	cloves garlic, minced	6
¼ cup	onion, diced	60 mL
2 Tbsp	Dijon Mustard	30 mL
¼ cup	Lindemans Bin 65 Chardonnay	60 mL
½ cup	cream cheese	125 mL
½ cup	whipping 35% cream	125 mL
2 Tbsp	soft goat cheese	30 mL
2 Tbsp	fresh chives, chopped	30 mL
	Salt and pepper, to taste	

THE BURGER

1½ lb	ice-cold ground veal	675 g
3 Tbsp	Orgasmic Onion Burger Seasoning (p. 44)	45 mL
¼ cup	corn flake crumbs	60 mL
	Nonstick cooking spray	
4	egg buns	4

King oyster mushrooms are great for grilling. They are firm-fleshed and have a sweet and nutty flavor that blends well with veal.

KING OYSTER MUSHROOM CREAM SAUCE: Preheat grill to medium-high, 450–550°F (230–280°C).

• Slice king oyster mushrooms in half or in three, lengthways, depending on the thickness of the stem, and place in a bowl. Season with olive oil, rice vinegar, salt and freshly ground black pepper.

• Grill slices of king oyster mushrooms for 4 to 5 minutes per side, until lightly charred and tender. Remove from grill and allow mushrooms to cool.

• Take half of the grilled mushrooms and set aside for garnishing your burger. Drizzle with a little olive oil and rice vinegar to keep moist. Take the remaining half of the grilled king oyster mushrooms and dice into ¼-inch (.5 cm) cubes. Set aside.

• In medium saucepot over medium-high, melt the butter. Add the garlic and onion and sauté for 1 to 2 minutes, until tender. Add the reserved diced king oyster mushrooms and continue to sauté for 1 to 2 more minutes. Add Dijon mustard and stir. Add white wine. Bring mixture to a boil and stir in cream cheese and heavy cream. Bring to boil again, lower heat to simmer and allow mixture to reduce and thicken, stirring occasionally to keep from burning. Remove from heat once thick and creamy and stir in goat cheese and chives and season to taste with salt and freshly ground black pepper.

• Set aside and keep warm.

THE BURGER: In a bowl, combine ground veal, Orgasmic Onion Burger Seasoning and corn flake crumbs. Mix well and form into four 6-oz (180 g) burgers. Place on a plate, cover and refrigerate for 1 hour.

• Preheat grill to medium-high, 450–550°F (230–280°C).

• Spray burgers with nonstick cooking spray.

• Grill burgers for 5 to 6 minutes per side, until well-done but still moist and juicy.

• Toast buns.

ASSEMBLE YOUR BURGERS! Bun bottom, burger, reserved slices of grilled king oyster mushrooms, King Oyster Mushroom Cream Sauce, and finish with bun top.

MAKES 4 BURGERS

GREEN CHILI BASIL PESTO VEAL BURGER
WITH PANCETTA & TALEGGIO CHEESE

GREEN CHILI BASIL PESTO

2	bunches basil	2
8	cloves garlic	8
1–2	green chili pepper, seeds and membrane removed and minced	1–2
¼ cup	pine nuts	60 mL
½ cup	olive oil	125 mL
2 Tbsp	lemon juice	30 mL
	Salt and pepper, to taste	

THE BURGER

1½ lb	ice-cold ground veal	675 g
3 Tbsp	Better Butter Burger Seasoning (p. 39)	45 mL
3 Tbsp	green chili basil pesto	45 mL
¼ cup	panko (Japanese-style) bread crumbs	60 mL
1	egg	1
	Nonstick cooking spray	
8	slices pancetta	8
8	thick slices Taleggio cheese	8
4	ciabatta buns	4

GREEN CHILI BASIL PESTO: In a food processor, pulse basil, garlic, chili pepper and pine nuts. With the machine running, add oil in a steady stream, until oil is emulsified and mixture is smooth. Add in lemon juice, season with salt and pepper to taste and set aside.

THE BURGER: In a bowl, combine ground veal, Better Butter Burger Seasoning, green chili basil pesto, panko bread crumbs and egg. Mix well and form into four 6-oz (180 g) burgers. Place on a plate, cover and refrigerate for 1 hour.

• Preheat grill to medium high, 450–550°F (230–280°C).

• Spray burgers with nonstick cooking spray.

• Grill burgers for 5 to 6 minutes per side, until well-done but still moist and juicy.

• While the burgers are grilling, grill the pancetta for 1 to 2 minutes per side, until crispy.

• Set aside and keep warm.

• Spread the top of each burger with about a tablespoon (15 mL) of Green Chili Basil Pesto. Top with Taleggio cheese and close lid, allowing cheese to melt.

• Toast buns.

ASSEMBLE YOUR BURGERS! Bun bottom, burger with pesto and Taleggio, pancetta, bun top. Serve immediately.

MAKES 4 BURGERS

NOTE: It's not always easy to find Taleggio cheese. If you can't find it, substitute with Buffalo Mozarella, grated Fontina, or Gorgonzola.

BBQ VEAL BURGER
WITH POKER CHIP SALAD

POKER CHIP SALAD

2 cups	orange carrots, thinly sliced in rounds	500 mL
2 cups	yellow, red, candy cane or maroon carrots, thinly sliced in rounds (you will find multicolored carrots in specialty produce stores)	500 mL
2 cups	seedless cucumber, thinly sliced in rounds	500 mL
1 cup	red radish, thinly sliced in rounds	250 mL
1 cup	daikon radish, thinly sliced in rounds	250 mL
¼ cup	sweet onion, finely diced	60 mL
2	green onions, finely chopped	2

BBQ DRESSING

¼ cup	Ted's World Famous BBQ Crazy Canuck Sticky Chicken and Rib Sauce or your favorite gourmet-style BBQ sauce	60 mL
¼ cup	tomato chili sauce	60 mL
1 oz	Jack Daniel's Tennessee Whiskey	30 mL
1 Tbsp	prepared horseradish	15 mL
3 Tbsp	cider vinegar	45 mL
3 Tbsp	olive oil	45 mL
Dash	hot sauce	Dash
Dash	Worcestershire sauce	Dash
1 tsp	Bone Dust™ BBQ Seasoning (p. 39)	5 mL

THE BURGER

2¼ lb	ice-cold ground veal	1 kg
2 Tbsp	butter, softened	30 mL
3 Tbsp	Bone Dust™ BBQ Seasoning (p. 39)	45 mL
¼ cup	Ted's World Famous BBQ Crazy Canuck Sticky Chicken and Rib Sauce or your favorite gourmet-style BBQ sauce	60 mL
3 Tbsp	panko (Japanese-style) bread crumbs	45 mL
2 tsp	Worcestershire sauce	10 mL
Big Splash	Jack Daniel's Tennessee Whiskey	Big Splash

Little burgers, fast grilling and lots of crunchy vegetables.

POKER CHIP SALAD: When buying the vegetables for this salad, purchase ones with a similar diameter so that when you slice them in rounds, they look like different-colored poker chips.

• Bring 6 cups (1.5 L) of water to a rolling boil. Add sliced carrots and blanch for 2 to 3 minutes, until the carrots are just starting to soften. Drain and rinse under cold, running water to cool. Drain again. In a large bowl, combine the blanched carrots, cucumber, red radish, daikon radish, diced sweet onion and green onions. Set aside.

BBQ DRESSING: In a separate bowl, whisk together the BBQ sauce, chili sauce, Jack Daniel's, horseradish, cider vinegar and olive oil. Season to taste with a dash of hot sauce, a dash of Worcestershire sauce and Bone Dust™ BBQ Seasoning. Pour half the dressing over the Poker Chip Salad, gently mix, cover and refrigerate for at least 1 hour to marinate. Transfer remaining dressing to a small container and reserve for basting your burgers.

MAKES APPROXIMATELY 1 CUP

THE BURGER: In a bowl, combine ice-cold ground veal, softened butter, Bone Dust™ BBQ Seasoning, BBQ sauce, bread crumbs and Worcestershire sauce. Add a big splash of Jack Daniel's and mix.

• Form into twelve 3-oz (100 g) burgers, approximately 1 inch (2.5 cm) thick and 3 inches (7.5 cm) in diameter. Place on a parchment-paper-lined plate and refrigerate for a minimum of 1 hour.

• Preheat grill to medium-high, 450–550°F (230–280°C).

• Spray burgers with nonstick cooking spray.

• Grill burgers for 4 to 6 minutes per side, basting with reserved BBQ dressing, until fully cooked but still moist and juicy.

• Remove from grill.

ASSEMBLE YOUR BURGERS! Poker Chip Salad topped with 2 Barbecue Veal Burgers.

MAKES 12 BURGERS

Jack Daniel's is a registered trademark ©2010.
Your friends at Jack remind you to drink responsibly.

Lamb Burger with Grilled Haloumi Cheese and
Kalamata Olive Tapenade (p. 166)

LAMB BURGERS

LAMB ROTI BURGER

CURRIED POTATOES

2 lb	Yukon Gold potatoes, cut into 1-inch to 2-inch (2.5–5 cm) chunks	907 g
2 Tbsp	olive oil	30 mL
3 Tbsp	yellow curry powder	45 mL
1	medium onion, diced	1
4	cloves garlic, minced	4
1 Tbsp	fresh thyme, chopped	15 mL
	Salt and freshly ground black pepper, to taste	
6 cups	chicken stock	1.5 L

WEST INDIAN HOT PEPPER SAUCE

2-4	Scotch Bonnet peppers, stems removed	2-4
¼ cup	cane vinegar	60 mL
1 tsp	sugar	5 mL
1 tsp	salt	5 mL

THE BURGER

1½ lb	ice-cold ground lamb	675 g
1 cup	onion, minced	250 mL
4	cloves garlic, minced	4
1 tsp	fresh ginger, chopped	5 mL
2	green onions, finely chopped	2
1 Tbsp	fresh thyme, chopped	15 mL
2 Tbsp	Bone Dust™ BBQ Seasoning (p. 39)	30 mL
1 Tbsp	yellow curry powder	15 mL
½ cup	bread crumbs	125 mL
1	small egg	1
	Nonstick cooking spray	
2	plum tomatoes, sliced into small wedges	2
1	small white onion, sliced	1
½	seedless cucumber, thinly sliced	½
2	green onions, chopped	2
1 Tbsp	fresh cilantro, chopped	15 mL
Drizzle	olive oil	Drizzle
Drizzle	cane vinegar	Drizzle
	Salt and pepper to taste	
8	precooked roti breads	8

You can find baked roti dough in ethnic and West-Indian grocery stores.

CURRIED POTATOES: Preheat oven to 375°F (190°C).

• Place the diced potatoes in a large bowl. Add olive oil, curry powder, onion, garlic and thyme. Season to taste with salt and freshly ground black pepper. Pour potatoes into an ovenproof dish approximately 4 inches (10 cm) deep. Add chicken stock and cover tightly with aluminum foil.

• Place in oven and bake for 50 to 60 minutes, until the potatoes are fork-tender and the liquid is mostly absorbed.

• Remove from oven and keep warm.

WEST INDIAN HOT PEPPER SAUCE: In a food processor, combine the Scotch Bonnet peppers, cane vinegar, sugar and salt. Pulse until smooth. Transfer to a small saucepot and heat slowly over medium heat, stirring occasionally, until mixture reaches a boil. Using a hand blender, purée until smooth; allow to cool. Transfer to a clean container and refrigerate until needed.

THE BURGER: In a bowl, combine ground lamb, onion, garlic, ginger, green onions, thyme, Bone Dust™, curry powder, bread crumbs and egg. Mix well and form into twelve 2-oz (60 g) burgers approximately ½ to 1 inch (2–2.5 cm) thick and 2 inches (5 cm) in diameter. Place on a plate, cover and refrigerate for 1 hour.

• Preheat grill to medium-high, 450–550°F (230–280°C).

• Spray burgers with nonstick cooking spray.

• Grill burgers for 4 to 6 minutes per side, until well-done but still moist and juicy.

• While the burgers are grilling, combine in a large bowl the tomatoes, onion, cucumber, green onions and cilantro. Drizzle with a little olive oil and cane vinegar, and season to taste with salt and freshly ground black pepper. Set aside.

• Warm roti bread until crisp and heated through.

ASSEMBLE YOUR BURGERS! Place a roti on a plate. Top with a cup (250 mL) of warmed Curried Potatoes and top with three lamb burgers. Drizzle with West Indian Hot Pepper Sauce. Top with tomato-cucumber-onion salad and finish with roti top. Serve immediately.

MAKES 4 BURGERS

LAMB BURGER
WITH GRILLED HALOUMI CHEESE AND KALAMATA OLIVE TAPENADE

KALAMATA OLIVE TAPENADE

1 cup	kalamata olives, pitted	250 mL
3	cloves garlic, minced	3
1 Tbsp	ouzo	15 mL
1	anchovy	1
1 Tbsp	fresh oregano, chopped	15 mL
1 Tbsp	lemon juice	15 mL
1	green onion, chopped	1
2 Tbsp	olive oil	30 mL
	Salt and freshly ground black pepper, to taste	

THE BURGER

1¼ lb	ice-cold ground lamb	500 g
6	cloves garlic, minced	6
1 Tbsp	Dijon mustard	15 mL
2 Tbsp	fresh rosemary, chopped	30 mL
	oregano	
Splash	Worcestershire sauce	Splash
1 tsp	black pepper, freshly ground	5 mL
	Kosher salt, to taste	
4 + 4	slices Haloumi cheese, approximately 2 inches (5 cm) square and ½ inch (1.5 cm) thick	4 + 4
	Nonstick cooking spray	
4	Greek-style pitas	4
	Olive oil	
	Vine-ripened tomatoes, sliced	

Haloumi cheese, is a wonderful grilling cheese. Its firmness allows for good grilling as it doesn't completely melt through the grill.

KALAMATA OLIVE TAPENADE: In a food processor, place the kalamata olives, garlic, ouzo, anchovy, oregano, lemon juice, green onion and olive oil. Put on lid and purée until smooth. Transfer mixture to a bowl, and season to taste with salt and freshly ground black pepper. Cover and refrigerate until needed.

THE BURGER: In a large bowl, combine ground lamb, garlic, mustard, rosemary and oregano. Season to taste with a splash or two of Worcestershire sauce, freshly ground black pepper and kosher salt. Gently mix.

• Portion burger mixture into 8 equal-sized balls, pressing the meat gently together so it adheres. Form each ball into a 1- to 1 ½-inch (2.5–3.5 cm) thick oval-shaped burger patty.

• Place four patties on a flat work surface. Place a slice of Haloumi cheese on top of each patty, and place a second burger patty on top of that. Flatten and crimp the edges to seal, creating a stuffed burger. Place on burger patty paper, cover and refrigerate for a minimum of 1 hour, to allow the meat to rest.

• Preheat grill to medium-high, 450–550°F (230–280°C).

• Spray burgers with nonstick cooking spray.

With the grill lid open, grill the burgers for 5 to 6 minutes per side, until fully cooked but still moist and juicy.

• While the burgers are grilling, lightly spray the reserved 4 slices of Haloumi cheese with nonstick cooking spray. Grill cheese for 1 to 2 minutes per side, until warmed and lightly charred.

• Brush pitas lightly with olive oil and season to taste with salt and freshly ground black pepper. Grill to toast.

• Remove burgers from grill.

ASSEMBLE YOUR BURGERS! Grilled pita, Kalamata Olive Tapenade, sliced tomato, burger and grilled Haloumi cheese.

MAKES 8 BURGERS

Serve with Lindemans Bin 40 Merlot.

STUFFED BISTRO LAMB BURGER

WITH SMOKED GRUYÈRE, MASHED POTATO CRUST, AND RED WINE SHALLOT GRAVY

RED WINE SHALLOT GRAVY

¼ cup	butter	60 mL
3 cups	shallots, sliced	750 mL
4	cloves garlic, minced	4
1 Tbsp	fresh rosemary, chopped	15 mL
¼ cup	all-purpose flour	60 mL
1½ cups	lamb or beef stock	375 mL
½ cup	Lindemans Bin 45 Cabernet Sauvignon	125 mL
½ cup	steak sauce (HP or similar)	125 mL
1 tsp	Worcestershire sauce	5 mL
	Salt and pepper, to taste	

THE BURGER

2 lb	ice-cold ground lamb	907 g
2	cloves garlic, minced	2
3	shallots, finely chopped	3
3 Tbsp	Ted's World Famous BBQ Crazy Canuck Sticky Chicken and Rib Sauce	45 mL
1 Tbsp	fresh rosemary, chopped	15 mL
	Salt and black pepper, to taste	
2 cups	smoked Gruyère cheese, grated	500 mL
2 cups	Creamy Mashed Potatoes (p. 105)	500 mL
6	sourdough burger buns	6
	butter, melted	

My friend Christine Chamberlaine shared this recipe with me. Lamb burgers topped with mashed potatoes and gravy—to die for!

RED WINE SHALLOT GRAVY: In a medium saucepan, melt the butter over medium heat. Sauté the shallots and garlic for 10 to 15 minutes, stirring occasionally, until the shallots are tender and caramelized golden brown. Add the rosemary and flour and cook, stirring constantly, for 4 to 5 minutes, being careful not to burn the flour. Add the lamb stock ½ cup (125 mL) at a time, stirring constantly, until smooth and thickened. Stir in the red wine and steak sauce and reduce heat to low. Simmer for 15 minutes, stirring occasionally. Season to taste with salt and pepper. Keep warm until needed.

THE BURGER: In a large bowl, combine the ice-cold ground lamb, garlic, shallots, BBQ sauce and rosemary. Season to taste with salt and black pepper.

• Form into twelve 3-oz (90 g) uniform patties.

• Form the grated smoked Gruyère cheese into six 2-oz (60 g) pucks a little smaller than the diameter of the patty, pressing firmly.

• Place a puck of cheese on 6 of the patties, cover with the remaining patties and press the edges together to seal and encase the smoked Gruyère cheese. Cover and refrigerate for 1 hour, to allow the meat to set.

• Preheat grill to medium-high, 450–550°F (230–280°C).

• Grill burgers for 6 to 8 minutes per side for medium-well.

• Brush burger buns with melted butter and grill, cut-side down, until crisp and golden brown.

ASSEMBLE YOUR BURGERS! Place a stuffed burger on the base of each toasted bun. Top with a scoop of Creamy Mashed Potatoes (p. 105). Ladle Red Wine Shallot Gravy over the potatoes and burgers. Eat with a knife and fork.

MAKES 12 BURGERS

KARELA COCONUT LAMB BURGER

POMEGRANATE GLAZE

¼ cup	pomegranate molasses	60 mL
¼ cup	frozen blueberries	60 mL
¼ cup	honey	60 mL
1 oz	Chambord Black Raspberry Liqueur	30 mL

THE BURGER

1½ lb	ice-cold ground lamb	675 g
1 Tbsp	pomegranate molasses	15 mL
4	cloves garlic, minced	4
1	small onion, diced	1
1 Tbsp	Worcestershire sauce	15 mL
1–2	hot green chili peppers, minced	1–2
2 Tbsp	fresh cilantro, chopped	30 mL
2 tsp	black pepper, ground	10 mL
1 tsp	cumin, ground	5 mL
2 tsp	curry powder	10 mL
¼ cup	golden raisins	60 mL
¼ cup + ½ cup	unsweetened coconut, grated	60 mL + 125 mL
	Salt, to taste	
	Golden Delicious apple slices, 4½ inches (1.5 cm) thick	
	Nonstick cooking spray	
½ cup	goat mozzarella, diced	125 mL

I created this recipe while traveling through the spice region of India.

POMEGRANATE GLAZE: In a small saucepan, combine pomegranate molasses, frozen blueberries, honey and Chambord Liqueur. Bring mixture to a boil over medium heat, stirring occasionally to keep from scorching. When mixture is thick, purée until smooth and strain. Season with salt to taste and set aside.

THE BURGER: Preheat grill to medium-high, 450–550°F (230–280°C).

• In a large bowl, mix the ground lamb, 1 Tbsp (15 mL) pomegranate molasses, garlic, onion, Worcestershire sauce, green chili peppers and cilantro. Add black pepper, cumin, curry powder, raisins and ¼ cup (60 mL) shredded coconut. Season to taste with salt.

• Form into four 6-oz (180 g) round burger patties approximately 1½ inches (3.5 cm) thick and 4 inches (10 cm) in diameter. Roll burgers around the edge in the remaining shredded coconut to form a crust.

• Grill burgers for 4 to 5 minutes per side, basting with Pomegranate Glaze, for burgers that are done medium-well but are still moist and juicy.

• While burgers are grilling, spray the apple slices with nonstick cooking spray and grill for 3 to 4 minutes per side, until lightly charred and tender.

ASSEMBLE YOUR BURGERS! Grilled apple, Coconut Lamb Burger, extra Pomegranate Glaze and goat mozzarella. Serve immediately.

MAKES 4 BURGERS

ROSEMARY AND ROASTED GARLIC LAMB BURGER
WITH GOAT CHEESE GUNK

ROASTED GARLIC GOAT CHEESE GUNK

8	cloves garlic, roasted	8
½ cup	creamy goat cheese, softened	125 mL
½ cup	mayonnaise	125 mL
1 Tbsp	lemon juice	15 mL
1 tsp	fresh rosemary, chopped	5 mL
	Salt and freshly ground black pepper, to taste	

MARINATED OLIVES

½ cup	kalamata olives	125 mL
½ cup	small green olives	125 mL
½ cup	stuffed green olives	125 mL
3 Tbsp	olive oil	45 mL
2 Tbsp	lemon juice	30 mL
1 Tbsp	fresh oregano, chopped	15 mL
12	cloves garlic, roasted	12
1 tsp	red chile pepper flakes, crushed	5 mL
1 tsp	kosher salt	5 mL
½ tsp	freshly ground black pepper	2.5 mL

THE BURGER

1½ lb	ice-cold ground lamb	675 g
12	cloves garlic, roasted, minced	12
1	small onion, diced	1
¼ cup	Dijon mustard	60 mL
1 Tbsp	Worcestershire sauce	15 mL
2 Tbsp	fresh rosemary, chopped	30 mL
	Salt and freshly ground black pepper, to taste	
4	fresh pocket-style pita breads	4
	Olive oil	
1	bunch arugula, cleaned	1

ROASTED GARLIC GOAT CHEESE GUNK: In a bowl, mix the roasted garlic, goat cheese, mayonnaise, lemon juice and rosemary. Season to taste with salt and freshly ground black pepper. Transfer to a smaller container, cover and refrigerate until needed.

MAKES APPROXIMATELY 1½ CUPS (375 ML)

MARINATED OLIVES: In a bowl, combine kalamata olives, small green olives and stuffed green olives. Add olive oil, lemon juice, oregano, roasted garlic, pepper flakes, kosher salt and black pepper. Mix well and set aside to allow olives to marinate.

THE BURGER: Preheat grill to medium-high, 450–550°F (230–280°C).

• In a large bowl, mix the ground lamb, garlic, onion, mustard, Worcestershire sauce and rosemary. Season to taste with salt and freshly ground black pepper.

• Form into four 6-oz (180 g) round burger patties approximately 1½ inches (3.5 cm) thick and 4 inches (10 cm) in diameter.

• Grill burgers for 4 to 5 minutes per side, for medium-well doneness but burgers that are still moist and juicy.

• Brush pita with olive oil and grill until warmed and lightly charred.

ASSEMBLE YOUR BURGERS! Pita, arugula, burger, Roasted Garlic Goat Cheese Gunk and marinated olives.

MAKES 4 BURGERS

Serve with Lindemans Bin 65 Chardonnay.

TIP: If you're not a fan of a certain type of meat, switch it up with what you like. There are no rules, just your great taste!

GAME BURGERS

GREAT CANADIAN MOOSE BURGER

YUKON JACK GLAZE

¼ cup	Yukon Jack Canadian Liqueur	60 mL
½ cup	Map-o-Spread or maple syrup	125 mL
½ cup	corn syrup	125 mL

THE BURGER

	Meat thermometer	
4 tsp + 1 Tbsp	olive oil	20 mL + 15 mL
3 cups	onions, sliced	750 mL
½ tsp + 2 Tbsp	Orgasmic Onion Burger Seasoning (p. 44)	2.5 mL + 30 mL
1½ lb	ice-cold moose meat, ground	675 g
½ lb	ice-cold pork, ground	225 g
2 Tbsp	Worcestershire sauce	30 mL
2	cloves garlic, minced	2
6	burger buns	6
1½ cups	aged white cheddar cheese, shredded	375 mL

As a crazy Canuck, this burger is my true Canadian heritage.

YUKON JACK GLAZE: In a bowl, whisk together the Yukon Jack, the Map-o-Spread and the corn syrup. Set aside.

THE BURGER: In a large skillet, heat 2 tsp (10 mL) of oil over medium heat. Add the onion and cook for about 10 minutes or until golden, stirring occasionally. Season with Orgasmic Onion Burger Seasoning. Set aside and keep warm.

• In a large bowl, combine moose meat, ground pork, Worcestershire sauce, garlic and remaining 2 Tbsp (30 mL) Orgasmic Onion Burger Seasoning. Mix well to combine and put aside, covered and refrigerated, for 1 hour to set.

• Remove burger mixture from fridge and form into six 6-oz (180 g) burger patties about 1 inch (2.5 cm) thick. Place on a tray with wax paper in between layers and refrigerate, covered, for another hour, allowing patties to rest and set.

• Preheat grill to medium-high, 450–550°F (230–280°C).

• Place patties on grill directly over medium heat and grill for 5 to 6 minutes per side, basting with Yukon Jack basting sauce and turning once halfway through grilling, until the meat is no longer pink and has reached an internal temperature of 160°F (75°C).

• While the patties cook, brush cut-sides of burger buns with remaining 1 Tbsp (15 mL) of olive oil. Place the burger buns on the grill directly over heat and grill for 2 to 3 minutes or until toasted, turning once halfway through the grilling time.

• Top each moose burger with ¼ cup (60 mL) of the cheese and allow cheese to melt, about 2 minutes.

ASSEMBLE YOUR BURGERS! Remove bun bottoms from grill. Top bun bottom with a cheesy moose burger, some warm onion mixture and finish with bun top. Repeat with remaining moose burgers and buns.

MAKES 6 BURGERS

NOTE: If you can't get moose meat, replace it with venison, bison or beef.

BRYN'S BISON BURGER
WITH ROASTED RED PEPPER RELISH AND OKA CHEESE

FIRE-ROASTED RED PEPPER RELISH

2	red peppers, cut in half and seeded	2
1	medium-sweet onion, sliced	1
2	red-hot banana peppers	2
1 Tbsp	olive oil	15 mL
2	cloves roasted garlic, minced	2
1 Tbsp	fresh thyme, chopped	15 mL
1 Tbsp	white balsamic vinegar	15 mL
	Salt and pepper, to taste	

THE BURGER

1½ lb	ice-cold bison (buffalo), ground	675 g
½ lb	ice-cold pork, ground	225 g
2 Tbsp	Orgasmic Onion Burger Seasoning (p. 44)	30 mL
1 Tbsp	Worcestershire sauce	15 mL
	Salt and freshly ground black pepper to taste	
4	slices Oka cheese	4
4	sesame seed hamburger buns	4
4 tsp	mayonnaise	20 mL
4	leaves Bibb lettuce	4

Bison is a lean meat. It's best when it is freshly ground so that you can grill bison burgers to a nice medium-rare or medium to keep them from drying out. My friend, Bryn, likes to add a little ground pork to increase the moisture and bring out the flavor in the bison.

FIRE-ROASTED RED PEPPER RELISH: Preheat grill to medium-high, 450–550°F (230–280°C).

• Season red peppers, onion and banana peppers with olive oil. Fire-roast for 10 to 15 minutes, until lightly charred and tender, turning occasionally to keep from burning.

• Remove from grill and cool.

• Dice red peppers, onion and banana peppers. Place in a bowl and add roasted garlic, thyme, 1 Tbsp of olive oil and white balsamic vinegar. Season with salt and freshly ground black pepper and set aside.

THE BURGER: In a bowl, combine ground bison, ground pork, Orgasmic Onion Seasoning, Worcestershire sauce. Season to taste with salt and pepper.

• Form into four 8-oz (225 g) burgers, cover and refrigerate for a minimum of 1 hour, allowing the burgers to rest.

• Preheat grill to medium-high heat, 450–550°F (230–280°C).

• Remove bison burger patties from fridge and place on grill. Grill for 8 to 10 minutes, until fully cooked but still moist and juicy.

• **NOTE:** Slow it down and don't squish these burgers. Bison is very lean, and keeping as many of the juices in the meat as possible is important for ending up with a moist and juicy burger.

• When the burgers are just about cooked, top each with a slice of Oka cheese; close lid and allow cheese to melt, about 1 minute.

• Toast buns.

ASSEMBLE YOUR BURGERS! Bun bottom, Bibb lettuce, Bison Burger with melted Oka cheese, Fire-Roasted Red Pepper Relish and bun top.

MAKES 4 BURGERS

ROASTED GARLIC BISON BURGER
WITH GRILLED PORTOBELLO MUSHROOMS

ROASTED GARLIC BUTTER

¼ lb	butter	60 mL
8	cloves roasted garlic, minced	8
1 Tbsp	fresh herbs (parsley, sage, rosemary, thyme, cilantro), chopped	15 mL
	Salt and pepper, to taste	
8	slices Texas Toast	8

THE BURGER

1½ l	ice-cold bison, ground	750 g
1	large white onion, diced	1
6	cloves roasted garlic, minced	6
2 Tbsp	fresh herbs (parsley, sage, rosemary, thyme, cilantro), chopped	30 mL
2 Tbsp	hot mustard	30 mL
1 Tbsp	Worcestershire sauce	15 mL
1 Tbsp	Balsamic Glazing Sauce (p. 63)	15 mL
4 Tbsp	unsalted butter, softened	60 mL
	Salt and pepper, to taste	
4	portobello mushrooms, stems removed and soaked in water	4
2 Tbsp	olive oil	30 mL
	Salt and pepper, to taste	
¼ cup	Balsamic Glazing Sauce (p. 63)	60 mL
2	balls buffalo mozzarella, sliced ½ inch (1.5 cm) thick	2

ROASTED GARLIC BUTTER: To prepare the garlic butter, in a small bowl combine softened butter, garlic and herbs. Season to taste with salt and pepper, spread evenly onto Texas Toast slices and set aside.

THE BURGER: In a large bowl, combine ground bison, white onion, roasted garlic, herbs, mustard, Worcestershire sauce, balsamic glaze and butter. Season to taste with salt and pepper.

• Using your hands, mix well until all ingredients are fully incorporated.

• Form bison mixture into 4 equal-sized balls. On a flat surface, flatten each ball and form into ½-inch (1.5 cm) thick squares, about the same size as the Texas Toast. Place onto a parchment-paper-lined tray, cover and refrigerate to allow bison patties to firm and set.

• Preheat grill to medium-high heat, 450–550°F (230–280°C).

• Remove portobello mushrooms from water and season with olive oil, salt and pepper. Place seasoned portobello mushrooms on grill, flesh-side up, and grill for 2 to 3 minutes. Turn over mushrooms and grill for an additional 2 to 3 minutes. Remove from grill and set aside, keeping warm.

• Remove bison burger patties from fridge and place on grill. Grill for 8 to 10 minutes, turning once and basting with balsamic glaze during the last few minutes of grilling.

• Place bison burgers onto top rack of grill. Place one grilled portobello mushroom onto each bison burger and top with a couple of slices of buffalo mozzarella.

• **NOTE:** Slow it down and don't squish these burgers. Bison is very lean, and keeping as many of the juices in the meat as possible is important for cooking up a moist and juicy burger.

• Meanwhile, grill toast. Place toast, butter-side down, onto grill and grill for 2 to 3 minutes, until golden brown and lightly charred. Flip toast over and grill for an additional 2 to 3 minutes to toast the other side.

ASSEMBLE YOUR BURGERS! Remove toast from grill and place 4 slices, butter-side down, onto a cutting board. Top each piece of toast with one bison burger, and top each burger with another slice of toast, butter side up. Add your favorite burger garnishes and serve immediately.

MAKES 4 BURGERS

NOTE: To roast garlic, place peeled garlic cloves in a small pot and cover cloves with olive oil. Over medium-low heat, slowly roast garlic until tender and golden brown. Remove from heat and allow to cool.

BLACK PEPPER–CRUSTED KANGAROO BURGER

FIRE-ROASTED BEET MASH

2	medium to large beets	2
1 Tbsp	butter	15 mL
1 Tbsp	honey	15 mL
1 Tbsp	fresh thyme, chopped	15 mL
	Salt and freshly ground black pepper, to taste	

GOLD COAST SLAW

4 cups	white cabbage, grated	1 L
3	green onions, thinly sliced	3
½ cup	white onion, grated	125 mL
½ cup	Manchego cheese, grated	125 mL
1	green apple, grated	1
1 Tbsp	lemon juice	15 mL
3 Tbsp	mayonnaise	45 mL
2 Tbsp	parsley, chopped	30 mL
Pinch	cayenne pepper	Pinch
	Salt and freshly ground black pepper, to taste	

Aussie burgers traditionally are made of beef and topped with a slice of cooked beet and a fried egg. This one has a twist— kangaroo meat with a mash of roasted beet purée and topped with a fried quail egg.

FIRE-ROASTED BEET MASH: Preheat grill to medium-high, 450–550°F (230–280°C).

• Place beets on upper grill rack, close lid and roast beets for 45 to 60 minutes, until fully cooked and tender.

• Remove from grill and allow beets to cool for 10 minutes.

• Peel beets. Place roasted peeled beets in a bowl, and mash using a potato masher or a fork. Add butter, honey, thyme, and season to taste with salt and pepper.

• Set aside and keep warm.

GOLD COAST SLAW: In a large bowl, combine grated cabbage, green onions, white onion, Manchego cheese, green apple, lemon juice, mayonnaise and chopped parsley. Add a pinch of cayenne pepper and season to taste with salt and freshly ground black pepper. Cover and refrigerate until needed. It is best if the slaw has a chance to chill for at least an hour before serving

MAKES APPROXIMATELY 6 CUPS (1.5 L)

NOTE: if you can't find ground kangaroo, try bison, venison, ostrich or beef

THE BURGER

	Napoleon Griddle Pan	
1 lb	ice-cold ground kangaroo meat	454 g
½ lb	ice-cold ground pork	225 g
Splash	Lindemans Bin 50 Shiraz	Splash
2 Tbsp	Dijon mustard	30 mL
2	cloves garlic, minced	2
2 Tbsp	chopped fresh chives	30 mL
1 Tbsp	Sweet and Smoky BBQ Burger Seasoning (p. 43)	15 mL
	Black pepper, ground	
2 Tbsp	butter	30 mL
4	quail eggs	4
4	crusty dinner rolls, halved	4
	Nonstick cooking spray	

THE BURGER: In a bowl, combine ice-cold ground kangaroo and pork with a splash of Shiraz red wine. Add Dijon mustard, garlic, chopped fresh chives and Sweet and Smoky BBQ Burger Seasoning.

• Form into four 6-oz (180 g) baseball-shaped burgers, pressing the top and bottom flat so you have burgers that have been squished a little and bulge in around the middle, but that remain quite thick, approximately 2 inches (2.5 cm). Place on a parchment-paper-lined plate, cover and refrigerate, allowing the burgers to rest for at least 1 hour.

• Preheat grill to medium-high, 450–550°F (230–280°C), and place a Napoleon Griddle Pan over one burner, keeping the burner underneath on low.

• Spread black pepper evenly onto the surface of a plate. Remove burgers from refrigerator and roll the bulge part of each burger around in the ground black pepper.

• Spray burgers with nonstick cooking spray.

• Grill burgers for 6 to 8 minutes per side, until fully cooked but still moist and juicy. Drizzle burgers as they grill with a little Shiraz, if you so desire. Because these burgers are thick, they will take a bit of time to cook.

NOTE: Slow it down, and don't squish these burgers. Kangaroo is very lean, and keeping as many of the juices in the meat as possible is important for ending up with a moist and juicy burger. I like these burgers grilled to medium-rare or medium. As long as the kangaroo is freshly ground, go for it.

• When the burgers are just about cooked, top each burger with an even layer of Fire-Roasted Beet Mash.

• On a Napoleon Griddle Pan or in a fry pan, melt a little butter. Fry quail eggs either sunny-side up or over-easy (your choice).

• Warm buns.

ASSEMBLE YOUR BURGERS! Bun bottom, Gold Coast Slaw, kangaroo burger topped with Fire-Roasted Beet Mash, quail egg and bun top. Serve with Lindemans Bin 50 Shiraz.

MAKES 4 BURGERS

BLUEBERRY VENISON BURGER

BLUEBERRY CHUTNEY

1 cup	frozen blueberries	250 mL
1	Bartlett pear, ripe but firm, diced ¼ inch (.5 cm)	1
¼ cup	sugar	60 mL
1 tsp	ginger, minced	5 mL
1 oz	Chambord Black Raspberry Liqueur	30 mL
Pinch	cinnamon, ground	Pinch
Pinch	cayenne pepper	Pinch
1	sprig fresh thyme	1
	Salt and freshly ground black pepper, to taste	

CARROT SLAW

4	large carrots, peeled	4
¼ cup	sweet onion, minced	60 mL
2 tsp	ginger, freshly grated	10 mL
1	seedless orange, peeled and segmented, reserving 3 Tbsp (45 mL) of the juice as well	
1 tsp	fresh thyme, chopped	5 mL
1	green onion, finely chopped	
2 Tbsp	honey	30 mL
2 Tbsp	rice vinegar	30 mL
1 Tbsp	Thai sweet chili sauce	15 mL
2 Tbsp	vegetable oil	30 mL
	Salt and freshly ground black pepper, to taste	

THE BURGER

1½ lb	ice-cold ground venison	675 g
2 Tbsp	soft butter	30 mL
1 cup	frozen blueberries	250 mL
¼ cup	onion, minced	60 mL
1 tsp	ginger, minced	5 mL
¼ cup	panko (Japanese-style) bread crumbs	60 mL
Pinch	cinnamon, ground	Pinch
	Salt and freshly ground black pepper, to taste	
	Nonstick cooking spray	

BLUEBERRY CHUTNEY: In a small saucepan, combine frozen blueberries, diced pear, sugar, ginger and Chambord. Add a pinch of cinnamon and cayenne pepper and a sprig of fresh thyme. Heat over medium-low heat, stirring occasionally, until the mixture reaches a low boil. Simmer for 10 to 15 minutes, stirring occasionally, until the mixture is slightly thick. Remove from heat, remove sprig of thyme and discard and season to taste with salt and freshly ground black pepper. Set aside to cool.

MAKES APPROXIMATELY 2 CUPS (500 ML)

CARROT SLAW: Grate the carrots and place in a large bowl. Add minced sweet onion, ginger, orange segments and reserved orange juice, thyme, green onion, honey, rice vinegar, sweet chili sauce and oil. Season to taste with salt and freshly ground black pepper. Mix gently to combine. Cover and refrigerate until needed.

MAKES APPROXIMATELY 4 TO 6 CUPS (1–1.5 L)

THE BURGER: In a bowl, combine ground venison, soft butter, frozen blueberries, onion, ginger, bread crumbs and a pinch of cinnamon. Generously season to taste with salt and freshly ground black pepper.

• Form into four 6-oz (180 g) two-inch (5 cm) thick round burgers. Place on a parchment-paper-lined plate, cover and refrigerate, allowing the burgers to rest for at least 1 hour.

• Preheat grill to medium-high, 450–550°F (230–280°C).

• Spray burgers with nonstick cooking spray.

• Grill burgers for 6 to 8 minutes per side, until fully cooked but still moist and juicy.

• Note: These burgers are thick and will take a bit of time to cook. Slow it down and don't squish the burgers. Venison is very lean, and keeping as many of the juices in the meat as possible is important for a moist and juicy burger. Me, I like to have these burgers grilled to medium-rare or medium.

• When the burgers are just about cooked, top each burger with a round slice of camembert cheese, close lid and allow cheese to warm and melt for about 1 to 2 minutes.

ASSEMBLE YOUR BURGERS! Carrot Slaw, Venison Burger topped with Camembert and Blueberry Chutney.

MAKES 4 BURGERS

Chambord is a registered trademark © 2010.
Please Drink Responsibly.

GRILLED OSTRICH BURGER

GRILLED VEGETABLE SALAD

Napoleon Multi-Grill Basket

½	bunch asparagus spears, halved	½
12	cipolini onions, peeled	12
1	medium green zucchini, halved lengthways and cut on the bias into 1-inch (1.5 cm) thick chunks	1
1	medium red bell pepper, cut into 2-inch (5 cm) chunks	1
1	medium orange bell pepper, cut into 2-inch (5 cm) chunks	1
12	small cremini mushrooms	12
1	small bulb fennel, cut into 1-inch (2.5 cm) thick strips	1
3 Tbsp	olive oil	45 mL
3 Tbsp	balsamic vinegar	45 mL
	Kosher salt and freshly ground black pepper, to taste	
1 Tbsp	fresh cilantro, chopped	45 mL

GRILLED VEGETABLE SALAD: Place all vegetables in a large bowl. Add olive oil and balsamic vinegar and season to taste with kosher salt and freshly ground black pepper. Gently mix to evenly coat.

• Transfer to a Napoleon Multi-Grill Basket. Set aside.

• Preheat grill to medium-high, 450–550°F (230–280°C).

• Grill vegetables for 8 to 10 minutes per side, turning occasionally, until vegetables are lightly charred and tender.

• Remove from grill and carefully transfer to a large bowl. Add chopped fresh cilantro and adjust seasoning with a little more balsamic vinegar and salt and ground black pepper.

• Set aside. Serve either hot or cold—it's your choice.

SERVES 4

THE BURGER

1½ lb	ice-cold ground ostrich	675 g
2 Tbsp	soft butter	30 mL
2 Tbsp	Bone Dust™ BBQ Seasoning (p. 39)	30 mL
3 Tbsp	panko (Japanese-style) bread crumbs	45 mL
1 Tbsp	fresh cilantro, chopped	15 mL
1 Tbsp	soy sauce	15 mL
	Salt and freshly ground black pepper, to taste	
4	medium caps shiitake mushrooms	4
1 cup	water	250 mL
2 Tbsp	rice vinegar	30 mL
1 Tbsp	soy sauce	15 mL
1 Tbsp	sugar	15 mL
	Nonstick cooking spray	
4	slices Tilset cheese	4
4	blackberries	4

THE BURGER: In a bowl, combine ground ostrich, soft butter, Bone Dust™ Seasoning, panko bread crumbs, cilantro and soy sauce. Generously season to taste with salt and freshly ground black pepper.

• Form into four 6-oz (180 g) two-inch (5 cm) thick round burgers. Place on a parchment-paper-lined plate, cover and refrigerate, allowing the burgers to rest for at least 1 hour.

• In a small saucepan, combine the shiitake mushrooms, water, rice vinegar, soy sauce and sugar. Bring mixture to a boil, reduce heat to low and simmer for 5 minutes. Remove from heat and allow mushrooms to steep in the water-soy mixture until cool.

• Remove mushrooms from cooking liquid (reserving cooking liquid) and pat dry with paper toweling. Set aside.

• Preheat grill to medium-high, 450–550°F (230–280°C).

• Spray burgers and mushrooms with nonstick cooking spray.

• Grill burgers for 6 to 8 minutes per side, until fully cooked but still moist and juicy.

NOTE: These burgers are thick and will take a bit of time to cook. Slow it down, and don't squish the burgers. Ostrich is very lean, and keeping as many of the juices in the meat as possible is important for ending up with a moist and juicy burger. I like to have these burgers grilled to medium-rare or medium as long as the ostrich is freshly ground. Go for it!

• At the same time as you're grilling the burgers, grill the mushrooms for 3 to 5 minutes per side, basting with reserved cooking liquid to keep the mushrooms moist.

• Turn the mushrooms gill-side up and top each cap with a thick slice of Tilset cheese. Close lid and allow the cheese to melt, about 1 minute.

ASSEMBLE YOUR BURGERS! Burger, Tilset-topped shiitake mushrooms garnished with a fresh blackberry. Serve with grilled vegetables.

MAKES 4 BURGERS

CHICKEN BURGERS

BUFFALO CHICKEN WING BURGER
WITH BLUE CHEESE CELERY SALAD

CELERY AND BLUE CHEESE TOPPING

½ cup	celery, chopped	125 mL
2 Tbsp	red onion, chopped	30 mL
¼ cup	blue cheese, crumbled	60 mL
1–2 Tbsp	mayonnaise	15–30 mL
1 tsp	lemon juice	5 mL
	Sea salt and freshly ground black pepper, to taste	

THE BURGER

8	jumbo chicken wings, winglet and drumette attached, tip removed, or boneless skin on small chicken thighs	8
¾ lb	ice-cold ground chicken	375 g
½ lb	boneless skinless chicken breast meat, chopped	225 g
¼ cup	panko (Japanese-style) bread crumbs	60 mL
1	green onion, chopped	1
¼ cup	red onion, finely chopped	60 mL
2 Tbsp	Hot and Spicy Bone Dust™ BBQ Seasoning (p. 43)	30 mL
1 Tbsp	lemon juice	15 mL
Dash	hot sauce	Dash
1 tsp	black pepper, freshly ground	5 mL
	Kosher salt, to taste	
	Nonstick cooking spray	

HOT WING SAUCE

½ cup	hot sauce	125 mL
2 Tbsp	butter	30 mL
1 Tbsp	lemon juice	15 mL

THE GARNISH

4	hamburger buns	4
2 cups	iceberg lettuce, shredded	500 mL

I was at a local butcher shop, and they had some mighty big chicken wings. Beside them was some freshly ground chicken meat. I got to thinking—if I deboned those mighty big wings and filled them with some ground chicken, it might just make for one incredible burger, so I bought the wings and the ground chicken.

The preparation seemed a lot easier than it was.

I'm pretty good with a knife (I hope so!) and I was able to nicely debone each wing in three to five minutes.

If you don't want to spend time on that crazy deboning business, use boneless skin on chicken thighs instead.

CELERY AND BLUE CHEESE TOPPING: In a bowl, combine celery, red onion, blue cheese, mayonnaise and lemon juice. Season to taste with salt and freshly ground black pepper. Cover and refrigerate until needed.

THE BURGER: Using a sharp knife, debone the jumbo chicken wings. Your first cut should be from the tip of the drumette to the winglet joint. Using the tip of the knife, cut down along the side of the wing bone. Next, slide the tip of the knife under one end of the bone from one side to the other. Carefully cut along the length of the bone, cutting through at the tip. Scrape the meat down to the winglet joint. Cut through the joint to remove the drumette bone. Whew! That was a bit of work, and just think—there are seven and a half wings still to do. Repeat the process on the winglet portion of the wing. Repeat with remaining wings.

• Next, lay each wing flat on a work surface with skin-side down. Using the tip of the knife, butterfly to expose the meat inside. Whew—even more work! Cover and refrigerate.

• In a large bowl, combine ground and chopped chicken, bread crumbs, onions, Hot and Spicy Bone Dust™ BBQ Seasoning, lemon juice and hot sauce. Season to taste with salt and freshly ground black pepper. Gently mix.

• Divide burger mixture into 8 equal parts. Set aside.

• Season deboned chicken wings with Hot and Spicy Bone Dust™ BBQ Seasoning. Lay one deboned chicken wing on a flat work surface, skin-side down.

• Place one portion of chicken burger mixture on top of the seasoned boneless wing. Push the mixture to the edges of the wing, keeping a uniform thickness.

• Top with a second deboned wing, now with the skin-side up. Press firmly and shape into an oval burger.

• Place on burger patty paper and repeat with remaining wings and ground-chicken mixture. Cover and refrigerate for a minimum of 1 hour, to allow the meat to rest.

• In a small saucepan over medium heat, combine hot sauce, butter and lemon juice; heat, stirring occasionally. Set aside.

• Preheat grill to medium-high, 450–550°F (230–280°C).

• Spray burgers with nonstick cooking spray.

• With the grill lid open, grill the burgers for 6 to 8 minutes per side, until fully cooked but still moist and juicy, basting with reserved Hot Wing Sauce.

• Toast buns.

• Remove burgers from grill.

ASSEMBLE YOUR BURGERS! Bun bottom, lettuce, burger, Celery and Blue Cheese Topping, bun top. Repeat with remaining burgers.

MAKES 8 BURGERS

PLANKED CHICKEN BURGER
WITH PEACH AND BOURBON CHUTNEY

PEACH AND BOURBON CHUTNEY

12	fresh ripe peaches	12
1 cup	white vinegar	250 mL
½ cup	white sugar	125 mL
½ cup	plump golden raisins	125 mL
1	small sweet onion, finely diced	1
1	yellow bell pepper, seeded and finely diced	1
1	clove garlic, minced	1
2 tsp	fresh ginger, minced	10 mL
1 tsp	red chili peppers, crushed	5 mL
1 tsp	pure vanilla extract	5 mL
2 tsp	salt	10 mL
2 oz	bourbon	60 mL

Most chicken burgers end up spongy and never really have great texture. My recipe calls for thin strips of fresh chicken-breast meat. They give the burger a nice firm bite.

PEACH AND BOURBON CHUTNEY: To help with peeling the peaches, bring a large pot of water to a rolling boil.

• Carefully place the peaches into the water to blanch for 30 seconds.

• Using a pair of tongs or a wire mesh strainer, remove the peaches from the boiling water and plunge into a bowl of ice water. This will stop the cooking process.

• Peel peaches. Cut each peach in half and remove seeds.

• Slice peaches into ½-inch (1.5 cm) thick slices. You will need approximately 4 cups (1 L) of sliced peaches.

• Place sliced peaches in a medium saucepan. Add vinegar, sugar, raisins, onion, yellow pepper, garlic, ginger, chilies, vanilla extract and salt.

• Over medium-high heat, and stirring continuously, bring mixture to a boil; reduce heat to low and simmer for 15 to 20 minutes, stirring frequently, until the mixture is thick.

• Remove from heat, stir in the bourbon and transfer mixture to container. Allow to cool, cover and refrigerate for up to 2 weeks. Use with your favorite grilled burgers.

TIP: Planking burgers is burger grilling made easy. No turning, flipping, squishing or pressing. Set it and almost forget it. Dead easy!

MAKES APPROXIMATELY 5 CUPS (1.25 L)

THE BURGER

1	cedar plank, 24 inches long by 12 inches wide by ½ inch thick (60 cm by 30 cm by 1.5 cm), soaked in water for 1 hour	1
2 lb	ice-cold ground chicken	907 g
1 lb	boneless skinless chicken breasts, thinly sliced into strips	454 g
¼ cup	Parmesan cheese, grated	60 mL
½ cup	panko (Japanese-style) bread crumbs	125 mL
1	large egg	1
1 Tbsp	fresh parsley, chopped	15 mL
1 Tbsp	Bone Dust™ BBQ Seasoning (p. 39)	15 mL
¾ cup	crispy fried onion pieces (available in Asian grocery stores)	180 mL
1	medium sweet onion, diced	1
4	cloves garlic, minced	4
1 Tbsp	olive oil	15 mL
8	balls bocconcini cheese, frozen	8
8	grape tomatoes	8

NOTE: Putting the cheese in the freezer keeps it from melting too quickly when grilling your burgers.

• In a large bowl, combine ground chicken, sliced chicken-breast meat, Parmesan cheese, bread crumbs, egg, parsley, Bone Dust™ BBQ Seasoning, crispy fried onion pieces, sweet onion, garlic and olive oil. Mix well.

• Form into 8 equal-sized baseball-shaped burgers.

• Push a hole into the center of each burger to make a well. Place a frozen bocconcini ball of cheese in the center of each burger and fold the meat around to seal it in. Cover and place burgers in refrigerator for 1 hour.

• Preheat grill to medium-high, 450–550°F (230–280°C).

• Evenly space burgers on a 2-foot (60 cm) soaked cedar plank.

• Place in grill, close lid and plank-bake for 30 to 40 minutes, until chicken burgers are fully cooked, moist and juicy.

• When the burgers are just about completed, grill 8 grape tomatoes until lightly charred and tender. Place 1 charred tomato on top of each planked chicken burger.

• Remove from grill and serve immediately with your favorite bun and burger condiments.

MAKES 8 BURGERS

SWEET AND SASSY
ULTIMATE CHICKEN BURGER

SWEET AND SASSY BBQ SAUCE

¼ cup	honey	60 mL
¼ cup	Southern Comfort	60 mL
2 Tbsp	Thai sweet chili sauce	30 mL
3 Tbsp	Ted's World Famous BBQ Crazy Canuck Sticky Chicken and Rib Sauce or your favorite gourmet-style BBQ sauce	45 mL

THE BURGER

6	boneless, skinless chicken breasts (4 oz/120 g)	6
1 + 2 Tbsp	Bone Dust™ BBQ Seasoning (p. 39)	15 + 30 mL
1 cup + Big Drizzle	Southern Comfort	250 mL + Big Drizzle
½ cup	orange juice	125 mL
2 Tbsp	olive oil	30 mL
3	cloves garlic, minced	3
2 Tbsp	fresh cilantro, chopped	30 mL
2	hot small red peppers, minced	2
1 tsp	cracked black pepper	5 mL
½ lb	Monterey Jack cheese	225 g
1 lb	ice-cold ground chicken	454 g
¼ cup	Parmesan cheese, grated	60 mL
2 Tbsp	bread crumbs	30 mL
2	green onions, chopped	2
½ cup	onion, finely diced	125 mL
2 Tbsp	fresh herbs (parsley & sage), chopped	30 mL
1	large egg	1
	Nonstick cooking spray	
6	multi-grain hamburger buns	6
1 pint	onion sprouts	500 mL
1	tomato, sliced	1
1	avocado	1

SWEET AND SASSY BBQ SAUCE: In a small bowl, whisk together the honey, Southern Comfort, Thai sweet chili sauce and BBQ sauce. Set aside for basting.

THE BURGER: Using a sharp knife, butterfly each chicken breast. Cut from top to bottom, down one side of the breast, splaying out the meat to butterfly.

• Place chicken breasts, one at a time, between 2 sheets of plastic wrap and, using a meat mallet or rolling pin, gently pound the meat to a uniform ½-inch (1.5 cm) thickness, keeping the breast whole and intact. Repeat for remaining chicken breasts.

• Season both sides with Bone Dust™ BBQ Seasoning and place in a large bowl.

• Add Southern Comfort, orange juice, olive oil, garlic, cilantro, hot chili peppers and black pepper. Mix well to evenly coat all the chicken breasts. Cover and refrigerate for 4 hours.

• Cut the Monterey Jack cheese into ½-inch (1.5 cm) cubes. Freeze for 1 hour.

NOTE: Freezing the cheese allows it to melt slowly, so that when the meat is cooked, the cheese is soft.

• In a bowl, combine the ground chicken, Bone Dust™ BBQ Seasoning, Parmesan, big drizzle of Southern Comfort, bread crumbs, green onions, onion, herbs and egg. Mix well until incorporated.

• Break apart the frozen cheese so that each cube is separated. Add frozen cheese to meat mixture and mix well to incorporate.

• Scoop the ground chicken mixture into approximately 6 balls, using a 3-oz (100 mL) ice-cream scoop. With your hands, pat the burgers to remove excess air. Press and form into a 3-inch (7.5 cm) diameter and ½-inch (1.5 cm) thick burger patty.

• Place on a wax-paper-lined tray and place in the freezer for 15 minutes to help the meat set and rest.

• Place 1 flattened, marinated chicken breast on a plate. Top with 1 burger. Wrap the chicken breast around the patty, encasing the burger in the breast. Repeat with remaining chicken breasts and patties. Wrap and refrigerate for 1 hour.

• Preheat grill to high, 550°F (280°C).

• Brush wrapped chicken burgers with oil.

• Grill for 2 to 3 minutes per side to sear.

• Reduce heat to low, less than 250°F (120°C).

• Baste burgers with Sweet and Sassy BBQ Sauce. Close grill lid and continue to cook for 15 to 20 minutes, basting with extra Sweet and Sassy BBQ Sauce until fully cooked. When checked with a thermometer placed in the center of the burger, the temperature should read a minimum of 160°F (70°C).

ASSEMBLE YOUR BURGERS! Bun bottom, burger, onion sprouts, tomato, avocado, bun top.

MAKES 6 BURGERS

CHICKEN SLIDERS
WITH CHARRED CORN RELISH

CHARRED CORN RELISH

4	ears peaches-and-cream or bicolor corn, shucked	4
1	large sweet onion, peeled and sliced into ½-inch (1.5 cm) thick rounds	4
1	large red bell pepper, cut in half lengthways and seeded	1
2 Tbsp	olive oil	30 mL
1 Tbsp	Bone Dust™ BBQ Seasoning (p. 39)	15 mL
½ cup	green cabbage, finely diced	125 mL
½ cup	malt vinegar	125 mL
¼ cup	sugar	60 mL
1 tsp	salt	5 mL
1 tsp	celery seed	5 mL
2 Tbsp	all-purpose flour	30 mL
1 tsp	turmeric	5 mL
2 tsp	mustard powder	10 mL

MINI CORN MUFFINS

	Mini muffin tin	
	Nonstick cooking spray	
1 cup	all-purpose flour	250 mL
¾ cup	cornmeal	380 mL
1 Tbsp	granulated sugar	15 mL
3 Tbsp	baking powder	45 mL
1 tsp	salt	5 mL
1	large egg	1
⅔ cup	milk	160 mL
1/3 cup	butter, unsalted and softened	80 mL

CHARRED CORN RELISH: Preheat grill to medium-high, 450–550°F (230–280°C).

• In a bowl, toss ears of corn, onion and pepper with olive oil and Bone Dust™ BBQ Seasoning. Grill for 8 to 10 minutes, until lightly charred and tender.

• Remove from grill and allow mix to cool slightly.

• Using a sharp knife, cut the kernels of corn from the cob. You will need approximately 2 cups (500 mL) of kernels. Place in a medium saucepan.

• Finely chop the charred onion and bell pepper and add to corn kernels.

• Add cabbage, malt vinegar, sugar, salt and celery seed. Place on stovetop over medium heat.

• In a small bowl, combine flour, turmeric and mustard powder with 2–3 Tbsp of water. Stir until it forms a smooth paste.

• Add to corn mixture on stovetop and continue to cook, stirring occasionally, until the mixture comes to a low boil. Reduce heat to low and simmer, stirring occasionally to keep from scorching, for 15 minutes.

• Remove from heat and transfer to container. Allow to cool, cover and refrigerate for up to 2 weeks. Use with your favorite grilled burgers.

MAKES ABOUT 6 CUPS (1.5 L)

MINI CORN MUFFINS: Prepare grill for indirect grilling. Turn on one side of grill to low heat (about 250°F/120°C) and the other side to high heat (about 550°F/280°C).

• Grease mini muffin tin and set aside.

• In a large bowl, sift together flour, cornmeal, sugar, baking powder and salt.

• In a small bowl, with a fork beat together egg, milk and butter.

• Pour egg mixture into flour mixture. Stir just until flour is moistened.

• Pour a little batter into each mini muffin and place on grill on side preheated to low.

• Bake for 15 to 20 minutes, or until golden brown and a toothpick inserted into the center of the cornbread pulls out clean.

• Cut into squares and serve with butter.

MAKES 12 TO 16 MINI MUFFINS

THE BURGER

1½ lb	ice-cold ground chicken	675 g
5 Tbsp	Better Butter Burger Seasoning (p. 39)	75 mL
¼ cup	Lindemans Bin 65 Chardonnay	60 mL
1	small red onion, finely diced	1
½ cup	coarse white bread crumbs	125 mL
¼ cup	Parmesan cheese, grated	60 mL
3 Tbsp	olive oil	45 mL
12	slices provolone cheese	12
12	Mini Corn Muffins	12
	Mayonnaise	
1	bunch Bibb lettuce leaves	1

THE BURGER: In a bowl, mix ground chicken, Better Butter Burger Seasoning, Chardonnay, onion, bread crumbs and Parmesan cheese. Form into 12 equal-sized small burger patties, about 2 inches (5 cm) in diameter and 1 inch (1.5 cm) thick. Cover and refrigerate for 1 to 2 hours.

• Preheat grill to medium-high (450–550°F/230–280°C).

• Brush burgers lightly with olive oil. Grill 4 to 5 minutes per side, or until juices run clear and burgers are fully cooked and well-done. (Using an instant-read meat thermometer, check internal temperature. It should be 165°F/75°C.)

• When the burgers are just about done, top each with a slice of provolone cheese, close grill lid and allow cheese to melt.

• Cut the tops off the muffins.

ASSEMBLE YOUR BURGERS! Muffin bottom, mayonnaise, Bibb lettuce, Charred Corn Relish, burger, muffin top.

MAKES 12 BURGERS

RED NECK CHICKEN BURGER
WITH BACON AND CHEDDAR FLAPJACKS

RED NECK WHITE SAUCE

½ cup	cream cheese, softened	125 mL
½ cup	sour cream	125 mL
½ cup	The Special Sauce (p. 55)	125 mL
1 Tbsp	prepared hot horseradish	15 mL
1 Tbsp	white vinegar	15 mL
1	anchovy fillet, minced	1
1 clove	garlic, minced	1
1 tsp	Bone Dust™ BBQ Seasoning (p. 39)	5 mL
Splash	Worcestershire sauce	Splash
Dash	hot sauce	Dash
	Freshly ground black pepper, to taste	

BACON AND CHEDDAR FLAPJACKS

Sometimes a bun is just too much for a burger, so these burgers are served between bacon and cheddar pancakes.

	Napoleon Griddle	
1 cup	flour	250 mL
1 tsp	baking soda	5 mL
½ tsp	salt	2.5 mL
¼ cup	corn flour	60 mL
1	large egg	1
1 cup	whole milk	250 mL
1	green onion, minced	1
1	clove garlic, minced	1
1 tsp	Bone Dust™ BBQ Seasoning (p. 39)	5 mL
1 cup	cheddar cheese, grated	250 mL
4	slices of bacon, fully cooked and chopped	4
	Salt and pepper, to taste	
4 Tbsp	butter	60 mL

RED NECK WHITE SAUCE: In a bowl, combine cream cheese, sour cream, mayonnaise, horseradish, white vinegar, anchovy, garlic and Bone Dust™ BBQ Seasoning. Season to taste with a splash of Worcestershire sauce, a dash of hot sauce and freshly ground black pepper. Mix until smooth. Transfer to a container, cover and refrigerate until needed.

MAKES APPROXIMATELY 2 CUPS (500 ML)

BACON AND CHEDDAR FLAPJACKS: In a bowl, mix the flour, baking soda, salt and corn flour.

• In a separate bowl, whisk together the egg and milk.

• Slowly whisk the egg-milk mixture into the dry mix until fully incorporated and no lumps exist. Let rest for 2 hours.

• Fold into the batter the green onions, garlic, Bone Dust™ BBQ seasoning, cheese and bacon. Season to taste with salt and pepper.

• Set up grill with Napoleon Griddle Pan. Preheat griddle to medium-low, 250–350°F (120–175°C).

• Melt 1 Tbsp (30 mL) of butter in a Napoleon Griddle and ladle 2 oz (60 mL) of batter into the pan to make a pancake.

• Fry until the surface bubbles, turn over and continue to fry for 1 to 2 minutes, until golden brown and cooked. Repeat until all the batter is used up.

MAKES 12 FLAPJACKS

THE BURGER

1 lb	ice-cold ground chicken	454 g
1 lb	chicken breasts, boneless skinless, coarsely chopped	454 g
3 Tbsp	Red Neck White Sauce	45 mL
1 cup	crushed ranch-flavor tortilla chips	250 mL
½ cup	white onion, finely diced	125 mL
1 Tbsp	fresh parsley, chopped	15 mL
3 Tbsp	Orgasmic Onion Burger Seasoning (p. 44)	45 mL
2	poblano peppers, halved and seeded	2
6	slices pepper jack cheese	6
6	slices thick-sliced smoked bacon, fried crisp	6
6	leaves lettuce	6
6	slices ripe tomato	6

THE BURGER: In a bowl, combine ice-cold ground and chopped chicken, Red Neck White Sauce, tortilla chips, onion, parsley and Orgasmic Onion Burger Seasoning.

• Mix well and form into six 6-oz (180 g) burgers patties, approximately 1 inch (2.5 cm) thick and 4 inches (10 cm) in diameter. Place burgers on a plate, cover and refrigerate for at least 1 hour, until required.

• Preheat grill to medium-high, 450–550°F (230–280°C).

• Grill poblano peppers for 4 to 5 minutes per side, until lightly charred and tender.

• Grill burgers for 6 to 8 minutes per side, until fully cooked but still moist and juicy. Top each burger with a slice of pepper jack cheese, reduce heat to low and allow cheese to melt.

• While the burgers are grilling, prepare the flapjacks.

ASSEMBLE YOUR BURGERS! Flapjack, lettuce, tomato, burger, Red Neck White Sauce, poblano pepper and flapjack.

MAKES 6 BURGERS

GRILLED CHICKEN BURGER
WITH HOT BUTTERED LOVE BBQ DIP

HOT BUTTERED LOVE BBQ DIP

1 cup	Ted's World Famous BBQ Crazy Canuck Sticky Chicken and Rib Sauce	250 mL
1 cup	chicken stock	250 mL
¼ cup	honey	60 mL
¼ cup	Jack Daniel's Tennessee Whiskey	60 mL
1 Tbsp	Sri Racha Vietnamese hot sauce	15 mL
2 tsp	Bone Dust™ BBQ Seasoning (p. 39)	10 mL
½ lb	cold butter, cut into cubes	225 g

THE BURGER

1 lb	ice-cold ground chicken	454 g
1 lb	chicken breasts, boneless skinless, diced	454 g
2 Tbsp	butter, softened	30 mL
1 cup	panko (Japanese-style) bread crumbs	250 mL
½ cup	white onion, finely diced	125 mL
1 Tbsp	Sriracha Vietnamese hot sauce	15 mL
1 Tbsp	fresh cilantro, chopped	15 mL
3 Tbsp	Bone Dust™ BBQ Seasoning (p. 39)	45 mL
2 cups	Emmenthal cheese, shredded	500 mL
6	onion buns	6
	Hand-leafed lettuce	
	Ripe tomato, sliced	
	White onions, thinly sliced	

These burgers are sure to have you stripping down to your skivvies just to save on dry cleaning. The chicken burger is a sticky, gooey mess, but well worth the number of napkins you have to use. For an added effect, mold the burgers into heart shapes.

HOT BUTTERED LOVE BBQ DIP: In a medium saucepan, combine the BBQ sauce, chicken stock, honey, Jack Daniel's, hot sauce and Bone Dust™. Bring mixture to a low boil and reduce heat to low. Using a whisk, stir in the cold butter a little bit at a time so that it emulsifies; set aside.

MAKES ABOUT 3 CUPS (750 ML)

THE BURGER: In a bowl, combine ice-cold ground and diced chicken, butter, bread crumbs, onion, hot sauce, cilantro and Bone Dust™ BBQ Seasoning. Mix well and form into six 6-oz (180 g) burgers patties, approximately 1 inch (2.5 cm) thick and 4 inches (10 cm) in diameter.

• Place burgers on a plate, cover and refrigerate for at least 1 hour, until required.

• Preheat grill to medium-high, 450–550°F (230–280°C).

• Grill burgers for 6 to 8 minutes per side, until fully cooked but still moist and juicy.

• Take burger and dip it into reserved Hot Buttered Love BBQ Dip, return to grill and top with a handful of shredded Emmenthal cheese, close lid and let cheese melt.

• Warm buns.

ASSEMBLE YOUR BURGERS! Bun bottom, lettuce, tomato, onion, burger and bun top. Serve everyone a ramekin of warm Hot Buttered Love BBQ Dip for dipping their burger before every bite. These chicken burgers are for sure a sticky, gooey mess!

MAKES 6 BURGERS

TANDOORI BURGER
WITH CUCUMBER MINT RAITA

CUCUMBER MINT RAITA

1	ripe tomato, peeled, seeded and chopped	1
1	medium cucumber, peeled, halved, seeded and grated	1
2	cloves garlic, minced	2
¼ cup	fresh mint, chopped	60 mL
Pinch	cayenne	Pinch
½ tsp	cumin	2.5 mL
2 Tbsp	lemon juice	30 mL
1 cup	yogurt	250 mL
½ cup	sour cream	125 mL
½ cup	red onion, diced	125 mL
	Salt and pepper, to taste	

TANDOORI BBQ SAUCE

2 Tbsp	vegetable oil	30 mL
3 Tbsp	Tandoori Burger Seasoning (p. 40)	45 mL
3	red chili peppers, minced	3
3	cloves garlic, minced	3
½	small onion, diced	½
¼ cup	sugar cane vinegar or cider vinegar	60 mL
½ cup	ketchup	125 mL
½ cup	honey	125 mL

THE BURGER

1½ lb	ice-cold ground chicken	675 g
3 Tbsp	Tandoori Burger Seasoning (p. 40)	45 mL
2	cloves garlic, minced	2
2	green chilies, minced	2
4 tsp	ginger, minced	20 mL
¼ cup	yogurt	60 mL
1 Tbsp	vegetable oil	15 mL
1 Tbsp	lemon juice	15 mL
2 Tbsp	fresh cilantro, chopped	30 mL
4	pieces naan bread (found in ethnic food stores and bakeries)	4
½ cup	olive oil	125 mL
	Salt and pepper, to taste	
2 cups	iceberg lettuce, shredded	500 mL

CUCUMBER MINT RAITA: With a sharp knife score the tomato and score its bottom. Blanch in boiling water for 5 to 10 seconds. Cool and peel off the skin. Chop tomatoes and set aside.

• In a bowl, mix the peeled tomato, cucumber, garlic, mint, cayenne, cumin, lemon juice, yogurt, sour cream and onion. Season to taste with salt and pepper. Cover and refrigerate for 1 hour.

MAKES APPROXIMATELY 2 CUPS (500 ML)

TANDOORI BBQ SAUCE: Heat oil in a medium saucepan over medium-high heat. Add Tandoori Burger Seasoning and stir continuously for 30 seconds to lightly scorch the spices. Add chilies, garlic, onion and continue to stir until onions are tender. Reduce heat to low and add cane vinegar, ketchup and honey. Bring to a low boil; simmer for 10 minutes. Purée sauce and strain to remove particles. Set aside and keep warm.

THE BURGER: In a bowl, combine ground chicken, Tandoori Burger Seasoning, garlic, chilies, ginger, yogurt, oil, lemon juice and cilantro. Mix well but gently.

• Form into twelve 2-oz (60 g) mini burgers. Place on a plate, cover and refrigerate for 2 hours, to allow flavors to develop fully.

• Preheat grill to medium-high 450–550°F (230–280°C).

• Grill mini tandoori chicken burgers for 3 to 4 minutes per side, basting liberally during the last half of grilling with the reserved Tandoori BBQ Sauce.

• While the burgers grill, brush the naan bread with olive oil. Season to taste with salt and pepper. Grill-toast naan for 1 to 2 minutes per side, until lightly golden and hot. Cut naan bread in half.

ASSEMBLE YOUR BURGERS! Naan, Cucumber Mint Raita, shredded lettuce and Tandoori Burgers. Drizzle with extra Tandoori BBQ Sauce and serve immediately.

MAKES 12 BURGERS

FAJITA BURGER

GUACAMOLE

2	avocados, peeled and seeded	2
2 Tbsp	lime juice	30 mL
1 Tbsp	olive oil	15 mL
1 Tbsp	fresh cilantro, chopped	15 mL
1	green onion, finely chopped	1
	Salt and freshly ground black pepper, to taste	

FIRE-ROASTED FOUR-PEPPER SALSA

2	red bell peppers, halved and seeded	2
1	yellow bell pepper, halved and seeded	1
1	green bell pepper, halved and seeded	1
1	red onion, peeled and quartered	1
2 Tbsp	olive oil	30 mL
1 Tbsp	smoked chipotle chilies in adobo sauce, puréed	15 mL
1 Tbsp	garlic, chopped	15 mL
1 Tbsp	fresh cilantro, chopped	15 mL
1 Tbsp	lime juice	15 mL
	Salt and coarsely ground black pepper, to taste	

SALSA VERDE

6	tomatillos, chopped	6
1	poblano pepper, roasted, peeled, seeded and diced	1
2	jalapeño peppers, seeded and finely chopped	2
1	small yellow onion, finely diced	1
4	cloves garlic, minced	4
4	green onions, finely chopped	4
¼ cup	fresh cilantro, chopped	60 mL
2 Tbsp	white vinegar	30 mL
2 Tbsp	olive oil	30 mL
Pinch	ground cumin	Pinch
	Salt and pepper, to taste	

GUACAMOLE: In a bowl, mash the avocados with a fork. Stir in the lime juice, olive oil, cilantro and green onion. Season to taste with salt and freshly ground black pepper. Cover and refrigerate.

MAKES ABOUT 2 CUPS (500 ML)

FIRE-ROASTED FOUR-PEPPER SALSA: Preheat grill to high, 550°F (280°C).

• On a lightly greased grill, roast the red, yellow and green peppers and the red onion until charred all over and tender.

• Peel any loose skin from the peppers. Dice the peppers and onion; place in a large bowl.

• Add the olive oil, puréed chipotle chilies, garlic, cilantro, lime juice, salt and pepper. Mix thoroughly, cover and refrigerate at least 1 hour.

MAKES 2 TO 3 CUPS (500–750 ML)

SALSA VERDE: In a bowl, mix the tomatillos, poblano and jalapeño peppers, onion, garlic, green onions, cilantro, vinegar and olive oil. Season to taste with cumin, salt and pepper.

MAKES ABOUT 2 CUPS (500 ML)

LIME BEER BASTING SAUCE

½	bottle Honey Lager beer	½
¼ cup	butter	60 mL
1 Tbsp	lime juice	15 mL

THE BURGER

2 lb	ice-cold ground chicken	907 g
2 Tbsp	Bone Dust™ BBQ Seasoning (p. 39)	30 mL
2 tsp	cumin, ground	10 mL
2 tsp	chili powder	10 mL
2 Tbsp	lime juice	30 mL
1 Tbsp	vegetable oil	15 mL
1 cup	corn tortilla chips, crushed	250 mL
½ cup	onion, minced	125 mL
4	cloves garlic, minced	4
2	jalapeño peppers, finely chopped	2
	Nonstick cooking spray	
8	flour tortillas	8
2 cups	iceberg lettuce, shredded	500 mL
2 cups	pepper jack cheese, shredded	500 mL
1 cup	refried beans (optional)	250 mL
2 cups	cooked yellow rice (optional)	500 mL

LIME BEER BASTING SAUCE: In a small saucepan over medium heat, combine the beer, butter and lime juice. Heat until butter has melted. Remove from heat. Set aside and keep warm.

THE BURGER: In a bowl, combine ice-cold ground chicken, Bone Dust™, cumin, chili powder, lime juice, vegetable oil, tortilla chips, onion, garlic and jalapeño.

• Mix well and form into eight 4-oz (120 g) rectangular-shaped burgers about 1 inch (2.5 cm) thick. Cover and refrigerate for 2 hours, to allow the burgers to set and the flavors to mix.

• Preheat grill to medium-high, 450–550°F (230–280°C).

• Spray burgers with nonstick cooking spray.

• Grill burgers for 5 to 6 minutes per side, basting liberally with Lime Beer Basting sauce.

• Warm flour tortillas.

ASSEMBLE YOUR BURGERS! Flour tortilla, refried beans and/or yellow rice if prepared, shredded lettuce, Fajita Chicken Burger, shredded cheese, salsa and guacamole. Serve immediately.

MAKES 8 BURGERS

TURKEY BURGERS

PLANKED KENTURKEY DERBY BURGER
WITH MINT JULEP GLAZING SAUCE

2	maple or oak or cedar planks, 12 inches long by 8 inches wide by ½ inch thick (30 cm by 12 cm by 1.5 cm), soaked in water for a minimum of 1 hour	

MINT JULEP GLAZING SAUCE

1 cup	brown sugar	250 mL
¼ cup	water	60 mL
2	cloves garlic, minced	2
½ cup	mint jelly (the bright green stuff)	125 mL
½	bunch fresh mint, chopped	1/2
¼ cup	bourbon	60 mL
	Salt and freshly ground black pepper, to taste	

THE BURGER

1 lb	ice-cold ground turkey	454 g
½ lb	turkey breast meat, finely chopped	225 g
½ cup	corn flake crumbs	125 mL
1	small egg	1
1	small onion, diced	1
¼ cup	Parmesan cheese, grated	60 mL
1 tsp	cracked black pepper	5 mL
¼ tsp	cayenne pepper	1 mL
2 tsp	salt	10 mL
1 Tbsp	fresh sage, chopped	15 mL
1 Tbsp	fresh mint, chopped	15 mL
1 oz	bourbon	30 mL

This is a burger that should be served at the Kentucky Derby.

MINT JULEP GLAZING SAUCE: In a small pot, combine brown sugar, water, garlic and mint jelly. Bring mixture to a boil over medium heat, stirring occasionally. Reduce heat to low and add chopped fresh mint and bourbon. Remove from heat and let stand for 15 minutes so flavors infuse. Season to taste with salt and freshly ground black pepper. Set aside.

MAKES APPROXIMATELY 2½ CUPS (625 ML)

THE BURGER: In a bowl, combine ground turkey and chopped turkey breast meat with corn flake crumbs, egg, onion, Parmesan cheese, black pepper, cayenne pepper, salt, sage, mint and bourbon.

• Mix well and form into 8 baseball-shaped round burgers. (Note: Do not flatten the burgers; leave them shaped like baseballs. This will help keep your burgers moist and juicy.) Place burgers on a tray or plate, cover and refrigerate for 1 hour. This will allow the meat to rest.

• Preheat grill to medium-high, 450–550°F (230–280°C).

• Evenly space 4 burgers on each plank. Place on grill and close lid. Plank-bake for 25 to 30 minutes, basting with reserved Mint Julep Glazing Sauce during the last 15 minutes of planking, until the burgers are fully cooked but still moist and juicy.

• Remove burgers from grill.

ASSEMBLE YOUR BURGERS and serve with a knife and fork, or serve on your favorite buns with all your favorite burger condiments.

MAKES 8 BURGERS

TURKEY BURGER SHASHLIK

CURRY HONEY BASTE

2 tsp	yellow curry powder	10 mL
¼ tsp	cayenne pepper	1 mL
1 tsp	fresh ginger, chopped	5 mL
2	cloves garlic, minced	2
½ cup	lime juice	125 mL
1 Tbsp	fresh cilantro, chopped	15 mL
½ cup	liquid honey	125 mL
	Salt and freshly ground black pepper, to taste	

GOAT CHEESE DUNK

¼ cup	mayonnaise	60 mL
¼ cup	plain yogurt	60 mL
¼ cup	soft creamy goat cheese	125 mL
2	cloves garlic, minced	2
1 tsp	fresh mint, chopped	5 mL
2 tsp	lemon juice	10 mL
1	green onion, finely chopped	1
	Salt and freshly ground black pepper, to taste	

SHASHLIK SALSA

2	plum tomatoes, diced	2
½ cup	red onion, diced	125 mL
½ cup	green pepper, diced	125 mL
2	green onions, chopped	2
1	hot green chile pepper, minced	1
1 Tbsp	fresh cilantro, chopped	15 mL
2 Tbsp	olive oil	30 mL
2 tsp	lime juice	10 mL
	Salt and freshly ground black pepper, to taste	

CURRY HONEY BASTE: In a small saucepan over medium-low heat, combine curry, cayenne, ginger, garlic, lime juice, cilantro and honey, and season to taste with salt and freshly ground pepper. Heat slowly until mixed. Set aside and keep warm.

GOAT CHEESE DUNK: In a bowl, combine mayonnaise, yogurt, goat cheese, garlic, mint, lemon juice and green onion. Season to taste with salt and freshly ground black pepper. Set aside.

SHASHLIK SALSA: In a bowl, combine tomatoes, red onion, green pepper, green onions, chili pepper, cilantro, olive oil and lime juice. Season to taste with salt and freshly ground black pepper. Set aside.

THE BURGER

6	large metal Napoleon Barbecue Skewers	
	Heavy-duty foil wrap	
1½ lb	ice-cold ground turkey	675 g
½ lb	turkey breast meat, finely chopped	225 g
1 Tbsp	fresh ginger, minced	15 mL
1 Tbsp	garam masala	15 mL
4 tsp	yellow curry powder	20 mL
2 tsp	cracked black pepper	10 mL
1 tsp	salt	5 mL
¼ cup	fresh cilantro, chopped	60 mL
4	cloves fresh garlic, minced	4
6	large fresh pitas	6
	Olive oil	
2 cups	iceberg lettuce, shredded	500 mL
	Nonstick cooking spray	

THE BURGER: Combine ground turkey, chopped turkey breast and spices in a bowl and mix well.

• Divide meat mixture into 6 equal portions. Mold mixture tightly around the skewer to form a long tight sausage shape with skewer ends protruding.

• Spray lengths of foil with nonstick cooking spray, then wrap foil snugly around each skewer and crimp ends. Place wrapped skewers back in refrigerator to chill for at least 30 minutes. Mixture must be very cold when placed on the grill.

• Preheat grill to medium-high heat, 450–550°F (230–280°C).

• Place foil packages of Turkey Burger Shashlik on the grill and grill for 2 to 3 minutes per side to start the kebabs cooking. Remove foil, return skewers to grill and continue to cook for 3 to 5 minutes more per side, basting with Curry Honey Baste, until lightly charred. Remove from grill and allow to rest for 1 to 2 minutes.

• Meanwhile, brush the pitas with a little olive oil and season to taste with salt and freshly ground black pepper. Warm pitas on grill.

ASSEMBLE YOUR BURGERS! Warmed pita, Goat Cheese Dunk, lettuce, Shashlik Salsa, Turkey Burger Shashlik and more Dunk if you desire.

MAKES 6 BURGERS

PRIMANTI BROS. TURKEY BURGER

SMOKY RUSSIAN DRESSING

½ cup	honey	125 mL
½ cup	ketchup (p. 75, or store-bought)	125 mL
¼ cup	white vinegar	60 mL
1 Tbsp	lemon juice	15 mL
2 tsp	smoked paprika	10 mL
1 tsp	mustard powder	5 mL
1 tsp	celery salt	5 mL
½ tsp	cayenne pepper	2.5 mL
1 cup	vegetable oil	250 mL
	Salt and pepper, to taste	

PRIMANTI BROS. SLAW

½	head green cabbage, thinly sliced	1/2
2	large carrots, peeled and grated	2
1	small onion, finely chopped	1
4	green onions, chopped	4
2 Tbsp	sugar	30 mL
1 Tbsp	malt vinegar	15 mL
½ tsp	salt	2.5 mL
½ cup	mayonnaise	125 mL
2 tsp	mustard powder	10 mL
1 tsp	black pepper	5 mL
1 tsp	smoked paprika	5 mL
¼ tsp	cayenne pepper	1 mL

SHOESTRING FRIES

4–8	large russet potatoes	4–8
	Peanut or vegetable oil	
	Bone Dust™ BBQ Seasoning (p. 39)	

Primanti Bros. is an iconic Pittsburg Depression-era restaurant, and today is a local favorite. What makes Primanti Bros. special is that they serve all their burgers with French fries. Not on the side, the way a normal restaurant would, but right on the sandwich. Next time you're in Pittsburg, stop in and try one of theirs.

SMOKY RUSSIAN DRESSING: In a medium bowl, whisk together the honey, ketchup, vinegar, lemon juice, smoked paprika, mustard powder, celery salt, cayenne and vegetable oil. Season to taste with salt and freshly ground black pepper. Transfer to a sealed container and refrigerate until needed. It will keep up to 1 week.

MAKES ABOUT 2 1/2 CUPS (625 ML)

PRIMANTI BROS. SLAW: In a large bowl, combine the cabbage, carrots, onion, green onions, sugar, malt vinegar and salt. Let marinate for 1 to 2 hours, tossing occasionally.

• Mix in the mayonnaise, mustard powder, black pepper, smoked paprika and cayenne. Season to taste with salt. Refrigerate until ready to serve.

SERVES 6

SHOESTRING FRIES: For the fries, you can use store-bought frozen fries (to make this recipe a little easier); or, if you wish, make your own fries. For best results use a store-bought deep fryer to cook your fries and follow the manufacturer's instructions.

• Wash the potatoes under cold water to remove dirt and grit. Using either a fry cutter or a knife, cut the potatoes into shoestrings, approximately 3 to 4 inches (7.5–10 cm) in length and ¼ inch (5 cm) thick.

• Place cut potatoes in a large bowl and place in the sink. Run cold water over them for 5 to 10 minutes to rinse off excess starch. Drain and pat dry with paper towel to remove excess water. Set aside.

• Fill fryer with oil, following manufacturer's instructions. Heat to 250°F (125°C).

• Blanch cut potatoes in small batches for 2 minutes and 30 seconds. Drain and place on a paper-towel-lined cookie sheet to absorb excess oil.

• Once all the shoestring potatoes have been blanched, increase fryer temperature to 365°F (180°C). Place a handful or two of the fries in the basket and fry for 4 to 6 minutes, until fries are golden brown and crisp. Drain and transfer to a bowl.

• Season to taste with Bone Dust™ BBQ Seasoning, then set aside and keep warm.

THE BURGER

1½ lb	ice-cold ground turkey	675 g
1½ lb	ice-cold turkey breast meat, finely chopped	675 g
¾ cup	corn flake crumbs	175 mL
1	large egg	1
2 Tbsp	mayonnaise	30 mL
1 cup	red onion, minced	250 mL
2	green onions, minced	2
½ cup	Romano cheese, grated	125 mL
1 tsp	cracked black pepper	5 mL
½ tsp	cayenne pepper	2.5 mL
2 tsp	salt	10 mL
2 Tbsp	fresh sage, chopped	30 mL
12	slices provolone or smoked provolone cheese	12
12	thick slices marble rye bread	12
6 tsp	mayonnaise	30 mL
6	thick slices ripe beefsteak tomato	6
1	medium red onion, super thinly sliced	1

THE BURGER: In a bowl, combine ground turkey and chopped turkey breast meat with corn flake crumbs, egg, mayonnaise, red onion and green onions, Romano cheese and black pepper, cayenne pepper, salt and sage.

• Mix well and form into twelve 4 oz (120 g) round burgers approximately 1 inch (2.5 cm) thick and 4 inches (10 cm) in diameter. Place burgers on a tray or plate, cover and refrigerate for 1 hour. This will allow the meat to rest.

• Preheat grill to medium-high, 450–550°F (230–280°C).

• Grill turkey burgers for 3 to 5 minutes per side, until well-done but still moist and juicy. Top each burger with a slice of provolone cheese, close lid and allow cheese to melt.

• Meanwhile, prepare the shoestring fries per method above.

• Remove burgers from grill.

ASSEMBLE YOUR BURGERS! Marble rye, Smoky Russian Dressing, one burger patty, a handful of crispy, hot shoestring fries, a second burger patty, thick slice of tomato, a scoop of slaw, thinly sliced red onion and top it. Repeat with remaining burgers.

MAKES 6 BURGERS

THANKSGIVING SLIDERS
WITH CRANBERRY ICE WINE RELISH

CRANBERRY ICE WINE RELISH

1 tsp	butter	5 mL
1 Tbsp	fresh shallot, chopped	15 mL
1 tsp	fresh thyme, chopped	5 mL
1½ cups	fresh or frozen cranberries	375 mL
½ cup	sugar	125 mL
¼ cup	dried cranberries, soaked in warm water for 15 minutes	60 mL
½ cup	ice wine	125 mL
1 tsp	lemon juice	5 mL
	Salt and pepper, to taste	

THE STUFFING

½ to ¾ lb	butter, melted	225–350 g
1	loaf stale enriched white bread, broken into crumbs	1
1	small onion, diced	1
1	rib celery, diced	1
2 Tbsp	fresh savory or sage, chopped	30 mL
	Salt and pepper, to taste	

When I first made these sliders, it was the day after Thanksgiving. I took the leftover turkey, diced it up and mixed it with ground turkey to make the burgers. Add your leftover cranberry relish and stuffing mixture and the recipe becomes pretty easy. This is a great way to use up leftovers.

CRANBERRY ICE WINE RELISH: In a medium saucepan, over medium-low heat, melt the butter. Sautée the shallot and thyme for 1 to 2 minutes, until tender.

• Add the fresh or frozen cranberries and, while stirring continuously, cook until the berries start to soften and split—about 4 to 5 minutes.

• Add sugar, drained soaked cranberries and ice wine. Bring to a boil. Add lemon juice. Season to taste with salt and pepper.

• Reduce heat to low and simmer for 10 minutes, until thick. Set aside and keep warm.

THE STUFFING: In a saucepan, melt the butter.

• In a large bowl, combine the bread crumbs, onion and celery. Sprinkle with plenty of dried savory, salt and pepper.

• Pour the butter over the bread crumb mixture and mix well to moisten. The stuffing mixture should be moist but not wet.

• Take a 2-foot (60 cm) long piece of aluminum foil and place it on a flat work surface.

• Pour stuffing mixture onto foil and form into a 4-inch (10 cm) thick cylinder. Tip gently; squish the moist stuffing together so that it holds its shape. Roll from the bottom up to make a nice sealed tube of stuffing.

• Preheat grill to medium heat, 350–450°F (175–230°C).

• Place the cylinder of stuffing on the top rack of your grill and close lid. Grill-bake the stuffing 30 to 35 minutes, rotating a quarter turn every 10 minutes, until stuffing mixture is hot.

• Remove from grill and set aside to cool. Transfer to the refrigerator and allow to set.

THE BURGER

1 lb	ice-cold ground turkey	454 g
1 lb	ice-cold turkey breast meat, finely chopped	454 g
½ cup	panko (Japanese-style) bread crumbs	125 mL
1	large egg	1
6	cloves garlic, minced	6
1	small sweet onion, finely diced	1
1 Tbsp	fresh savory or sage, chopped	15 mL
½ tsp	black pepper	2.5 mL
2 tsp	salt	10 mL
	Nonstick cooking spray	
2 cups	Swiss cheese, shredded	500 mL
1	fresh baguette, cut into sixteen 1-inch (2.5 cm) thick rounds	
	Mayonnaise	
	Radish, thinly sliced	
	Onion, thinly sliced	

THE BURGER: In a bowl, combine ground turkey and chopped turkey breast meat with panko bread crumbs, egg, garlic, onion, sage, black pepper and salt. Mix well.

• Form into sixteen 2-oz (60 g) round burgers. Make these burgers nice and thin, approximately 2 inches (5 cm) in diameter. Place burgers on a tray or plate, cover and refrigerate for 1 hour. This will allow the meat to rest.

• Remove turkey stuffing tube from the refrigerator and slice into sixteen 1-inch (2.5 cm) thick discs. Spray liberally with nonstick cooking spray. Set aside.

• Preheat grill to medium-high, 450–550°F (230–280°C).

• Grill turkey burgers for 2 to 3 minutes per side, until well done but still moist and juicy. At the same time, grill the slices of stuffing mixture just to warm.

• Top each burger with a little shredded Swiss cheese and close lid, allowing the cheese on the burgers to melt.

• Warm slices of baguette on the grill.

ASSEMBLE YOUR BURGERS! Brush each slice of baguette with a little mayonnaise. Top with warmed slice of stuffing, top with turkey burger slider, a little Cranberry Ice Wine Relish and garnish with a slice of fresh radish and onion. Serve immediately.

MAKES 16 SLIDERS

CALIFORNIA-SMOKED TURKEY BURGER

SMOKY MAPLE BASTE

¼ cup	maple syrup	60 mL
2 Tbsp	brown sugar	30 mL
½ cup	Ted's World Famous BBQ Crazy Canuck Sticky Chicken and Rib Sauce or your favorite gourmet-style sweet BBQ sauce	125 mL
2–3	drops hickory liquid smoke	2–3
2 Tbsp	butter, melted	30 mL

THE BURGER

1½ lb	ice-cold ground turkey	675 g
½ lb	ice-cold turkey breast thinly sliced in strips	225 g
1	small egg	1
1 Tbsp	mayonnaise	15 mL
1 cup	sweet onion, finely diced	250 mL
1 cup	crushed BBQ flavor Fritos® Corn Chips	250 mL
1 Tbsp	Bone Dust™ BBQ Seasoning (p. 39)	15 mL
1 tsp	smoked paprika	5 mL
1	smoked chipotle pepper in adobo sauce, minced	1
8	slices pepper jack cheese	8
8	sourdough hamburger buns	8
1	ripe avocado, peeled seeded and sliced into 16 thin wedges	1
1 lb	smoked turkey breast, deli shaved	454 g
	Alfalfa sprouts	

This turkey burger is sweet and smoky. I love the contrast in textures that comes from having ground turkey with thinly sliced strips of turkey in it. The burger has more bite, and with the added deli shaved smoked turkey, it becomes a decadent eating experience.

SMOKY MAPLE BASTE: In a bowl, combine maple syrup, brown sugar, BBQ sauce and liquid smoke. While stirring continuously, add the melted butter 1 Tbsp at a time. Set aside until needed.

THE BURGER: In a bowl, combine ground turkey and thinly sliced turkey breast meat with egg, mayonnaise, onion, corn chips, Bone Dust™ BBQ Seasoning, smoked paprika and chipotle pepper. Mix well.

• Form into eight 4-oz (120 g) round burgers approximately 1 inch (2.5 cm) thick and 4 inches (10 cm) in diameter. Place burgers on a tray or plate, cover and refrigerate for 1 hour. This will allow the meat to rest.

• Preheat grill to medium-high, 450–550°F (230–280°C).

• Grill turkey burgers for 4 to 5 minutes per side, basting with Smoky Maple Baste, until well-done but still moist and juicy.

• Top each burger with a slice of pepper jack cheese, close lid and allow cheese to melt.

• Warm buns.

ASSEMBLE YOUR BURGERS! Brush bun bottom with mayonnaise. Top with burger. Garnish each with 2 slices of avocado, 2 oz (60 g) of deli shaved smoked turkey and alfalfa sprouts. Add bun top and drizzle with a little extra Smoky Maple Baste. Serve immediately.

MAKES 8 BURGERS

TRIPLE-DECKER TURKEY CLUBHOUSE BURGER

CLUB BASTING SAUCE

¼ cup	vegetable oil	60 mL
¼ cup	white vinegar	60 mL
1 tsp	white sugar	5 mL
2	cloves garlic, minced	2
1 Tbsp	fresh parsley, chopped	15 mL
1 Tbsp	fresh oregano, chopped	15 mL
1 tsp	kosher salt	5 mL
½ tsp	black pepper, coarsely ground	2.5 mL
½ tsp	red chilies, crushed	2.5 mL
½ tsp	celery salt	2.5 mL
½ tsp	mustard powder	2.5 mL

CHEESY PEPPERCORN RANCH DRESSING

¼ cup	sour cream	60 mL
¼ cup	mayonnaise	60 mL
¼ cup	cream cheese	60 mL
¼ cup	Parmesan cheese, grated	125 mL
1	lemon, juiced	1
1 Tbsp	fresh parsley, chopped	15 mL
1 Tbsp	cracked black pepper	15 mL
1 tsp	garlic, minced	5 mL
	Salt, to taste	
	Hot sauce	

One of my favorite sandwiches is the club. Two meaty turkey burgers between layers of Texas Toast, with all those favorite sandwich trimmings—lettuce, tomato, onions, cheese and, of course, bacon.

CLUB BASTING SAUCE: In a jar with a lid, combine the vegetable oil, vinegar, sugar, garlic, parsley, oregano, salt, black pepper, chilies, celery salt and mustard powder. Seal jar and shake. Set aside.

MAKES APPROXIMATELY ¾ CUP (175 ML)

CHEESY PEPPERCORN RANCH DRESSING: In a bowl, stir together the sour cream, mayonnaise, cream cheese, Parmesan cheese, lemon juice, parsley, black pepper and garlic. Season to taste with salt and a dash or two of hot sauce and set aside.

THE BURGER

1 lb	ice-cold ground turkey	454 g
1 lb	ice-cold turkey breast meat, finely chopped	454 g
1 cup	saltine cracker crumbs	250 mL
1	large egg	1
2 Tbsp	mayonnaise	30 mL
1 tsp	cracked black pepper	5 mL
½ tsp	cayenne pepper	2.5 mL
2 tsp	salt	10 mL
	Hot Sauce, to taste	
8	slices Muenster cheese	8
16	slices bacon, cooked until crisp, and drained	16
12	slices Texas Toast white bread	12
6 tsp	mayonnaise	30 mL
4	leaves green leaf lettuce	4
4	thick slices ripe beefsteak tomato	4
1	medium red onion, super thinly sliced	1

THE BURGER: In a bowl, combine ground turkey and chopped turkey breast meat with cracker crumbs, egg, mayonnaise, black pepper, cayenne pepper and salt. Season to taste with a dash or two of hot sauce.

• Mix well and form into eight 4-oz (120 g) square burgers approximately 1 inch (2.5 cm) thick and 4 inches (10 cm) across. Place burgers on a tray or plate, cover and refrigerate for 1 hour. This will allow the meat to rest.

• Shake up Club Basting Sauce.

• Preheat grill to medium-high, 450–550°F (230–280°C).

• Grill turkey burgers for 3 to 5 minutes per side, basting liberally with Club Basting Sauce until burgers are well-done but still moist and juicy.

• Top each burger with a slice of Muenster cheese, close lid and allow cheese to melt.

• Toast Texas Toast until golden brown.

• Remove burgers from grill.

ASSEMBLE YOUR BURGERS! One slice of toast brushed with ranch dressing, topped with a leaf of lettuce, the burger, bacon and tomato, a second slice of toast brushed with ranch dressing on the top side, topped with a second leaf of lettuce, another burger, bacon and tomato and finished with the last slice of toast.

MAKES 4 SANDWICHES

TURDUCKEN BURGER
WITH HONEY DEW ORANGE GLAZING SYRUP

SOUTHERN COMFORT HONEY DEW GLAZING SYRUP

¼ cup	frozen concentrated orange juice, thawed	60 mL
½ cup	honey	125 mL
2 Tbsp	brown sugar	30 mL
2 Tbsp	ketchup	30 mL
¼ tsp	Worcestershire sauce	1 mL
1 oz	Southern Comfort	30 mL

TURDUCKEN FOIE STUFFING MIX

½ lb	foie gras, cleaned of veins	225 g
Big Drizzle	Southern Comfort	Big Drizzle
½ cup	ground duck meat (grind it yourself using a meat grinder —see p. 20—or ask your butcher for ground duck)	125 mL
	Salt and pepper, to taste	

CHICKEN BURGER

¾ lb	ice-cold ground chicken breast meat	375 g
½ lb	ice-cold chicken breast meat, finely chopped	225 g
3 Tbsp	panko (Japanese-style) bread crumbs	45 mL
2 Tbsp	ground Parmesan cheese	30 mL
1 tsp	salt	5 mL
	Freshly ground black pepper	

Only a select group of butchers have mastered making a really great Turducken. A Turducken is a boneless chicken stuffed into a boneless duck, which is in turn stuffed into a boneless turkey. Between each bird layer is a stuffing made from ground sausage. The dish—a holiday extravaganza—is lots of work and can be very expensive. So instead, I make a Turducken Burger— a chicken burger stuffed with foie gras, then stuffed into a duck burger, which in turn is stuffed into a turkey burger.

SOUTHERN COMFORT HONEY DEW GLAZING SYRUP: In a bowl, whisk together the concentrated orange juice, honey, brown sugar, ketchup, Worcestershire sauce and Southern Comfort. Set aside.

MAKES APPROXIMATELY 1 CUP (250 ML)

TURDUCKEN FOIE STUFFING MIX: In a bowl, break apart the lobe of foie gras. Carefully remove any remaining veins. Drizzle with Southern Comfort and season with salt and freshly ground black pepper, cover and refrigerate for 1 hour.

• Remove from refrigerator and add ground duck meat to the foie gras. Working quickly, mix the seasoned marinated pieces of foie gras with the ground duck. Scoop tablespoon-sized (15 mL) balls onto a parchment-paper-lined flat surface. Loosely cover and place in the freezer for a minimum of 1 hour.

CHICKEN BURGER: In a bowl, combine ground chicken, chopped chicken, bread crumbs, Parmesan cheese and salt. Season liberally with ground black pepper. Mix well but gently.

• Divide mixture into 8 equal portions approximately 2 to 3 oz (60–100 g) each.

• On a piece of parchment paper or plastic wrap, press each portion into a flat 4-inch (10 cm) disc-shaped burger. Place a piece of frozen foie gras mix on top of each flattened chicken patty. Mold the chicken burger around the foie gras mix, packing it firmly into the shape of a small ball. Cover on a plate, and put in freezer.

• Next, make the Duck Burger.

DUCK BURGER

1½ lb	ice-cold ground duck	675 g
½ cup	corn flake crumbs	125 mL
1 Tbsp	apple butter	15 mL
1 tsp	orange zest, freshly grated	5 mL
1 Tbsp	fresh sage, chopped	15 mL
½ tsp	black pepper, ground	2.5 mL
¼ tsp	allspice, ground	1 mL
Pinch	cinnamon	Pinch
	Salt, to taste	

TURKEY BURGER

2	maple or oak or cedar planks, 12 inches long by 6 inches wide by 1/2 inch thick (30 cm by 15 cm by 1.5 cm), soaked in water for a minimum of 1 hour	
1 lb	ice-cold ground turkey	454 g
1 lb	turkey breast meat, finely chopped	454 g
½ cup	panko (Japanese-style) bread crumbs	125 mL
1	small egg	1
1	small onion, diced	1
¼ cup	Parmesan cheese, grated	60 mL
1 tsp	cracked black pepper	5 mL
¼ tsp	cayenne pepper	1 mL
2 tsp	salt	10 mL
1 Tbsp	fresh sage, chopped	15 mL

DUCK BURGER: In a bowl, combine ice-cold ground duck, corn flake crumbs, apple butter, orange zest, sage, black pepper, allspice and cinnamon. Season to taste with salt. Mix well but gently.

• Divide mixture into 8 equal portions approximately 3 to 4 oz (100–120 g) each.

• Working on a piece of parchment paper or plastic wrap, press each portion to a flat 4- to 5-inch (10–12.5 cm) disc-shaped burger. Take foie gras-stuffed chicken burgers from the freezer and place on top of each flattened duck patty. Mold the duck burger around the foie gras-stuffed chicken burger, packing it firmly and into the shape of a medium-sized ball. Place on a plate, cover and put back in freezer.

• Next, make the Turkey Burger.

TURKEY BURGER: In a bowl, combine ground turkey and chopped turkey breast meat with panko bread crumbs, egg, onion, Parmesan cheese, black pepper, cayenne pepper, salt and sage. Mix well but gently.

• Divide mixture into 8 equal portions approximately 4 to 5-oz (120–150 g) maximum each.

• Working on a piece of parchment paper or plastic wrap, press each portion to a flat 5- to 6-inch (12.5–15 cm) disc-shaped burger. Take foie gras-stuffed chicken stuffed duck burgers from the freezer and place on top of each flattened turkey patty. Mold the turkey burger around the foie gras-stuffed chicken stuffed duck burger, packing it firmly and into the shape of a large large-sized softball.

NOTE: Do not flatten the burgers; leave them shaped like baseballs. This will help keep your burgers moist and juicy, and keep all the layers intact when you cut into the burger.

• Place burgers on a tray or plate, cover and refrigerate for 1 hour to allow the meat to rest.

• Preheat grill to medium-high, 450–550°F (230–280°C).

• Evenly space 4 burgers on each plank. Place on grill and close lid. Plank-bake for 30 to 40 minutes, basting with reserved Honey Dew Glazing Syrup during the last 15 minutes of planking, until the burgers are fully cooked but still moist and juicy and have reached an internal temperature of 160°F (75°C).

• Remove burgers from grill.

ASSEMBLE YOUR BURGERS! Serve with a knife and fork, or serve on your favorite buns with all your favorite burger condiments.

MAKES 8 BURGERS

DUCK BURGERS

PLANKED PROSCIUTTO-WRAPPED DUCK BURGER
WITH APPLE BUTTER BASTE

APPLE BUTTER BASTE

½ cup	apple butter	125 mL
½ cup	brown sugar	125 mL
¼ cup	Gentleman Jack Rare Tennessee Whiskey	60 mL
¼ cup	apple juice	60 mL
¼ cup	dehydrated apple, finely diced	60 mL
2 tsp	ginger	10 mL
¼ tsp	cracked black pepper	1 mL
Pinch	cinnamon	Pinch
	Salt	

THE BURGER

2	apple wood or cedar, maple or oak planks, 12 inches long by ½-inch thick (30 cm by 1.5 cm), soaked in water for at least 1 hour	
1½ lb	ice-cold ground duck	675 g
¼ cup	apple butter	60 mL
½ cup	corn flake crumbs	125 mL
1 tsp	ginger, minced	5 mL
3	cloves garlic, minced	3
¼ cup	shallot, finely diced	60 mL
1 Tbsp	fresh thyme, chopped	15 mL
1 tsp	black pepper, coarsely ground	5 mL
2 tsp	salt	10 mL
6	slices prosciutto	6
6	toothpicks	6

APPLE BUTTER BASTE: In a small saucepan, combine apple butter, brown sugar, Gentleman Jack, apple juice, dehydrated apple, ginger, black pepper and cinnamon. Heat slowly over medium heat, stirring occasionally, until thick and sticky. Set aside and keep warm.

MAKES APPROXIMATELY 2 CUPS (500 ML)

THE BURGER: Place ice-cold ground duck into a large bowl. Add apple butter, corn flake crumbs, ginger, garlic, shallot, thyme, black pepper and salt. Mix well and form into six 4-inch (10 cm) high and 2-inch (5 cm) square tower-like burgers.

• Wrap each burger with a slice of prosciutto and secure with a toothpick. Place on a plate, cover and refrigerate for at least 1 hour.

• Preheat grill to medium, 350–450°F (175–230°C).

• Evenly space 3 burgers on each plank. Place on grill and close lid.

• Plank-roast duck burgers for 20 to 25 minutes, basting frequently with reserved Apple Butter Baste, until the burgers are fully cooked (have reached an internal temperature of 160°F/70°C) and the prosciutto is crisp.

• Baste with extra sauce.

• Remove from grill.

ASSEMBLE YOUR BURGERS! Suggestion: Multi-grain bun, burger, your favorite burger toppings and top with bun top.

MAKES 6 BURGERS

Gentleman Jack is a registered trademark ©2010
A gentleman knows his limits. Drink responsibly.

DUCK BURGER SLIDERS SALAD
WITH CHAMBORD AND BLUE CHEESE

BLOOD ORANGE DRESSING

4	blood oranges, peeled and segmented, juices reserved	4
2	shallots, finely chopped	2
¼ cup	honey	60 mL
¼ cup	blackberries, smashed	60 mL
¼ cup	raspberry vinegar	60 mL
1 oz	Chambord Black Raspberry Liqueur	30 mL
½ tsp	ginger, minced	2.5 mL
1 tsp	fresh tarragon, chopped	5 mL
	Salt and pepper, to taste	

THE BURGER

1½ lb	ice-cold ground duck	375 g
¼ cup	mashed blackberries	60 mL
½ cup	panko (Japanese-style) bread crumbs	125 mL
¼ cup	almonds, ground	60 mL
2	cloves garlic, minced	2
1 Tbsp	Bone Dust™ BBQ Seasoning (p. 39)	15 mL
Splash	Chambord Black Raspberry Liqueur	Splash
4	handfuls mixed baby greens (combination of radicchio, Belgium endive, arugula, Swiss chard, pea shoots and baby leaf lettuces)	4
½ cup	crumbled blue cheese or Stilton blue cheese	125 mL
¼ cup	toasted slivered almonds	60 mL
	Nonstick cooking spray	

This elegant burger salad made from succulent duck is a great way to start a backyard dinner party.

BLOOD ORANGE DRESSING: In a small saucepan, over medium heat, combine the blood orange segments and juices, shallots, honey, blackberries, raspberry vinegar, Chambord and ginger. Heat slowly, stirring occasionally, until warm. Add tarragon and season to taste with salt and freshly ground black pepper.

THE BURGER: In a bowl, combine duck, blackberries, bread crumbs, garlic and Bone Dust™ BBQ Seasoning. Add a splash of Chambord.

• Form into twelve 2-oz (60 g) mini burgers approximately ½ inch (2.5 cm) thick and 2 inches (5 cm) in diameter. Place on a plate, cover and refrigerate for a minimum of 1 hour.

• Preheat grill to medium-high, 450–550°F (230–280°C).

• Spray burgers with nonstick cooking spray.

• Grill burgers for 3 to 5 minutes per side, until they are just well-done but still moist and juicy.

• Place salad greens on four separate plates. Sprinkle with crumbled blue cheese and almonds.

• Place three mini duck burgers on each plate and drizzle liberally with Blood Orange Dressing. Serve immediately.

MAKES 12 SLIDERS

FOIE GRAS-PULLED PORK BURGER
WITH GREEN APPLE SLAW

GREEN APPLE SLAW

1	green apple, thinly sliced and cut into julienne strips	1
4	radishes, thinly sliced and cut into julienne strips	4
½	red onion, thinly sliced	½
1 Tbsp	fresh chives, chopped	15 mL
3 Tbsp	cider vinegar	45 mL
2 Tbsp	olive oil	30 mL

THE BURGER

	Napoleon Grill Topper	
3 cups	BBQ pulled-pork, shredded (p. 131)	750 mL
1	lobe ice-cold foie gras, cleaned of veins	1
1 Tbsp	apple butter	15 mL
½ cup	panko bread crumbs	125 mL
1 Tbsp	fresh thyme, chopped	15 mL
Splash	Jack Daniel's Tennessee Whiskey	Splash
	Salt and freshly ground black pepper, to taste	
Drizzle	honey	Drizzle
1	fresh baguette (French stick), sliced, into 16 rounds	1

GREEN APPLE SLAW: In a bowl, combine green apple, radishes, red onion, chives, cider vinegar and olive oil. Gently mix and season with salt and freshly ground black pepper. Cover and refrigerate until needed.

THE BURGER: Prepare the pulled-pork (see p. 131). Do not add any sauce to the recipe at this time; the smoked and shredded, pulled-pork is all you will need.

• Place the pulled-pork in a large bowl. Set aside.

• Break apart the lobe of foie gras and remove any remaining veins. You will need to add approximately half the foie gras to the pulled-pork mixture.

• Add apple butter, bread crumbs, thyme and a big splash of Jack Daniel's. Season to taste with salt and freshly ground black pepper. Quickly mix, breaking the foie gras into small pieces. Place bowl in refrigerator for 1 hour to keep cold.

• Remove meat mixture from refrigerator and form into sixteen 2-oz (60 g) mini burgers. Place on a parchment-paper-lined cookie sheet and again refrigerate for 1 hour.

• Preheat grill to medium-high, 450–550°F (230–280°C).

• Place Grill Topper on grill.

• Lightly toast the slices of baguette. Set aside.

• Place foie gras-pulled pork burgers on Grill Topper and close lid. These will not take long to heat up—approximately 8 minutes. Remember, foie gras is delicate and mostly fat, so be careful not to overcook or you will lose all the foie in the bottom of your grill.

• Remove from grill. Place one foie gras-pulled pork burger on top of each slice of baguette. Drizzle with honey and garnish with Green Apple Slaw. Serve immediately.

MAKES 16 MINI BURGERS

SEAFOOD BURGERS

CHILLED LOBSTER AND AVOCADO BURGER

THE BURGER

3	large, firm but ripe avocados, halved and pit removed	3
1 Tbsp	olive oil	30 mL
	Salt and pepper, to taste	
	Lemon or lime juice	
1 lb	cooked and chilled lobster meat, thawed and drained well if using frozen lobster meat	454 g
½ cup	diced—¼ inch (.5 cm)—white onion	125 mL
2	green onions, thinly sliced on the bias	2
1	small green pepper, diced ¼ inch (.5 cm)	1
1	small red pepper, diced ¼ inch (.5 cm)	1
1	jalapeño pepper, seeded and finely chopped	1
½ cup	mayonnaise	125 mL
1–2 Tbsp	cilantro, chopped	15–30 mL
1-2 Tbsp	lime, juiced	15–30 mL
1 tsp	Bone Dust™ BBQ Seasoning (p. 39)	5 mL
Dash	chipotle chile–flavored Tabasco	Dash
	Salt and pepper, to taste	
4	crusty dinner rolls	4
	Bibb lettuce	
	Ripe tomato, sliced	
	Red onion, sliced	

This burger does not get grilled. It is served cold! It looks like a burger but it is made from cooked lobster with chilled avocado.

• Preheat grill to high, 550°F (280°C).

• Brush avocado halves with olive oil and season with salt and freshly ground black pepper. Grill avocados over high heat for 1 to 2 minutes per side, until lightly charred.

• Remove from grill, cool quickly in refrigerator and brush with lemon or lime juice. Dice avocados.

• In a large bowl, mix the lobster meat, onion, green onions, red and jalapeño peppers, mayonnaise, diced avocado, cilantro, lime juice and Bone Dust™ BBQ Seasoning. Season to taste with a dash of chipotle Tabasco, salt and freshly ground pepper.

• Mix well to incorporate. Cover and refrigerate for 1 hour.

ASSEMBLE YOUR BURGERS! Roll bottom, Bibb lettuce, tomato, red onion, Lobster Avocado Burger, roll top.

TIP: Avocado flesh rapidly discolors when exposed to the air. To prevent discoloration, sprinkle with lemon or lime juice to keep from oxidizing

MAKES 6 BURGERS

GRILLED SALMON BURGER

HORSERADISH CREAM CHEESE SPREAD

½ cup	cream cheese, softened	125 mL
¼ cup	sour cream	60 mL
2 Tbsp	mayonnaise	30 mL
2 Tbsp	hot prepared horseradish	30 mL
½ cup	dill havarti cheese, shredded	125 mL
1 tsp	lemon juice	5 mL
	Salt and freshly ground black pepper, to taste	

CHARDONNAY BUTTER BASTE

¼ cup	butter	60 mL
¼ cup	Lindemans Bin 65 Chardonnay	60 mL
1 Tbsp	lemon juice	15 mL
1 Tbsp	Orgasmic Onion Burger Seasoning (p. 44)	15 mL

THE BURGER

	Meat grinder	
2 lb	ice-cold fresh Atlantic salmon, boneless and skinless	907 g
2	large shallots, finely chopped	2
2	green onions, finely chopped	2
1 Tbsp	fresh dill, chopped	15 mL
2 Tbsp	lemon juice	30 mL
1 oz	Lindemans Bin 65 Chardonnay	30 mL
1 Tbsp	hot prepared horseradish	15 mL
1	egg white	1
½ cup	panko (Japanese-style) bread crumbs	125 mL
1 tsp	Orgasmic Onion Burger Seasoning (p. 44)	5 mL
	Vegetable oil	
	Nonstick cooking spray	
6	pumpernickel bagels	6
6	slices cured or smoked salmon	6
	Dill sprigs	

HORSERADISH CREAM CHEESE SPREAD: In a bowl, whisk together the cream cheese, sour cream, mayonnaise, horseradish, dill havarti cheese and lemon juice. Season to taste with salt and freshly ground black pepper. Cover and refrigerate until needed.

MAKES APPROXIMATELY 2 CUPS (500 ML)

CHARDONNAY BUTTER BASTE: In a small saucepan, combine butter, Chardonnay wine, lemon juice and Orgasmic Onion Burger Seasoning. Stir to combine. Set aside and keep warm.

THE BURGER: Take half the salmon and, using a sharp knife, finely dice the salmon into 1/4-inch (1 cm) cubes. Cover and refrigerate to keep cold.

• Take the remaining salmon and grind it in a meat grinder. Add to diced refrigerated salmon. Transfer to a bowl.

• Combine chopped salmon, shallots, green onions, dill, lemon juice, Chardonnay, horseradish, egg white, panko bread crumbs and seasoning.

• Form into four 6-oz (180 g) patties as uniform in size as possible. A flatter burger will cook more evenly and faster than a ball-like burger. Cover with plastic wrap and refrigerate for 2 hours, to allow the burgers to set up.

NOTE: Get it cold! You can even place the burgers in the freezer to really set them up—for about 30 minutes; you do not want to freeze them.

• Preheat grill to medium-high, 450–550°F (230–280°C).

• Brush burgers with vegetable oil. Grill burgers for 6 to 8 minutes per side, basting liberally as they cook with the Chardonnay Butter Baste, for medium to medium-well doneness.

• Toast bagels.

ASSEMBLE YOUR BURGERS! Pumpernickel bagel, Horseradish Cream Cheese Spread, burger, more Horseradish Cream Cheese Spread, smoked salmon and dill. Serve with a wedge of lemon, some sea salt and vinegar chips.

MAKES 4 BURGERS

CHESAPEAKE CRAB CAKE BURGER

CUCUMBER CABBAGE SLAW

4 cups	white cabbage, grated	1 L
1	large seedless cucumber, grated and squeezed of excess moisture	1
1	small red onion, grated and squeezed of excess moisture	1
2	green onions, chopped	2
1 Tbsp	fresh herbs (a mix of parsley, dill and cilantro), chopped	15 mL
¼ cup	Miracle Whip®	60 mL
2 Tbsp	white vinegar	30 mL
1 Tbsp	lemon juice	15 mL
1 tsp	whole grain mustard	5 mL
1 tsp	Bone Dust™ BBQ Seasoning (p. 39)	5 mL
	Salt and freshly ground black pepper, to taste	

THE BURGER

1	cedar plank, 12 inches long by 8 inches wide by 1/2 inch thick (30 cm by 20 cm by 1.5 cm), soaked in water for a minimum of 1 hour	
1 lb	lump crabmeat	454 g
½	small red onion, finely diced	½
2	green onions, thinly sliced on the bias	2
¾ cup	mayonnaise	180 mL
1 Tbsp	prepared mustard	15 mL
2 Tbsp	chopped fresh herbs (a mix of parsley, dill and cilantro)	30 mL
1	red-hot chile pepper, minced	1
1	red bell pepper, diced	1
1 Tbsp	Bone Dust™ BBQ Seasoning (p. 39)	15 mL
1 Tbsp	lemon juice	15 mL
Dash	hot sauce	Dash
	Salt and pepper, to taste	
24	saltine crackers, coarsely broken	24
4	crusty rolls	4
	Onion sprouts	

The best crab cakes I ever had came from the Captain's Galley Restaurant in Crisfield, Maryland. I think this recipe surpasses that one.

CUCUMBER CABBAGE SLAW: In a bowl, combine white cabbage, cucumber, red onion, green onions, herbs, Miracle Whip®, vinegar, lemon juice and whole grain mustard and Bone Dust™. Season to taste with salt and freshly ground black pepper. Cover and refrigerate for at least an hour so the flavors combine.

MAKES APPROXIMATELY 6 CUPS (1.5 L)

THE BURGER: In a large bowl, combine crabmeat, red and green onions, mayonnaise, mustard, herbs, chile, red pepper, Bone Dust™ BBQ Seasoning and lemon juice. Mix well and season to taste with hot sauce, salt and pepper.

• Gently fold in crackers and combine, being careful not to over mix. The mixture should be a little moist.

• Pack crabmeat into 4 equal-sized balls, pressing excess air out of cake. Form into burgers approximately 1 to 1½ inches (2.5–3.5 cm) thick and 3 inches (7.5 cm) in diameter.

• Preheat grill to medium-high, 450–550°F (230–280°C).

• Place crab cakes on a plank. Close lid and plank-bake for about 20 to 25 minutes, until golden brown and heated through.

ASSEMBLE YOUR BURGERS! Crusty roll bottom, Cucumber Cabbage Slaw, planked crab cake burger, onion sprouts and crusty roll top.

MAKES 4 BURGERS

BACON-WRAPPED SCALLOP BURGER

GREEN MANGO SALAD

1	green mango, peeled and pitted	1
1	red bell pepper, cut into thin strips	1
1	green bell pepper, cut into thin strips	1
1	red onion, thinly sliced	1
3	green onions, thinly sliced	3
1 Tbsp	fresh cilantro, chopped	15 mL
¼ cup	Thai sweet chili sauce	60 mL
3 Tbsp	rice vinegar	45 mL
2 Tbsp	vegetable oil	30 mL
1 Tbsp	garlic, finely chopped	15 mL
2 tsp	sugar	10 mL
1 tsp	fresh ginger, finely chopped	5 mL
1 tsp	fish sauce	5 mL
	Salt and pepper, to taste	

GREEN MANGO SALAD: Cut the mango into thin strips about ¼ inch (.5 cm) thick and 3 inches (7.5 cm) long. Place in a large bowl. Add the red pepper, green pepper, red onion, green onion and cilantro.

• In a small bowl, whisk together the Thai sweet chili sauce, rice vinegar, vegetable oil, garlic, sugar, ginger and fish sauce.

• Pour the dressing over the mango mixture and season to taste with salt and pepper. Toss well. Chill and serve.

SERVES 6

THAI CHILI BUTTER BASTE

½ cup	Thai sweet chili sauce	125 mL
1 Tbsp	fish sauce	15 mL
1 Tbsp	lime juice	15 mL
3 Tbsp	butter	45 mL
1 Tbsp	Parmesan cheese	15 mL

THE BURGER

1	cedar plank, 12 inches long by 8 inches wide by ½ inch thick (30 cm by 20 cm by 1.5 cm), soaked in water for a minimum of 1 hour	
	toothpicks	
½ lb	ice-cold sea scallops	225 g
1 lb	bay scallops	454 g
½ cup	panko (Japanese-style) bread crumbs	125 mL
1 tsp	Bone Dust™ BBQ Seasoning (p. 39)	5 mL
1 Tbsp	lime juice	15 mL
1	egg white	1
	Sea salt and freshly ground black pepper, to taste	
6	slices double smoked bacon	6

THAI CHILI BUTTER BASTE: In a small saucepan, combine Thai sweet chili sauce, fish sauce, lime juice and butter. Heat slowly over medium-low heat, stirring occasionally. Remove from heat and stir in Parmesan cheese. Set aside and keep warm.

THE BURGER: Place sea scallops in a food processor and purée until smooth.

• Transfer to a large bowl. Add bay scallops, panko bread crumbs, mayonnaise, Bone Dust BBQ™ Seasoning, lime juice and egg white. Season with sea salt and freshly ground black pepper.

• Portion into six 4-oz (120 g) burger patties approximately 2 inches (5 cm) thick and 2 to 3 inches (5–7.5 cm) in diameter.

• Wrap each burger with a slice of thickly sliced double-smoked bacon. (Note: The thickness of the burger should be as close to the thickness of the bacon as possible.)

• Secure with a toothpick.

• Place on a parchment-paper-lined plate, cover and refrigerate for at least 1 hour. (Note: You can even place the burgers in the freezer to really set them up— for about 30 minutes; you do not want to freeze them.)

• Preheat grill to medium-high, 450–550°F (230–280°C).

• Place bacon-wrapped burgers on a plank. Close lid and plank-bake for about 18 to 20 minutes, basting with Thai Chili Butter Baste, until the bacon is crisp and the burgers are firm to the touch and heated through.

ASSEMBLE YOUR BURGERS! Green Mango Salad, Bacon-Wrapped Scallop Burger.

MAKES 6 BURGERS

PLANK-GRILLED COD CAKES
WITH ICE SHRIMP SALSA

ICE SHRIMP SALSA

1½ cups	baby ice shrimp, fully cooked	375 mL
½ cup	red onion, finely diced	125 mL
1 Tbsp	lemon juice	15 mL
1 Tbsp	prepared horseradish	15 mL
¼ cup	ketchup	60 mL
1 Tbsp	fresh parsley, chopped	15 mL
Dash	hot sauce	Dash
	Salt and freshly ground black pepper, to taste	

THE BURGER

1	regular apple wood or cedar plank, soaked in water for a minimum of 1 hour	
1 lb	salt codfish	454 g
½ lb	ice-cold sea scallops, chopped	225 g
2 cups	water	500 mL
2 Tbsp	butter	30 mL
½ cup	mayonnaise	125 mL
2	large egg yolks	2
3	cloves garlic, minced	3
2 Tbsp	lemon juice	30 mL
1 Tbsp	fresh cilantro, chopped	15 mL
3	green onions, thinly sliced	3
1	small red onion, diced	1
1 tsp	Bone Dust™ BBQ Seasoning (p. 39)	5 mL
	Salt, pepper and hot sauce, to taste	
2 cups	oyster crackers, coarsely crushed	500 mL
8	small crusty rolls	8

My dad's panfried cod cake recipe taken to the plank. Thanks, Dad!

ICE SHRIMP SALSA: In a bowl, combine baby ice shrimp, red onion, lemon juice, horseradish, ketchup, parsley and hot sauce. Season to taste with salt and pepper. Cover and refrigerate.

THE BURGER: Soak salt cod in water overnight, changing the water three times, until the codfish is hydrated. Drain, rinse and drain again.

• Place salt cod evenly into a 2-inch (5 cm) deep sauté pan. Pour 2 cups (500 mL) of water and add 2 Tbsp (30 mL) of butter. Slowly heat to boiling point and simmer for 5 to 10 minutes. Drain and allow salt cod to cool.

• In a large mixing bowl, whisk together the mayonnaise, egg yolks, garlic, lemon juice, cilantro, green onion, red onion and Bone Dust™ BBQ Seasoning.

• Add the chopped scallops and codfish to the mayonnaise mixture and season to taste with salt, pepper and a dash of hot sauce. Mix to incorporate. Next, add the oyster cracker crumbs and gently mix with your hands mix until everything binds together firmly.

• Form into eight 3-oz (100 g) cakes—you can use an ice-cream scoop to make this a little easier. Evenly space cod cakes on the presoaked plank.

• Preheat grill to medium, 350–450°F (175–230°C).

• Place the planked cod cakes on the grill, close lid and bake for 12 to 15 minutes, until fully cooked and heated through.

NOTE: If the plank catches fire, reduce heat and use a water spray bottle to put out the flames.

• Open grill lid and, using a spatula, carefully remove the cod cakes from the plank.

ASSEMBLE YOUR BURGERS: Roll bottom, leaf lettuce, Ice Shrimp Salsa, planked cod cake, a little more Ice Shrimp Salsa and roll top.

MAKES 8 BURGERS

PUTTING ON THE RITZ: GRILLED SCALLOP SLIDERS

MANGO AVOCADO SALSA

1	ripe mango, peeled and seeded and the flesh diced 1/4 inch	1
1	ripe avocado, peeled, pitted and the flesh diced 1/4 inch	1
½ cup	white onion, finely diced	125 mL
2 Tbsp	lime juice	30 mL
2 Tbsp	orange juice	30 mL
1 Tbsp	honey	15 mL
1 Tbsp	olive oil	15 mL
1 Tbsp	fresh cilantro, chopped	15 mL
2	green onions, chopped	2
1	jalapeño pepper, seeded and finely diced	1
Big Splash	Southern Comfort	Big Splash
	Salt and freshly ground black pepper, to taste	

MUSTARD HONEY DRIZZLE

1 Tbsp	old-fashioned grain mustard	15 mL
¼ cup	honey	60 mL
1 Tbsp	orange juice	15 mL

THE BURGER

	Napoleon Injector	
8	jumbo ice-cold fresh sea scallops, under 6 per lb (.5 kg) if you can find them	8
½ cup	butter, melted	125 mL
¼ cup	Southern Comfort	60 mL
8	Ritz Crackers	8
8	slices prosciutto	8

Fancy-shmancy burgers but oh so delicious!

MANGO AVOCADO SALSA: In a bowl, combine mango, avocado, white onion, lime and orange juice, honey, olive oil, cilantro, green onions and jalapeño pepper. Season to taste with a big splash of Southern Comfort, salt and freshly ground black pepper. Cover and refrigerate until needed.

MAKES ABOUT 3 CUPS (750 ML)

MUSTARD HONEY DRIZZLE: In a small bowl or cup, stir together the mustard, honey and orange juice. Set aside.

THE BURGER: Pat scallops dry with paper toweling. Set aside, refrigerated.

• In a small pot, over medium heat, melt the butter with the Southern Comfort.

• Suck up the melted butter mixture into the Napoleon Injector. Inject each scallop with a little butter–Southern Comfort mixture and place on parchment-paper-lined plate. Cover and place in the freezer for 10 minutes to chill. Reserve any leftover butter mixture for basting.

• Preheat grill to medium-high, 450–550°F (230–280°C).

• Remove burgers from freezer. Season burgers with salt and freshly ground black pepper.

• Grill burgers for 2 to 3 minutes per side, until just cooked through, the flesh is opaque and the outside lightly charred.

ASSEMBLE YOUR BURGERS! Ritz Cracker, prosciutto, grilled scallop, Mango Avocado Salsa. Drizzle with Mustard Honey Drizzle.

MAKES 8 AS AN APPETIZER OR 4 AS A MAIN COURSE

Southern Comfort is a registered trademark © 2010 Please Drink Responsibly.

STUFFED SOFT-SHELL CRAB BURGER

THE BURGER

Napoleon Griddle Pan

1 lb	ice-cold lump crabmeat	454 g
3 Tbsp	mayonnaise	45 mL
½ cup	panko (Japanese-style) bread crumbs	125 mL
2	green onions, diced	2
2	hard-boiled eggs, minced	2
½ cup	red onion, diced	125 mL
Splash	lemon juice	Splash
1 Tbsp	fresh parsley, chopped	15 mL
1 Tbsp	Bone Dust™ BBQ Seasoning (p. 39)	15 mL
	Hot sauce	
	Salt and freshly ground black pepper, to taste	
4	fresh jumbo soft shell crabs, trimmed of bile sack and eyes	4
1 cup	whipping (35%) cream	25 mL
1 cup	ranch dressing	250 mL
1	egg yolk	1
¼ cup	Parmesan cheese, grated	60 mL
½ cup	fine bread crumbs	125 mL
2 cups	panko (Japanese-style) bread crumbs	500 mL
	All-purpose flour	
3 Tbsp	butter	45 mL
¼ cup	vegetable oil	60 mL

There is nothing more special than soft-shell crabs. When in season, they are a special treat. This recipe is a bit of work, but well worth it. Have fun and go a little crazy.

THE BURGER: In a bowl, combine ice-cold crabmeat, mayonnaise, bread crumbs, green onions, hard-boiled eggs, red onion, lemon juice, parsley, Bone Dust™ BBQ Seasoning and a dash or two of hot sauce. Season to taste with salt and freshly ground black pepper.

• Using a 3-oz (100 mL) ice-cream scoop, scoop the crab mixture into 6 equal-sized balls.

• Season soft-shell crabs with salt and freshly ground black pepper.

• Place a crab cake ball on top of each soft-shell crab and press to lightly flatten so that the crab cake and crab adhere. Place on a parchment-paper-lined plate and put in the freezer for approximately 30 minutes.

• Pour whipping cream into a large bowl and add ranch dressing, egg yolk and Parmesan cheese. Whisk until smooth.

• Place fine bread crumbs and panko bread crumbs into a bowl.

• Take soft shell crab burger and dust evenly with all-purpose flour—not too heavily, just lightly.

• Dip the dusted soft-shell crab burgers into the whipping cream–ranch dressing mixture, coating completely. Next, dip them in the bread-crumb mixture, being sure to cover the entire burger and pressing so that the breading adheres. Place on a parchment-paper-lined cookie sheet. Set aside.

• Preheat grill to medium, 350–450°F (175–230°C).

• Place the Napoleon Griddle over the burner.

• Melt butter and oil on griddle pan. Griddle-fry the soft-shell crab burgers for 3 to 5 minutes per side, until the breading is golden brown and crisp. Place on upper grill rack, close lid and continue to cook for 5 to 8 minutes, until heated through. Brush with a little butter.

ASSEMBLE YOUR BURGERS! Serve with a salad.

MAKES 6 BURGERS

CEDAR-PLANKED TILAPIA SLIDERS
WITH PEAR AND RADISH SLAW

PEAR AND RADISH SLAW

¼ cup	red onion, thinly sliced into matchstick-sized strips	60 mL
2	Bartlett pears, grated	2
8	red radishes, thinly sliced and cut into matchstick-sized strips	8
2 Tbsp	olive oil	30 mL
2 Tbsp	fresh cilantro, chopped	30 mL
1 Tbsp	fresh lime juice	15 mL
	Salt and freshly ground black pepper, to taste	

THE BURGER

1	cedar plank, 12 inches long by 8 inches wide by ½ inch thick (30 cm by 20 cm by 1.5 cm), soaked in water for a minimum of 1 hour	1
1½ lb	ice-cold boneless tilapia	675 g
½ cup	red onion, finely diced	125 mL
2	green onions, finely chopped	2
2 Tbsp	Orgasmic Onion Burger Seasoning (p. 44)	30 mL
1 Tbsp	fresh dill, chopped	15 mL
1 tsp	fresh lemon juice	5 mL
½ cup	panko (Japanese-style) bread crumbs	125 mL
1	egg white	1
8	slices Emmenthal cheese	8
8	slices baguette	8
	Mayonnaise or tartar sauce	

PEAR AND RADISH SLAW: In a bowl, combine the red onion, pears, radishes, olive oil, cilantro and lime juice. Season to taste with salt and freshly ground black pepper. Cover and refrigerate until needed.

THE BURGER: Using a sharp knife, finely chop half the tilapia; then using a meat grinder, grind the remaining tilapia.

• In a bowl, mix the chopped and ground tilapia, red onion, green onions, cilantro, Orgasmic Onion Burger Seasoning, lemon juice, panko bread crumbs and egg white. The mixture should be a little moist and sticky, but not too dry.

• Using an ice-cream scoop, form into 8 mini burgers. Evenly space burgers on the presoaked cedar plank. Cover with plastic wrap and refrigerate for 1 to 2 hours.

• Preheat grill to medium-high, 450–550°F (230–280°C).

• Plank-grill tilapia burgers for 15 to 18 minutes, until just about cooked through, checking once or twice to ensure that the planks have not caught fire.

• During the last few minutes of plank-grilling, top each tilapia burger with a slice of Emmenthal cheese; close lid and allow the cheese to melt.

• Open grill and carefully remove the hot planks. Using a spatula, remove tilapia burgers from plank.

ASSEMBLE YOUR BURGERS! Fresh baguette, mayo or tartar sauce, burger. Top with Pear and Radish Slaw.

MAKES 8 BURGERS

SUSHI-TUNA BURGER

SUSHI RICE

1 cup	short grain rice	250 mL
2 cups	water	500 mL

THE BURGER

½ lb	ice-cold fresh sushi-grade tuna, finely chopped	250 g
1 Tbsp	coconut water	15 mL
1 Tbsp	lime juice	15 mL
Splash	Finlandia Vodka	Splash
	salt and freshly ground black pepper, to taste	
2	green onions, finely chopped	2
1 Tbsp	fresh cilantro, chopped	15 mL
	a few dashes of fish sauce	
2	4-oz (120 g) portions ice-cold fresh sushi-grade tuna cut into long 2-inch (5 cm) squares	2
1 Tbsp	Bone Dust™ BBQ Seasoning (p. 39)	15 mL
	Onion sprouts	
	Wasabi	
	Pickled ginger	
	Soy sauce	

You will need 1 lb of fresh sushi-grade tuna. Half is needed for grilling, half for tartar.

SUSHI RICE: Rinse rice well, 5 or 6 times, until water runs clear.

• Put the rice into a pot that has a tight-fitting lid. Add the water and bring to a boil, uncovered, over high heat.

• Cover and reduce heat to medium-low. Cook, covered, for 15 minutes.

• Remove from heat and allow rice to sit for 5 minutes, covered.

• Transfer the rice to a large Tupperware container or roasting pan. Spread the rice evenly to allow the steam to escape.

• Allow rice to cool. Cover and set aside.

THE BURGER: Using a sharp knife, finely dice 8 oz (250 g) of tuna, being careful not to over chop and make the tuna mushy.

• Place tuna in a large bowl. Add coconut water, lime juice and vodka, and season with salt and freshly ground black pepper to taste. Cover and marinate, refrigerated, for 15 minutes.

• Add the green onions, cilantro and fish sauce to the tuna mixture and gently mix. Form into 1- to 2-oz (30–60 g) mini tuna-tartar burgers. Place on a parchment-paper-lined plate and keep refrigerated.

• Preheat Napoleon Sizzle Zone™ to high, 1800°F (900°C).

• Season the 2 x 4 oz (125 g each) rectangles of sushi-grade tuna with Bone Dust™ BBQ Seasoning.

• Sear tuna on all 4 sides over the Sizzle Zone™ for about 30 seconds per side. Remove and slice on the bias into a ¼-inch (.5 cm) thick square.

ASSEMBLE YOUR BURGERS! Make a Sushi Rice ball and press to lightly flatten. Smear a little wasabi paste on top of the rice. Top with tuna tartar burger and finish with a slice of Bone Dust™–rubbed-seared tuna. Drizzle with soy sauce, and serve with pickled ginger and wasabi, if you so desire.

MAKES 12 BITE-SIZED BURGERS

Finlandia Vodka is a registered trademark ©2010 Keep your senses pure. Drink responsibly.

MOZZARELLA TUNA BURGER

CRAB AND AVOCADO SALSA

1/2 cup	lump crabmeat	125 mL
1	avocado, peeled and pitted and diced	1
2	green onions, diced	2
¼ cup	red onion, diced	60 mL
1 Tbsp	fresh chives, chopped	15 mL
1 Tbsp	lemon juice	15 mL
1 Tbsp	olive oil	15 mL
	Salt and freshly ground black pepper, to taste	

This is a rich and delicious burger. Make fresh and grill to medium-rare or medium for a moist and succulent burger.

CRAB AND AVOCADO SALSA: In a bowl, combine crabmeat, avocado, green onions, red onion, chives, lemon juice and olive oil. Gently mix. Season to taste with salt and freshly ground black pepper.

• Set aside, refrigerated.

CRISPY CRUST

4	cloves roasted garlic, minced	4
3 Tbsp	olive oil	45 mL
1 Tbsp	lemon juice	15 mL
½ tsp	kosher salt	2.5 mL
1 tsp	black pepper, freshly ground	5 mL
3 Tbsp	panko (Japanese-style) bread crumbs	45 mL

SAMBAL SOY

2 tsp	sambal chili sauce	10 mL
¼ cup	sashimi soy sauce	60 mL
1 Tbsp	green onion, minced	15 mL

THE BURGER

Meat grinder
Cookie Sheet

1 lb	ice-cold tuna	454 g
½ cup	frozen, partly skimmed mozzarella, finely diced	125 mL
1	egg white	1
1 cup	panko (Japanese-style) bread crumbs	250 mL
2 Tbsp	Orgasmic Onion Burger Seasoning (p. 44)	30 mL
2	green onions, minced	2
1 Tbsp	fresh flat-leaf parsley, chopped	15 mL
	Salt and freshly ground black pepper, to taste	
	Nonstick cooking spray	
2 cups	panko (Japanese-style) bread crumbs	500 mL

CRISPY CRUST: In a bowl, combine roasted garlic, olive oil, lemon juice, kosher salt and freshly ground black pepper. Add in the bread crumbs and stir until mixture forms a paste. You may need to add a few more panko bread crumbs to absorb most of the oil. Set aside.

SAMBAL SOY: In a bowl, combine sambal chili sauce, soy and green onion. Set aside.

THE BURGER: Using a meat grinder or food processor, grind half the tuna into a smooth paste. Transfer to a bowl. Set aside.

• Using a sharp knife, dice the other half of the tuna into ¼-inch (1 cm) dice. Add to bowl of ground tuna.

• Add frozen mozzarella cheese cubes. Add egg white, panko bread crumbs, Orgasmic Onion Burger Seasoning, green onions and parsley, and season to taste with salt and freshly ground black pepper.

• Form into six 3-oz (100 g) mini square or round burger patties approximately 1 to 1½ inches (2.5–3.5 cm) thick. Place on a parchment-paper-lined cookie sheet, cover and refrigerate, allowing the burgers to set.

• Preheat grill to medium, 350–450°F (175–230°C).

• Remove burgers from refrigerator and spray liberally with nonstick cooking spray. Roll burgers lightly in 2 cups (500 mL) of panko bread crumbs.

• Grill burgers for 3 to 5 minutes on one side, turn burgers over and top with a tablespoon of Crispy Crust mixture, reduce heat directly under the burgers, close lid and continue to cook for 3 to 5 minutes more, until the burger is crispy on the outside, moist and cheesy on the inside and heated through.

ASSEMBLE YOUR BURGERS! Burger with Crispy Crust, Crab and Avocado Salsa, onion sprouts, and drizzle with Sambal Soy.

MAKES 6 BURGERS

HALIBUT KING CRAB BURGER
WITH PANCETTA

THE BURGER

1½ lb	ice-cold fresh halibut, boneless and skinless	675 g
½ lb	Alaskan king crabmeat, chopped	225 g
½ cup	wild rice, fully cooked	125 mL
¼ cup	carrot, grated	60 mL
¼ cup	white onion, diced	60 mL
2	green onions, minced	2
1	clove garlic, minced	1
1 tsp	butter, softened	5 mL
2 Tbsp	Parmesan cheese, grated	30 mL
1	egg	1
¼ cup	panko (Japanese-style) bread crumbs	60 mL
2 Tbsp	Orgasmic Onion Burger Seasoning (p. 44)	30 mL
8	Brioche burger buns	8

THE BURGER: In a food processor or meat grinder, grind the halibut until smooth.

• Transfer to a bowl and add chopped crabmeat, wild rice, carrot, onion, green onion, garlic, butter, Parmesan cheese, egg, panko bread crumbs and Orgasmic Onion Burger Seasoning.

• Form into eight 4-oz (120 g) burger patties approximately 3 to 4 inches (7.5–10 cm) in diameter and 1 inch (2.5 cm) thick.

• Once you have made the 8 burgers, place a slice of pancetta on either side of the halibut burger and press firmly so that the pancetta sticks to the burger. Place on a parchment-paper-lined plate, cover and refrigerate for a minimum of 1 hour.

• Preheat grill to medium, 350–450°F (175–230°C).

• Grill burgers for 5 to 6 minutes per side, until fully cooked and the pancetta is crisp on the outside.

• Remove from grill.

ASSEMBLE YOUR BURGERS! Brioche bun, Mustard Coleslaw (p. 131), pancetta-crusted halibut burger and add Brioche bun top.

MAKES 8 BURGERS

LOBSTER ROLL BURGER

OLIVE POTATO SALAD

6	medium Yukon Gold potatoes	6
	Cold water, to cover	
1 tsp	salt	5 mL
1	rib celery, sliced	1
½	red pepper, diced	1/2
1	small onion, diced	1
2	green onions, thinly sliced	2
2	eggs, hard-boiled and diced	2
12	green pimento-stuffed olives, sliced	12
2 Tbsp	prepared mustard	30 mL
¾ cup	mayonnaise	180 mL
	Salt and pepper, to taste	

THE BURGER

3	2-lb (907 g) Atlantic cold-water lobsters	3
	Cold water	
	Kosher salt	
2 Tbsp	mayonnaise	30 mL
1 Tbsp	fresh dill, chopped	15 mL
	Salt, freshly ground black pepper and cayenne pepper to taste	
½ lb	ice-cold sea scallops	225 g
¼ cup	white onion, diced	60 mL
1	rib celery, finely diced	1
1 Tbsp	dill, chopped	15 mL
1 tsp	lemon juice	5 mL
½ cup	panko (Japanese-style) bread crumbs	125 mL
6	top-cut hot dog rolls	
	Hand-leafed lettuce	
	Nonstick cooking spray	

OLIVE POTATO SALAD: In a pot, boil potatoes in salted water until just cooked tender.

• Drain potatoes and cut into bite-sized chunks.

• In a bowl, combine potatoes, celery, red pepper, onion, green onions, eggs, and olives.

• Add mustard and mayonnaise. Mix well. Season with salt and pepper to taste.

• For best results, refrigerate overnight.

SERVES 8

THE BURGER: Bring a large pot of water to a boil. Add a handful of kosher salt for every gallon (4.5 L) of water. Boil lobsters for 6 to 8 minutes per pound (454 g). Remove from boiling water and let stand for 10 minutes to slightly cool.

• Crack and break apart the lobsters; carefully remove the meat, keeping the pieces as intact as possible.

• Separate the claws from the knuckle meat and tail. Cut the claws into 2 to 4 sections, depending on how big they are. Add mayonnaise, dill and lemon juice. Season to taste with salt and freshly ground black pepper and a pinch of cayenne pepper. Cover and refrigerate until required.

• Coarsely chop the tail meat and claw meat and place in a bowl.

• Place scallops in a food processor and pulse until smooth.

• In a bowl, combine lobster meat, scallops, diced onion, minced celery, dill, lemon juice and panko bread crumbs. Form into 6 cylinder-shaped lobster burgers. Wrap each lobster burger tightly in plastic wrap and refrigerate for 1 hour, allowing lobster meat to set.

• Preheat grill to medium, 350–450°F (175–230°C).

• Unwrap lobster burgers and spray with nonstick cooking spray.

• Grill burgers for 3 to 5 minutes per side, until fully cooked. Squeeze a little lemon juice over top just when they are cooked.

• Butter hot dog rolls and grill to toast lightly.

ASSEMBLE YOUR BURGERS! Bun, lettuce, Lobster Roll Burger and lobster salad. Serve with Olive Potato Salad.

MAKES 6 BURGERS

YING YANG FIREWORKS SHRIMP BURGER

8 + 8 pcs. jumbo shrimp (12 to 15   8 + 8
          per lb/454 g) peeled with tail on

FIREWORKS RED SHRIMP MARINADE

2 Tbsp	sambal chili sauce	30 mL
1 Tbsp	fish sauce	15 mL
2 tsp	Sri Racha hot sauce	10 mL
1 Tbsp	olive oil	15 mL
1 Tbsp	rice wine vinegar	15 mL
2 Tbsp	lime juice	30 mL

FIREWORKS GREEN SHRIMP MARINADE

2	jalapeño pepper	2
½	bunch cilantro, chopped	½
2	green onions	2
2 Tbsp	olive oil	30 mL
2 Tbsp	lime juice	30 mL
1 Tbsp	rice vinegar	15 mL
	Salt, to taste	

THE BURGER

1 lb	ice-cold fresh grouper or sea bass or halibut, boneless and skinless	454 g
1 lb	jumbo shrimp, peeled, deveined and chopped	454 g
¼ cup	white onion, diced	60 mL
2	green onions, minced	2
1 tsp	ginger, minced	5 mL
1 tsp	sambal chili sauce	5 mL
1 tsp	butter, softened	5 mL
2 Tbsp	Parmesan cheese, grated	30 mL
1	egg white	1
1 cup	panko (Japanese-style) bread crumbs	250 mL
1 Tbsp	Bone Dust™ BBQ Seasoning (p. 39)	15 mL

FIREWORKS RED SHRIMP MARINADE: In a bowl, combine sambal chili sauce, fish sauce, hot sauce, olive oil, vinegar and lime juice.

• Mix well and pour over 8 cleaned shrimp. Cover and refrigerate. Let marinate for 20 to 30 minutes.

FIREWORKS GREEN SHRIMP MARINADE: In a food processor, blend the jalapeño, cilantro, green onions, olive oil, lime juice and vinegar until smooth. Season to taste with salt.

• Mix well and pour over 8 cleaned shrimp. Cover and refrigerate. Let marinate for 20 to 30 minutes.

THE BURGER: In a food processor or meat grinder, grind the grouper (or other fish) until smooth.

• Transfer to a bowl and add chopped shrimp, onion, green onions, ginger, sambal chili sauce butter, Parmesan cheese, egg, bread crumbs and Bone Dust™ BBQ Seasoning.

• Form into eight 4-oz (120 g) burger patties approximately 3 to 4 inches (7.5–10 cm) in diameter and 1 inch (2.5 cm) thick.

• Once you have made the 8 burgers, take 1 red marinated shrimp and 1 green marinated shrimp and ying and yang them. Firmly push the two shrimp into the surface of one of the burgers so that they adhere. Repeat with remaining burgers and shrimp. Place burgers on a parchment-paper-lined plate, cover and refrigerate for a minimum of 1 hour.

• Preheat grill to medium, 350–450°F (180–230°C).

• Grill burgers for 5 to 6 minutes per side, until fully cooked.

• Remove from grill.

ASSEMBLE YOUR BURGERS! Burger with your choice of toppings.

MAKES 8 BURGERS

VEGETABLE BURGERS

RISOTTO MILANESE-STUFFED TOMATO BURGER

RISOTTO MILANESE

1	medium sweet onion, sliced	1
1	medium red bell pepper, cut in half and seeded	1
3 Tbsp	butter	45 mL
1	small onion, finely diced	1
1 cup	arborio rice	250 mL
1–2 tsp	saffron	5–10 mL
1 cup	Lindemans Bin 85 Pinot Grigio	250 mL
5 cups	chicken stock	1.25 L
2 Tbsp	Parmesan cheese	30 mL
½ cup	pearl bocconcini (fresh mozzarella balls)	125 mL
2 Tbsp	fresh herbs (thyme, parsley, chervil), chopped	30 mL
	Salt and pepper, to taste	
3	green onions, thinly sliced on the bias	3
¼ cup	frozen green peas, thawed	60 mL

THE BURGER

2	maple or oak or cedar planks, 12 inches long by 8 inches wide by ½ inch thick (30 cm by 20 cm by 1.5 cm), soaked in water for a minimum of 1 hour	
12	medium-sized vine-ripened tomatoes (not overly ripe— you need some stability to the tomato)	12
1	Calabrese baguette, sliced into rounds	1
	Olive oil	
1 Tbsp	fresh basil, chopped	15 mL

RISOTTO MILANESE: Preheat grill to high, 550°F (280°C).

• Grill sliced onion and red pepper for 5 to 6 minutes per side, until lightly charred and tender.

• Remove from grill and allow to cool.

• Dice grill-roasted onion and pepper and set aside.

• In a heavy pot, melt the butter over medium heat. Add the diced onions and cook for 3 to 5 minutes, until they are tender.

• Add the rice and the saffron. Stir well for about 1 minute to coat all the grains of rice in butter.

• Add the Pinot Grigio, stirring continuously, until most of the wine is absorbed.

• Reduce the heat to medium-low and add the chicken stock, 1 cup at a time, stirring slowly and constantly allowing the rice to absorb the liquid before each addition. Keep stirring until all the stock is absorbed and the rice is creamy and tender, about 20 to 25 minutes.

• Remove from heat. Season to taste with salt and pepper.

• Transfer risotto to a large bowl. Gently stir in the Parmesan cheese, pearl bocconcini, fresh herbs, green onions, green peas and reserved grill-roasted onion and red pepper. Adjust seasoning if required. Set aside.

THE BURGER: Using a sharp knife, cut off the top of the tomato, approximately ¼ inch (.5 cm) down from the top. Hollow out the tomato to make room for the risotto stuffing. (You may also need to cut a small portion of the tomato on the bottom so that the tomato will stand upright.)

• Using a small spoon, stuff each hollowed-out tomato with the cooled Risotto Milanese.

• Preheat grill to medium, 350–450°F (175–230°C).

• Place stuffed tomatoes on soaked grilling planks, six tomatoes per plank. Place plank on grill and close lid. Plank-grill the stuffed tomatoes for 30 to 45 minutes, until the rice stuffing is hot, the tomatoes are lightly charred and the skin is blistered.

• While the tomatoes are plank-grilling, brush the Calabrese baguette with olive oil.

• Grill, cut-side down, until golden brown and crisp.

• Remove bread from grill and rub liberally with a clove of fresh garlic. Season lightly with salt and freshly ground black pepper.

ASSEMBLE YOUR BURGERS! Toasted Calabrese baguette, Risotto Milanese-Stuffed Tomato Burger, and top with chopped fresh basil.

MAKES 6 BURGERS

GRILLED MUSHROOM RISOTTO BURGER
WITH STUFFED PORTOBELLO MUSHROOM CAPS

STUFFED PORTOBELLO MUSHROOMS

8	portobello mushroom caps	8
4 cups	hot water	1 L
¼ cup + ¼ cup	olive oil	60 mL + 60 mL
2 Tbsp + 2 Tbsp	balsamic vinegar	30 mL + 30 mL
1	small red onion, sliced	1
1 pint	red grape tomatoes	500 mL
1 pint	yellow grape or cherry tomatoes	500 mL
2 Tbsp	fresh basil, chopped	30 mL
1 cup	pearl bocconcini (fresh mozzarella balls)	250 mL
	Salt and pepper, to taste	

THE BURGER

	Napoleon Grill Topper	
2 Tbsp	Butter	30 mL
1 Tbsp	olive oil	15 mL
½ cup	white onion, diced	125 mL
4	cloves garlic, minced	4
2 cups	arborio rice	500 mL
1 cup	Lindemans Bin 65 Chardonnay	250 mL
6 cups	chicken stock	1.5 L
	Salt and pepper, to taste	
1 cup	shiitake mushrooms, sliced	250 mL
1 cup	cremini mushrooms	250 mL
1 cup	oyster mushrooms	250 mL
1 cup	button mushrooms	250 mL
2 Tbsp	olive oil	30 mL
1 Tbsp	balsamic vinegar	15 mL
¼ cup	cream	60 mL
¼ cup + ¼ cup	Parmesan cheese, grated	60 mL + 60 mL
½ cup	fontina cheese, grated	125 mL
	Nonstick cooking spray	

STUFFED PORTOBELLO MUSHROOMS: In a large bowl, soak portobello mushrooms in hot water for about 20 minutes.

• Preheat grill to medium (350–450°F/175–230°C).

• Remove portobello mushrooms from hot water and gently drain excess water. Toss drained portobello mushrooms in ¼ cup olive oil and 2 Tbsp of balsamic vinegar. Grill seasoned mushrooms until lightly charred and tender, about 10 to 12 minutes.

• Transfer mushroom caps to the top shelf of the grill and keep warm.

• Crank the grill to high, 550°F (280°C).

• Char-grill the onion for 3 to 5 minutes per side, until lightly charred and tender.

• Char-grill the red and yellow grape tomatoes until lightly charred and tender.

• Chop onion and in a bowl combine with charred red and yellow grape tomatoes. Add pearl bocconcini and season to taste with a little balsamic vinegar, olive oil, kosher salt and freshly ground black pepper.

• Spoon tomato-cheese mixture equally onto each grilled portobello mushroom cap. Set on top shelf of grill and keep warm.

THE BURGER: To make the risotto, in a heavy pot, melt the butter and oil over medium heat. Add the onion and garlic and cook for 3 to 5 minutes, until tender. Add the rice and stir. Add chardonnay, stirring until most of the wine is absorbed. Add smoked chicken stock, 1 cup at a time, stirring slowly and constantly allowing the rice to absorb the liquid before each addition. Keep stirring until all of the stock is absorbed and the rice is creamy and tender, about 20 to 25 minutes. Season to taste with salt and pepper and set aside.

• Preheat grill to medium-high (450–550°F/230–280°C).

• Toss shiitake, cremini, oyster and button mushrooms in olive oil and balsamic vinegar.

• Grill for 8 to 10 minutes, turning occasionally, until charred and tender. Remove from grill and coarsely chop.

• Add chopped, grilled mushrooms to cooked risotto and stir to incorporate.

• Add cream, ¼ cup (60 mL) of the Parmesan cheese and the fontina cheese. Stir to incorporate and cook for 1 to 2 minutes, until everything is hot.

• Remove from stove, transfer to a plastic-wrap-lined cookie sheet and allow mixture to cool.

• Divide the cooled Grilled Mushroom Risotto into 8 equal parts, approximately 4 oz (60 g) each.

• Moisten your hands with a little warm water and shape the risotto into 1½-inch (3.5) cm thick burger-like patties. Place on a plastic-wrap-lined cookie sheet and refrigerate for 1 hour so that the burgers set.

• Preheat grill to medium, 350–450°F (175–230°C).

• Place a Napoleon Grill Topper on grill.

• Spray risotto burgers with nonstick cooking spray.

• Grill burgers on Grill Topper for 5 to 6 minutes per side, until the outside of the risotto is crisp and golden brown and the burger is heated through.

ASSEMBLE YOUR BURGERS! Stuffed Portobello Mushrooms topped with Grilled Mushroom Risotto Burgers. Drizzle with balsamic vinegar, olive oil and chopped fresh basil and serve.

MAKES 8 BURGERS

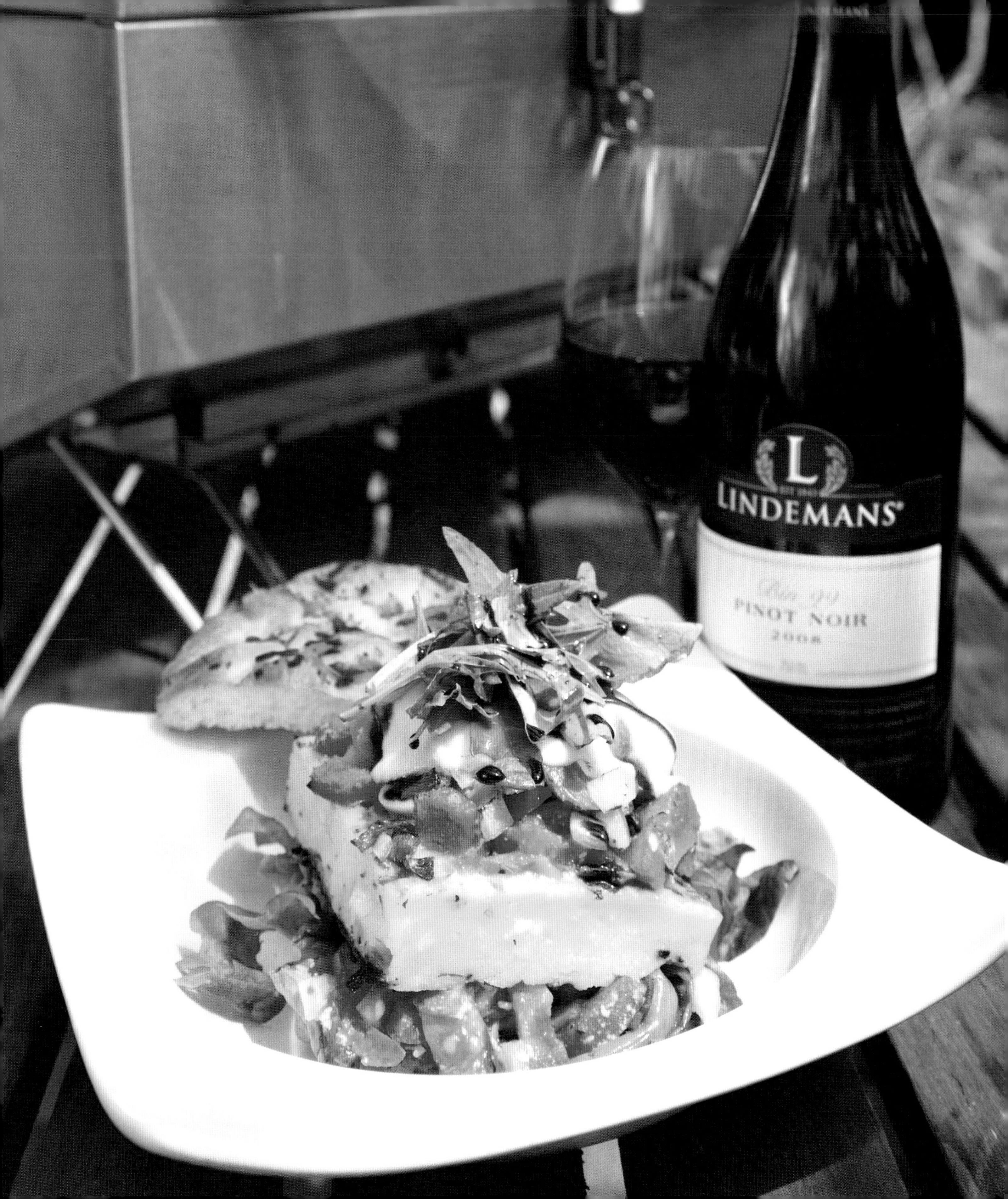
L
LINDEMANS
PINOT NOIR
2008

POLENTA BURGER
WITH FIRE-ROASTED BRUSCHETTA RELISH AND BUFFALO MOZZARELLA

FIRE-ROASTED BRUSCHETTA RELISH

3	ripe plum tomatoes, cut in half lengthways	3
1	medium red pepper, cut in half lengthways and seeded	1
1	medium sweet onion, peeled and sliced into ¼ inch (.5 cm) thick rounds	1
1	green onion	1
1	clove garlic, minced	1
1 Tbsp	Parmesan cheese, grated	15 mL
2 Tbsp	fresh basil, chopped	30 mL
¼ cup	green olives, chopped	60 mL
2 Tbsp	extra-virgin olive oil	30 mL
2 tsp	balsamic vinegar	10 mL
	Sea salt and freshly ground black pepper, to taste	

THE BURGER

3 cups	cold water	750 mL
1 tsp	salt	5 mL
1 cup	polenta (yellow cornmeal)	250 mL
1 Tbsp	butter	15 mL
1 Tbsp	fresh parsley, chopped	15 mL
2 Tbsp	Parmesan cheese, grated	30 mL
¼ cup	Gorgonzola cheese	60 mL
	Salt and pepper, to taste	
1	loaf, 4-inch by 4-inch (10 cm by 10 cm) squares of focaccia bread, cut in half through the middle	
2	handfuls arugula	2
1	large ball buffalo mozzarella, cut into 4 equal-sized rounds	1
	Balsamic vinegar	
	Olive oil	

FIRE-ROASTED BRUSCHETTA RELISH: Preheat grill to high, 550°F (280°C).

• Grill the tomatoes, red pepper, sweet onion and green onion for 5 to 8 minutes, turning occasionally, until everything is lightly charred and tender. Remove from grill and allow everything to cool.

• Coarsely chop the fire-roasted tomatoes, red pepper and onions and place in a bowl.

• Add garlic, Parmesan cheese, basil, chopped green olive, olive oil and balsamic vinegar. Season to taste with sea salt and freshly ground black pepper and set aside.

THE BURGER: In a medium saucepan, bring the water to a rapid boil. Add salt.

• Using a wire whisk and stirring continuously, add the cornmeal in a steady stream; reduce heat to low and continue stirring until the cornmeal is fully cooked and smooth, approximately 5 minutes.

• Remove from heat and stir in the butter, parsley, Parmesan and Gorgonzola cheeses. Season to taste with sea salt and freshly ground black pepper.

• Pour mixture into an 8-inch by 8-inch (20 cm by 20 cm) brownie tin, making sure mixture is approximately 1 inch (2.5 cm) thick. Smooth surface and allow mixture to cool. Cover with plastic wrap and refrigerate until the polenta (cooked cornmeal) has set.

• Unmold polenta. Cut into 4 equal-sized squares.

• Preheat grill to medium-high, 450–550°F (230–280°C).

• Brush polenta squares on both sides with olive oil. With the grill lid open, grill the polenta for 3 to 5 minutes per side, until lightly charred and hot.

• Top each Polenta Burger with a spoonful of Fire-Roasted Bruschetta, then top each with a slice of buffalo mozzarella. Close grill lid and allow cheese to melt for approximately 1 to 2 minutes.

• Meanwhile, brush focaccia bread with olive oil, and grill.

• Remove Polenta Burgers and focaccia from grill.

ASSEMBLE YOUR BURGERS! Focaccia, Polenta Burgers with Fire-Roasted Bruschetta Relish and Buffalo Mozzarella. Top with arugula and drizzle with balsamic vinegar and extra-virgin olive oil. Season with sea salt and freshly ground black pepper. Serve with Lindemans Bin 99 Pinot Noir.

MAKES 4 TO 8 BURGERS

GRILLED VEGETABLE BURGER

	Napoleon Grill Topper	
2 Tbsp	olive oil	30 mL
4	cloves garlic, minced	4
1	medium red onion, diced	1
8	pieces shiitake mushroom, thinly sliced	8
1	medium red bell pepper, diced	1
1	jalapeño pepper, finely chopped	1
1 cup	frozen corn kernels, thawed and drained	250 mL
1 cup	frozen green peas, thawed and drained	250 mL
1 Tbsp	fresh basil, chopped	15 mL
1	can (14 oz/398 mL) chickpeas, drained and mashed	1
¼ cup	Parmesan cheese, grated	60 mL
¼ cup	pine nuts, coarsely chopped	60 mL
¼ cup	tomato sauce	60 mL
1 Tbsp	balsamic vinegar	15 mL
¼–½ cup	bread crumbs	60–125 mL
	Salt, pepper and Cayenne pepper, to taste	
	Nonstick cooking spray	
2	balls buffalo mozzarella, sliced into 4	2
1 cup	tomato sauce	250 mL
8	hamburger buns	8

Although I'm a meatatarian, this is delicious!

• Over medium heat on the stove, heat oil in a large nonstick fry pan. Sauté garlic, red onion and mushrooms for 3 to 5 minutes, stirring occasionally until tender. Add in red pepper, jalapeño pepper, corn and green peas and continue to cook for 3 to 5 more minutes. Remove from heat and let cool.

• Add basil, mashed chickpeas, Parmesan, pine nuts, tomato sauce, balsamic vinegar and enough bread crumbs to bind firmly. Season to taste with salt, pepper and cayenne.

• Form into 8 equal-sized patties, cover and refrigerate for 2 hours, allowing the vegetable patties to become firm.

• Preheat grill to medium, 350–450°F (175–230°C).

• Spray Napoleon Grill Topper with nonstick cooking spray. Spray each vegetable burger with nonstick cooking spray.

• Grill burgers on topper for 4 to 5 minutes per side, until golden brown and heated through. Top with thinly sliced fresh mozzarella cheese and close lid, allowing the cheese to melt for about 1 minute.

• Lightly toast buns and serve with fresh vine-ripened tomatoes, alfalfa sprouts and a drizzling of extra tomato sauce.

MAKES 8 BURGERS

ZUCCHINI-WRAPPED MULTI-BEAN BURGER

	Napoleon Grill Topper	
2	hot banana peppers	2
1	sweet onion, sliced	1
1	red bell pepper, halved and seeded	1
1	orange bell pepper, halved and seeded	1
1	ear of corn	1
3	cloves garlic, minced	3
3 Tbsp	fresh herbs (parsley, thyme, rosemary), chopped	45 mL
1 cup	panko (Japanese-style) bread crumbs	250 mL
Splash	white balsamic vinegar	Splash
	Salt and freshly ground black pepper, to taste	
1	can (19 oz/540 mL) mixed beans, drained	1
½	can (14 oz/398 mL) refried beans	½
4	green zucchini, approximately 8 inches (20 cm) in length and 2 inches (5 cm) in diameter	4
8	slices fontina cheese	8
8	sesame seed buns	8
	Red leaf lettuce	
	Ripe tomato, sliced	
	Red onion, sliced	
	Nonstick cooking spray	

• Preheat grill to high, 550°F (280°C).

• Grill the banana peppers, onion, bell peppers and corn until lightly charred and tender, approximately 10 to 15 minutes, turning occasionally.

• Remove the stem and seeds from the banana peppers, chop the charred flesh and place in a large bowl.

• Chop the onions and bell pepper and add to the banana peppers.

• Using a sharp knife, cut the charred corn kernels from the ear and place in the bowl with the peppers.

• Add garlic, chopped herbs, panko bread crumbs; add a splash of white balsamic vinegar and season to taste with salt and pepper. Set aside.

• Place the bean medley in a bowl and mash lightly with a fork—just enough to squish the beans a little but not completely mush them. Add in the refried beans and stir to incorporate.

• Add the reserved grilled-vegetable mixture and mix well to form a thick paste-like consistency. Adjust seasoning with salt and freshly ground black pepper.

• Divide mixture into 8 equal parts. Form into 2-inch (5 cm) thick burger patties, approximately 3 inches (7.5 cm) in diameter. Place on a parchment-paper-lined plate, cover and refrigerate for 1 hour minimum so that the burgers can set.

• Using a slicer or a very sharp knife, cut the zucchini into long, thin (approximately ¼-inch/1 cm thick) strips. You will need approximately 40 long slices of zucchini.

• Bring a pot of water to a rolling boil.

• Fill a bowl with ice and cold water.

• Working with half a dozen strips of zucchini at a time, blanch the zucchini strips in the boiling water for 30 seconds, remove and plunge into the ice water to cool. Repeat until all the zucchini strips have been blanched and cooled. Drain and pat dry on paper toweling.

• Wrap each bean burger in 4 to 6 strips of thinly sliced blanched zucchini. Spray with nonstick cooking spray and return to the refrigerator to set for 1 hour.

• Turn grill down to medium heat, 350–450°F (175–230°C).

• Place a Napoleon Grill Topper on grill.

• Grill zucchini-wrapped bean burgers for 6 to 8 minutes per side, until lightly charred and heated through. When the burgers are just about done, top each burger with fontina cheese and close lid, allowing cheese to melt.

• Toast buns.

ASSEMBLE YOUR BURGERS! Bun bottom, lettuce, tomato, red onion, Zucchini-Wrapped Multi-Bean Burger with fontina cheese, bun top. Serve immediately.

MAKES 8 BURGERS

PLANKED MASHED POTATO BURGER
WITH MOLTEN CAMEMBERT

THE BURGER

2	regular cedar planks, 12 inches long by 8 inches wide by ½ inch thick (30 cm by 20 cm by 1.5 cm), soaked in cold water for a minimum of 1 hour	
2 lb	Yukon Gold potatoes	907 g
4	cloves garlic, minced	4
1 tsp	salt	5 mL
6 Tbsp	butter	100 mL
¼ cup	sour cream	60 mL
2 Tbsp	fresh parsley, chopped	30 mL
2 Tbsp	fresh chives, chopped	30 mL
	Salt and pepper, to taste	
	Nonstick cooking spray	

Pure decadence!

THE BURGER: Place potatoes in a large pot. Cover with cold water. Add garlic and bring to a boil over high heat. Reduce heat to medium-low and simmer for 20 to 30 minutes, or until potatoes are fully cooked and tender.

• Drain and return pan with potatoes to heat. Shake pan to remove excess moisture from potatoes and garlic. Remove from heat.

• Using a potato masher, mash potatoes and garlic until mixture is smooth.

• Add butter and sour cream to mashed potato mixture. Stir to combine.

• Transfer to a large bowl and cool fully. Once the potatoes have cooled, stir in the parsley and chives, and season to taste with salt and freshly ground black pepper.

• Using a 6-oz (180 mL) ice-cream scoop, scoop the cold mashed potato mixture into 8 equal-sized mounds. Mold each mound of mashed potatoes into a baseball-shaped burger. Cover and refrigerate for 1 hour, allowing the burgers to set.

• Preheat grill to medium, 350–450°F (175–230°C).

• Evenly space potato burgers on planks.

• Spray burgers evenly with nonstick cooking spray.

• Place on grill and plank-bake for 25 to 30 minutes, until the potato burgers are golden brown, crisp on the outside and hot on the inside.

• When the potato burgers are about halfway cooked, prepare the Molten Camembert.

TIP: Make your mashed-potato mixture 24 hours ahead.

MOLTEN CAMEMBERT

1   square cedar plank
      (about 6 inches long by
      6 inches wide/15 cm by
      15 cm), soaked in water

1   wheel Camembert cheese   1
      (about 5 to 6 oz/150–180 g)

      sea salt and freshly
      ground pepper, to taste

MOLTEN CAMEMBERT: Preheat grill to medium heat, 350–450°F (175–230°C).

• Place camembert on square plank and season with freshly ground black pepper.

• Place plank on grill and close lid. Plank-grill cheese for 15 to 18 minutes, until cheese is golden brown and the sides are beginning to bulge.

• Remove plank from grill.

• Remove mashed-potato burgers from grill and allow them to rest for 2 to 3 minutes

Now, this is the tricky part:

• Take a planked potato burger and turn it over. Using a small spoon, scoop out a portion of the hot mashed-potato mix; eat this if you wish—it will be delicious.

• Next, using a pair of tongs, peel back the top of the rind on the camembert cheese.

• Take a spoonful or two of Molten Camembert and spoon it into the scooped-out part of the potato burger.

• Season burgers with sea salt and freshly ground black pepper to taste. Serve immediately.

MAKES 8 BURGERS

BREAKFAST BURGERS

THE BREAKFAST BURGER

2	regular cedar planks, soaked in water for 1 hour	
6	toothpicks	

THE BURGER

1½ lb	ice-cold ground pork	675 g
¼ cup	panko (Japanese-style) bread crumbs	60 mL
2 Tbsp	Parmesan cheese, grated	30 mL
3 Tbsp	Bone Dust™ BBQ Seasoning (p. 39)	45 mL
2 Tbsp	honey mustard	30 mL
1	small onion, finely diced	1
6	slices thick sliced bacon	6
6	small eggs	6
4	English muffins	4

I first did this recipe for a local breakfast television show. The burgers are a true breakfast work of art.

• In a bowl, combine ground pork, bread crumbs, Parmesan cheese, Bone Dust™ BBQ Seasoning, honey mustard and finely diced onion.

• Form into four 6-oz (180 g) baseball-shaped burgers. Gently flatten slightly, pushing down on the center of the burger to form a well. This is where your egg will go. The well should be approximately 1 inch (2.5 cm) deep, allowing the egg to sit and cook evenly and not to run off the burger. Wrap each burger with a slice of bacon and secure with a toothpick. Cover and refrigerate, allowing the meat to rest.

• Preheat grill to medium-high, 450–550°F (230–280°C).

• Evenly space 3 burgers on each plank. Place planked breakfast burgers on grill and close lid. Plank-bake for 8 to 10 minutes to allow the outside of the meat to cook slightly.

• Top each burger with 1 egg. (I crack each egg into a small glass dish and pour the egg onto each burger. This is easier and less messy than trying to crack an egg over a hot grill.) Close lid and continue to cook for 15 to 20 minutes, until the burgers are fully cooked, the bacon a little crisp and the egg cooked but the yolk still a little runny.

• Remove from grill and serve on toasted English muffins.

MAKES 4 BURGERS

SAUSAGE BURGER
WITH BISCUITS & GRAVY

THE BURGER

1½ lb	ice-cold ground pork	675 g
1	small onion, diced	1
2 Tbsp	fresh sage, chopped	30 mL
1 tsp	black pepper, coarsely ground	5 mL
1 tsp	smoked paprika	5 mL
2 tsp	salt	10 mL
½ tsp	cayenne pepper	2.5 mL

SAUSAGE CREAM GRAVY

2 lb	ice-cold pork sausage meat	907 g
1 Tbsp	Bone Dust™ BBQ Seasoning (p. 39)	15 mL
2 Tbsp	oil	30 mL
1 tsp	dry sage	5 mL
½ tsp	salt	2.5 mL
1 tsp	mustard powder	5 mL
½ tsp	black pepper	2.5 mL
4 Tbsp	butter	60 mL
¼ cup	flour	60 mL
1½ cups	whole milk	375 mL
1½ cups	heavy (18%) cream	375 mL
	Salt and pepper, to taste	
	Worcestershire and hot sauce, to taste	

A good southern breakfast isn't complete without sausage cream gravy—creamy and rich and loaded with crumbled sausage meat. Pour it over fresh-baked sour cream and chive biscuits with grilled sausage patties and scrambled eggs. Now, that's the way to start the day!

THE BURGER: In a bowl, combine ice-cold ground pork, onion, sage, black pepper, smoked paprika, salt and cayenne pepper. Mix well.

• Form into six 4-oz (120 g) burger patties shaped into 1-inch (2.5 cm) thick rounds approximately 3 inches (7.5 cm) in diameter.

• Place on a plate and refrigerate for a minimum of 1 hour, allowing the burgers to rest.

SAUSAGE CREAM GRAVY: In a bowl, combine the sausage meat and Bone Dust™ BBQ Seasoning.

• In a large, deep fry pan, heat the oil over high heat. Fry the sausage meat in small batches until fully cooked. Drain, reserving fat. Set aside cooked sausage meat.

• Using a wooden spoon, scrape the little bits of cooked sausage meat from the bottom of the pan.

• Add 2 Tbsp (30 mL) of butter and 2 Tbsp (30 mL) of the reserved sausage fat to the fry pan over medium heat.

• Add flour and stir until the flour is completely blended with the butter mixture.

• Add the milk ½ cup (125 mL) at a time, stirring continuously, until the mixture has no flour lumps.

• Add the cream and continue stirring until fully mixed and smooth.

• Add cooked sausage meat. Bring mixture to a low boil, stirring frequently.

• Reduce heat to low and simmer, stirring occasionally, for 30 minutes, until sauce is thick and smooth, with a nice sausage flavor.

• Season to taste with salt, pepper, fresh sage, Worcestershire and hot sauce. Set aside and keep warm.

MAKES APPROXIMATELY 4 CUPS (1 L)

SOUR CREAM AND CHIVE BISCUITS

1	rolling pin	
1	3-inch (7.5 cm) round cookie cutter	
2½ cups	sifted all-purpose flour	625 mL
1 Tbsp	baking powder	15 mL
1 tsp	salt	5 mL
½ cup	butter	125 mL
1 cup	sour cream	250 mL
2 Tbsp	fresh chives, chopped	30 mL
Pinch	pepper	Pinch
Pinch	cayenne pepper	Pinch

SCRAMBLED EGGS

	Napoleon Griddle Pan	
6	large eggs	6
¼ cup	heavy (18%) cream	60 mL
1 Tbsp	fresh chives, chopped	15 mL
	Salt and freshly ground pepper, to taste	
2 Tbsp	butter	
6	slices mozzarella or Swiss cheese	6
	Nonstick cooking spray	

SOUR CREAM AND CHIVE BISCUITS: Preheat oven to 425°F (220°C).

• Sift flour, baking powder and salt into a bowl.

• Blend in butter using your hands or a tool, until the mixture looks like coarse cornmeal.

• Stir in sour cream and chives and mix until dough is soft but not gluey and sticky.

• Dump onto a floured work surface and knead 15 to 20 times.

• Roll the dough out to a thickness of 1½ inches (3.5 cm). Cut with a biscuit cutter into 3-inch (7.5 cm) rounds. Place on a greased parchment-paper-lined baking sheet.

• Bake for 12 to 15 minutes, until golden brown.

• Remove from oven and set aside.

MAKES ABOUT 12 BISCUITS

SCRAMBLED EGGS: Crack eggs into a medium bowl; add heavy cream, chives and season to taste with a little salt and pepper. Whisk. Set aside.

• Place a seasoned Napoleon Griddle Pan on your grill.

• Preheat your grill to medium-high, 450–550°F (230–280°C), with the burner under the griddle pan set to medium-low.

• Remove burgers from refrigerator and spray burgers lightly with nonstick cooking spray.

• Grill burgers for 5 to 6 minutes per side, until done medium-well but still moist and juicy.

• Top each burger with slice of mozzarella or Swiss cheese and allow cheese to melt.

• While the burgers are grilling, melt butter in griddle pan and scramble eggs until just cooked and light and fluffy. Turn burner under griddle pan off, keeping scrambled eggs warm.

ASSEMBLE YOUR BURGERS! Cut biscuits in half. Place a cheese-topped sausage patty on the bottom of a warm biscuit, follow with one-sixth of the scrambled egg mixture, then spoon warmed Sausage Cream Gravy over the eggs. Complete with the Sour Cream and Chive Biscuit top. Repeat with remaining biscuits and serve immediately.

MAKES 6 BURGERS

CAPTAIN CRUNCH WAFFLE BURGER

WAFFLE BURGER

	Napoleon Griddle Pan	
	Waffle Iron	
2 lb	ice-cold regular ground beef	907 g
½ lb	ice-cold ground pork	225 g
¼ cup	Bone Dust™ BBQ Seasoning (p. 39)	60 mL
1 cup	Captain Crunch Cereal, crushed	250 mL
16	slices Canadian back bacon or Canadian peameal bacon	16
2 Tbsp	butter	30 mL
4	large eggs	4
1½ cups	mozzarella cheese, shredded	380 mL
1½ cups	yellow cheddar cheese, shredded	380 mL

CAPTAIN CRUNCH WAFFLES

2 cups	sifted all-purpose flour	500 mL
1 Tbsp	baking powder	15 mL
2 Tbsp	white sugar	30 mL
1 tsp	salt	5 mL
Pinch	cayenne pepper	Pinch
3	large eggs, separated	3
1¼ cups	buttermilk	300 mL
4 Tbsp	melted shortening	60 mL
1½– 2 cups	Captain Crunch Cereal	375– 500 mL
	Nonstick cooking spray	

WAFFLE BURGER: In a bowl, combine ice-cold ground beef and pork with Bone Dust™ and crushed Captain Crunch cereal. Gently mix.

• Take your cold waffle iron and spray both sides with nonstick cooking spray.

• Divide the burger mixture into 4 equal parts approximately 10-oz (300 g) each.

• Spread 1 portion of the burger mixture over the bottom of the waffle iron, reaching all the crevasses and keeping the mixture uniformly thick—about 1½ inches (2.5–3.5 cm). Close waffle iron lid and press firmly. Open lid and carefully remove burger. Your burger will now look like a giant waffle.

• Repeat with remaining ground meat. Place on a parchment-paper-lined cookie sheet and refrigerate for 1 hour.

• Clean waffle iron according to manufacturer's instructions. Prepare waffles.

CAPTAIN CRUNCH WAFFLES: Sift all-purpose flour, baking powder, sugar, salt and cayenne pepper.

• In a separate bowl, beat egg yolks. Add buttermilk and melted shortening and continue to beat for 1 to 2 minutes to incorporate.

• Add to dry ingredients, whisking quickly.

• Beat the egg whites stiff and gently fold into the waffle batter. Cover and refrigerate until needed.

• Preheat waffle iron according to manufacturer's instructions.

• Remove waffle batter from refrigerator. Fold in the Captain Crunch Cereal and let stand for 5 minutes.

• Spray waffle iron evenly with nonstick cooking spray. Pour in enough waffle batter to fill all the nooks and grannies. Close lid and bake until fully cooked and golden brown, following the manufacturers usage instructions.

• Open lid and carefully remove. Set aside to cool. Repeat with remaining batter.

MAKES 4 WAFFLES

- Preheat grill to medium high, 450–550°F (230–280°C).

- Place the Napoleon Griddle Pan over one burner and turn heat to low.

- Remove waffle burgers from refrigerator and spray with nonstick cooking spray.

- Grill burgers for 8 to 10 minutes per side, until fully cooked but still moist and juicy.

- While the burgers are grilling, grill the back bacon for 1 to 2 minutes per side, until fully cooked. Transfer to warming grill rack.

- Melt a little butter on the griddle pan and fry the eggs, over easy or sunny side up, your choice. Turn heat off under griddle pan.

- Mix mozzarella and cheddar cheeses.

- Warm waffles on grill and top each waffle with a handful of shredded cheese. Close lid and allow cheese to melt.

ASSEMBLE YOUR BURGERS! Captain Crunch Waffles, Waffle Burger, grilled back bacon and fried egg.

MAKES 4 BURGERS

SMOKED SALMON BURGER

RED ONION DILL SALSA

½	red onion, diced	½
½ cup	diced cucumber	125 mL
1 Tbsp	capers	15 mL
1 Tbsp	fresh dill, chopped	15 mL
1 Tbsp	lemon juice	15 mL
1 tsp	prepared horseradish	5 mL
1 Tbsp	olive oil	15 mL
	Salt and freshly ground black pepper, to taste	

THE BURGER

1	cedar plank, 12 inches long by 8 inches wide by ½ inch thick (30 cm by 20 cm by 1.5 cm), soaked in water for a minimum of 1 hour	1
1 lb	ice-cold ground salmon	454 g
2 cups	smoked salmon, chopped	500 mL
½ cup	panko (Japanese-style) bread crumbs	125 mL
2	green onions, chopped	2
¼ cup	red onion, diced	60 mL
1 Tbsp	fresh dill, chopped	15 mL
1 Tbsp	lemon juice	15 mL
1 Tbsp	mayonnaise	15 mL
2 Tbsp	cream cheese	30 mL
1 Tbsp	Bone Dust™ BBQ Seasoning (p. 39)	15 mL
1	egg white from a small egg	1
1	lemon, halved	1
4	bagels	4
½ cup	cream cheese	125 mL
	Bibb lettuce	
4	slices smoked salmon	4
4	dill sprigs	4

A perfect brunch burger that adds a twist to smoked salmon.

RED ONION DILL SALSA: In a bowl, combine red onion, cucumber, capers, dill, lemon juice, horseradish, and olive oil. Season to taste with salt and freshly ground black pepper. Cover and refrigerate until needed.

MAKES APPROXIMATELY 1½ CUPS (375 ML)

THE BURGER: In a bowl, combine ground salmon, smoked salmon, bread crumbs, green onions, red onion, dill, lemon juice, mayonnaise, cream cheese and Bone Dust™ BBQ Seasoning. Add egg white and gently mix.

• Form into four 5-oz (150 g) burgers approximately 1 inch (2.5 cm) thick and 3 to 4 inches (7.5–10 cm) in diameter. Place on a parchment-paper-lined plate, cover and refrigerate for at least 1 hour.

• Preheat grill to medium, 350–450°F (175–230°C).

• Evenly space salmon burgers on soaked plank. Place on grill, close lid and plank-bake for 20 to 30 minutes, until fully cooked and heated through. Squeeze a little fresh lemon juice over top of the burgers and remove from grill.

• Toast bagels.

• Spread cream cheese onto the bottom half of the bagels.

ASSEMBLE YOUR BURGERS! Bagel bottom spread with cream cheese, lettuce, Smoked Salmon Burger, Red Onion Dill Salsa, and garnish with a slice of smoked salmon and a sprig of dill, and add bagel top.

MAKES 4 BURGERS

STEAK 'N' EGGS BURGER
WITH BBQ HOLLANDAISE

BBQ HOLLANDAISE

1 cup	butter	250 mL
1	bottle of your favorite beer	355 mL
4	egg yolks	4
2 Tbsp + ¼ cup	Ted's World Famous BBQ Crazy Canuck Sticky Chicken and Rib Sauce or your favorite gourmet-style BBQ sauce	30 mL + 60 mL
1 Tbsp	fresh parsley, chopped	15 mL
1 tsp	Bone Dust™ BBQ Seasoning (p. 39)	5 mL
1 tsp	lemon juice	5 mL
Big Dash	hot sauce	Big Dash
Dash	Worcestershire sauce	Dash
	salt and pepper, to taste	

THE BURGER

1 lb	ice-cold ground sirloin steak	454 g
3 Tbsp	Bone Dust™ BBQ Seasoning (p. 39)	45 mL
	Nonstick cooking spray	
1	bottle of your favorite beer	1
4	slices peameal bacon (each about 2 oz/60 g)	4
4	slices aged white cheddar cheese	4
3 cups	water	750 mL
1–2 Tbsp	white vinegar	15–30 mL
4	large eggs	4
2	English muffins, sliced in half horizontally	2

BBQ HOLLANDAISE: Heat the butter to a low boil and carefully skim any foam from the surface until you have golden and clear-clarified-butter. Set aside and keep warm.

• Pour off 2 tablespoons of beer and reserve.

• In a sauce pan, add the remaining beer and 6–8 cups of water and bring to a boil. This will be the mixture you will poach your eggs in later.

• Place the egg yolks in a stainless steel bowl and add the reserved 2 tablespoons of beer.

• In a medium bowl, whisk the egg yolks and beer reduction. Place over the pot of simmering beer-water mixture that you will use to poach your eggs in later and whisk constantly until the mixture is thick enough to form a ribbon when drizzled from the whisk. Be careful not to turn this into scrambled eggs. Remove from heat.

• Whisking constantly, slowly add clarified butter a little at a time until all the butter has been absorbed. Season with 2 Tbsp (30 mL) BBQ sauce, chopped parsley, Bone Dust™ BBQ Seasoning, lemon juice, a big dash of hot sauce, Worcestershire sauce and salt and pepper to taste. Set aside.

THE BURGER: In a bowl, combine ground sirloin steak and Bone Dust™ BBQ Seasoning.

• Mix and form into four 4-oz (120 g) burgers. Place on a parchment-paper-lined plate, cover and refrigerate for a minimum of 1 hour.

• Preheat grill to medium-high, 450–550°F (230–280°C).

• Remove burgers from refrigerator and spray with nonstick cooking spray.

• Grill burgers for 6 to 8 minutes per side, drizzling with a little extra cream ale, until fully cooked but still moist and juicy.

• While the burgers are grilling, grill the peameal bacon for 1 to 2 minutes per side.

• Top each burger with a slice of aged white cheddar cheese.

• In a medium-sized saucepan, combine 1 bottle beer, 3 cups (750 mL) of water and 2 Tbsp (30 mL) of white vinegar. Bring to a boil. Once it comes to a boil, reduce the heat to medium-low for a gentle simmer.

• Return beer-water pot to a boil.

- Crack each egg into a small cup or dish, taking care not to break the yolk.

- Stir the beer-water pot to create swirling action. Set aside, maintaining simmer.

- Grill peameal bacon for 2 to 4 minutes per side, basting with BBQ sauce, until fully cooked and lightly charred but still juicy. Set aside and keep warm.

- Now poach the eggs. Slip the eggs into swirling simmering beer water one at a time, leaving room for them to move around and float to poach. Poach for 2 to 3 minutes for runny yolks and firm whites. Poach longer for a more well done egg. Using a slotted spoon, remove eggs from pot and drain well. I like to gently pat the eggs with a piece of paper toweling to absorb excess moisture.

- Toast English muffins and butter them.

ASSEMBLE YOUR BURGERS! Half an English muffin, burger, cheddar cheese, peameal bacon, poached egg, BBQ Hollandaise. Repeat.

MAKES 4 BURGERS

DESSERT BURGERS

PEANUT BUTTER AND BANANA BURGER

DRUNKEN BERRIES

½ pint	raspberries	250 mL
½ pint	blueberries	250 mL
½ pint	blackberries	250 mL
1 Tbsp	sugar	15 mL
1 oz	Gentleman Jack Rare Tennessee Whiskey	30 mL
1 Tbsp	fresh mint, chopped	
	Black pepper, freshly ground	

THE BURGER

1	regular cedar plank	
¾ cup	smooth or crunchy peanut butter	180 mL
1	ripe banana, mashed	1
2 Tbsp	butter, softened	30 mL
1 cup + 2 cups	icing sugar	250 mL + 500 mL
3 cups	Rice Krispies	750 mL
1	banana, sliced into rounds	1
	Caramel Sauce (p. 294)	
	thyme	
¾ cup	peanuts, crushed	180 mL

DRUNKEN BERRIES: In a bowl, combine raspberries, blueberries, blackberries and sugar. Add Gentleman Jack and chopped mint, and season with a little freshly ground black pepper. Set aside.

THE BURGER: In a food processor, blend peanut butter, banana, butter and icing sugar. Transfer to a large bowl. Stir in ¾ of a cup (180 mL) of crushed peanuts and the Rice Krispies.

• Using a small 2-oz (60 mL) ice-cream scoop, scoop the mixture onto a parchment-paper-lined cookie sheet; cover and refrigerate for 1 hour.

• Remove peanut butter–banana scoops from the refrigerator and, while wearing rubber gloves, shape the scoops into 1-inch (2.5 cm) thick burger patties approximately 2 inches (5 cm) in diameter.

• Working with one burger at a time, roll the peanut butter–banana burgers in crushed peanuts, pressing gently so that the peanuts stick to the burgers. Place on a grilling plank and put into the freezer for 1 hour.

• Preheat grill to medium, 350–450°F (175–230°C).

• Place planked peanut butter–banana burgers on the grill and plank-bake for 10 to 15 minutes, until heated through.

• Carefully remove from grill.

• Place a burger on a plate. Top with a slice of fresh ripe banana. Spoon over Drunken Berries. Drizzle with Caramel Sauce (p. 294). Garnish with a little fresh thyme and serve immediately.

MAKES 12 BURGERS

BUTTER TART CHEESECAKE BURGER
WITH DOUBLE-SMOKED BACON AND CARAMEL SAUCE

CARAMEL SAUCE

2 cups	sugar	500 mL
1 cup	water	250 mL
1 Tbsp	lemon juice	15 mL
1 oz	Jack Daniel's Tennessee Whiskey	30 mL
½ cup	whipping cream	125 mL

CRUST

	Muffin Tin	
1¼ cups	graham cracker crumbs	310 mL
¼ cup	butter, melted	60 mL

CHEESECAKE BURGER MIX

2	packages cream cheese, 8 oz (225 g) each	2
¼ cup	sugar	60 mL
3	large eggs	3
1 cup	sour cream	250 mL
1 tsp	vanilla extract	5 mL
¼ tsp	salt	1 mL

BUTTER TART MIX

1	large egg	1
1/3 cup	corn syrup	80 mL
3 Tbsp	sugar	45 mL
1½ Tbsp	butter, melted	20 mL
Few Drops	vanilla extract	Few Drops

THE BURGER

1	regular cedar plank	1
6	thick slices double-smoked bacon	6

Okay, it's not really a burger, but it's oh so worth eating with your hands that it's like a burger.

CARAMEL SAUCE: Mix sugar, water, lemon juice and Jack Daniel's. Bring to a boil. Boil until it has an amber color. Don't stir or touch.

• Add whipping (35%) cream carefully—it will splatter. Stir and let cool at room temperature.

CRUST: Combine graham cracker crumbs and melted butter. Press mixture into the base of a large muffin tin.

CHEESECAKE BURGER MIX: Cream the cream cheese with the sugar.

• Add one egg at a time—make sure it's well combined. Scrape side of bowl.

• Then add sour cream, vanilla and salt. Mix well. Set aside.

BUTTER TART MIX: In a bowl, stir together to combine the egg, corn syrup, sugar, butter and vanilla. Set aside.

THE BURGER: Preheat grill to medium heat, 350–450°F (175–230°C). I suggest that the burners under the muffin tin be off and you bake on the grill using indirect heat with the lid closed.

• Pour 1- to 2-Tbsp of Butter Tart Mix onto the Crust. Fill remaining muffin cup with Cheesecake Burger Mix.

• Place on grill and grill-bake for 10 minutes. Open grill lid and spoon a heaping tablespoon (15 mL) of butter tart mix over top of the cheesecake.

• Rotate muffin tin, close lid and grill-bake for another 10 to 15 minutes. The butter tart mixture will sink into the cheesecake mix.

• Remove from grill and let cool at room temperature, then completely cool in fridge before you unmold cooled cheesecakes from the muffin tin.

• Remove cheesecakes from muffin tin. Place on a cedar plank. Place on grill on the top rack to warm the cakes.

• Grill thick slices of double-smoked bacon until crisp. Pat dry with paper toweling to remove the excess fat and dice.

• To serve, top with grilled bacon and drizzle on Caramel Sauce.

MAKES 12 BURGERS

CUPCAKE BURGER

THE CUPCAKE

	muffin tin	
1¾ cup	all-purpose flour	430 mL
2 tsp	baking soda	10 mL
1 tsp	cream of tartar	5 mL
½ tsp	salt	2.5 mL
¾ cup	milk	175 mL
¼ cup	sour cream	60 mL
½ cup	butter, softened	125 mL
⅔ cup	sugar	160 mL
1	egg	1
1	egg yolk	1

THE BROWNIE

1	9-inch (22.5 cm) square brownie tin	1
4 oz	dark chocolate	120 g
¼ cup + 2 Tbsp	butter, unsalted	60 mL + 30 mL
2	large eggs, room temperature	2
1 cup	sugar	250 mL
¼ cup + 2 Tbsp	all-purpose flour	60 mL + 30 mL

THE CUSTARD

½ cup	cornstarch	125 mL
6 Tbsp	sugar	100 mL
2 cups	milk	500 mL
4	egg yolks	4
1	vanilla bean	1

A lot of work but for kids we will make them anytime.

THE CUPCAKE: In a bowl, sift together the flour, baking soda, cream of tartar and salt. Set aside.

• In another bowl, whisk the milk and sour cream. Set aside.

• Cream together the room-temperature butter and sugar. Blend in egg and egg yolk.

• Add sour cream-milk mixture and blend until mixed.

• Add in dry ingredients and stir until smooth.

• Grease a muffin tin.

• Preheat grill to medium, 350–450°F (175–230°C).

• Fill muffin cups ¾ full with muffin mixture.

• Grill-bake over indirect heat for 20 to 25 minutes, until fully baked and a toothpick inserted in the middle comes out clean.

• Remove from grill and allow cupcakes to cool at room temperature.

• Unmold and place in an airtight container to keep nice and moist.

MAKES 12 MUFFINS

THE BROWNIE: Melt chocolate and butter over a double boiler or in the microwave.

• Cream together eggs and sugar in mixer until light and creamy.

• Mix in chocolate until just combined and fold in flour, stirring lightly.

• Preheat grill for indirect grilling to medium heat, 350–450°F (175–230°C).

• Pour batter into brownie tin and bake for 25 to 30 minutes, until a toothpick inserted in the middle comes out clean.

• Remove from grill and cool.

• Unmold brownies. Cut brownies with a 2-inch to 3-inch (5–7.5 cm) cookie cutter. Set aside.

THE CUSTARD: In a bowl, mix the cornstarch and the sugar. Add a ½ cup (125 mL) from the milk to the mix and add egg yolks. Set aside.

• Bring the rest of the milk and the vanilla bean to a boil. Whisk in the cornstarch–egg yolks mix and bring to a low boil while whisking constantly.

THE FILLING

1 pint	fresh strawberries, sliced	500 mL
1 Tbsp + ¾ cup	sugar	30 mL + 375 g
1 lb	softened butter	454 g
	Yellow and green food coloring	

• Strain into a bowl, cover with plastic wrap and cool completely.

THE FILLING: In a bowl, combine strawberries and 1 Tbsp (30 mL) sugar; gently mix and set aside.

• Cream the rest of the sugar and the butter with mixer until light and fluffy.

• Divide mix into two.

• In one batch, add a drop or two of yellow food coloring and mix to combine. Set aside.

• In the second batch, add a drop or two of green food coloring and mix to combine. Set aside.

ASSEMBLE YOUR BURGERS! Cut a muffin in half through the middle. Spread a layer of yellow icing on the cut side of the muffin bottom. Top with a spoonful of thick custard. Top with a brownie. Top with a layer of green icing. Add muffin top. Repeat with remaining muffins and serve immediately.

MAKES 12 BURGERS

ICE CREAM-SANDWICH BURGER

SMOKED CHOCOLATE

	Napoleon Charcoal Tray	
2 lb	chocolate bars—milk, dark, bittersweet or white (the bars should be at least 1 inch/ 2.5 cm thick)	907 g
3 cups	hickory smoking chips	750 mL
	Charcoal briquettes	
	Tin foil	
	Ice and cold water	

SMOKED-CHOCOLATE ESPRESSO ICE CREAM

2 cups	half-and-half (10%) cream	500 mL
3 cups	whipping (35%) cream	750 mL
2	vanilla beans, split lengthwise	2
1 oz	espresso, good and strong	30 mL
1½ cups	sugar	375 mL
12	large egg yolks	12
2 cups	smoked-chocolate pieces	500 mL

SMOKED CHOCOLATE: Place the chocolate bars in the freezer and freeze for a minimum of 1 hour.

• Place the Napoleon Charcoal Tray on one side of your grill.

• Prepare 5 to 8 charcoal briquettes.

• While the briquettes are heating, fill a bowl or foil pan with ice and a few cups of cold water. The ice and cold water will help keep your grill temperature low and the smoke cool.

• To prepare the smoked chocolate, cover the top grill rack of your Napoleon Grill with tin foil. Place the chocolate bars on the wrapped grill. You should only smoke chocolate on a top rack, as far away from the heat source as possible.

• When the charcoal is hot, carefully transfer it to the base of the smoker. With the lid on, heat the smoker to 135°F (60°C).

NOTE: When you initially place the hot coals in the grill, the temperature may go over 400°F (200°C), depending on how much charcoal has been added.

• Remove lid and allow the charcoal to cool.

• At the right temperature, place the chocolate-topped grill in the smoker and place lid on top.

• Add a handful of smoking chips to the hot coals and begin smoking.

• Maintain your grill temperature. If it gets too high, remove the cover to allow the heat to escape. Do not worry that you will lose a lot of smoke—it does not take a lot of smoke to add flavor to chocolate.

• Smoke chocolate for 35 to 45 minutes.

• Remove from grill and let chocolate completely cool. Store in self-sealing plastic bags.

SMOKED-CHOCOLATE ESPRESSO ICE CREAM: In a heavy saucepan, mix the half-and-half, the whipping cream and the espresso. Scrape the seeds from the vanilla bean and add bean. Slowly bring mixture to a boil. Remove from heat and let cool slightly.

• In a large bowl, whisk together the sugar and egg yolks until thick and smooth. Gradually beat in heated cream mixture. Return to medium heat and cook while stirring constantly, until the custard thickens and leaves a path on a wooden spoon when a finger is drawn across—about 8 to 10 minutes. Strain through a fine mesh strainer and set aside to keep warm.

PLANKED CHOCOLATE CHIP COOKIES

5	regular maple planks, soaked in water for at least 1 hour	
2 cups	oatmeal	500 mL
2 cups	all-purpose flour, sifted	500 mL
½ tsp	salt	2.5 mL
1 tsp	baking powder	5 mL
1 tsp	baking soda	5 mL
2	large eggs	2
1 tsp	vanilla extract	5 mL
1 cup	unsalted butter	250 mL
½ cup	sugar	125 mL
1½ cups	brown sugar	375 mL
2 cups	chocolate chips	500 mL
1½ cups	pecans, coarsely chopped	375 mL
¼ cup	honey	60 mL

• Melt the chocolate in a double boiler. Whisk the warm chocolate into the warm custard mixture to incorporate. Cool fully.

• Prepare ice cream in an ice-cream machine according to manufacturer's instructions.

• Freeze.

MAKES ABOUT 8 CUPS (2 L)

PLANKED CHOCOLATE CHIP COOKIES: Preheat grill to medium-high, 450–550°F (230–280°C).

• Blend oatmeal in food processor until it is a fine powder. Add flour, salt, baking powder, and baking soda. Mix well and set aside.

• In a small bowl, whisk eggs until frothy. Add vanilla and set aside.

• In a large bowl, cream together butter, white sugar and brown sugar. Add eggs-and-vanilla mixture to bowl and mix well to combine.

• Add flour mixture to butter mixture and mix thoroughly until blended. Add chocolate chips and pecans.

• Remove planks from water.

• Scoop out about 1 tsp (5 mL) of cookie dough and roll into a small ball. Flatten dough ball slightly with your hands and place on plank. Repeat with remaining dough until planks are full, spacing balls about 1 inch (2.5 cm) apart on the planks.

• Place planks on grill and bake for 10 to 12 minutes, or until cookies are golden brown and fully cooked. Depending on how many planks you can fit onto your grill, you may have to plank cookies in two batches.

• Carefully remove planks from grill and place on a metal baking sheet. Allow cookies to cool slightly.

• Using a spatula, remove cookies from planks and place on wire racks or platter to cool further.

• Drizzle with warm honey before serving.

ASSEMBLE YOUR BURGERS! Planked cookie, scoop of Smoked-Chocolate Espresso Ice Cream, planked cookie. Serve immediately.

MAKES ABOUT 2 DOZEN COOKIES

SHAKES

SARSAPARILLA JACK FLOAT

2	glass mugs, approximately 12 oz each	2
1 cup	heavy whipping cream 35%	250 mL
2 x 1½ oz shots	Jack Daniel's Tennessee Whiskey, chilled	2 x 45 mL
2 x ½ oz shots	Butterscotch Schnapps, chilled	2 x 45 mL
2–3 cups	icy cold Root Beer	500-750 mL
4 x 2 oz scoops	Butterscotch Ripple Ice Cream	4 x 60 mL
Drizzles	chocolate fudge sauce, store bought works great and it's easy	
2	long straws	2

This recipe reminds me of my childhood only way better now!
Tip: Place the bottles of Jack Daniel's Tennessee Whiskey and Butterscotch Schnapps into the freezer for at least one hour prior to making this tasty beverage.

• Place the mugs into the freezer for at least 1 hour prior to preparing this drink. A frosty mug truly makes this drink a brain freezer.

• Whip the whipping cream until it forms stiff peaks, refrigerate.

• Remove mugs from freezer.

• Working quickly, pour half of the Jack Daniel's and half of the Butterscotch Schnapps into each glass. Top with icy cold root beer. Note: Leave a couple of inches from the rim so the drinks don't over flow when you add the ice cream.

• Top each with a large scoop of butterscotch ripple ice cream, a large spoonful of fresh whipped cream. Drizzle with chocolate fudge sauce, insert straw and serve immediately.

MAKES 2 TASTY BEVERAGES

• Serve this with The Jackinator Burger recipe on page 81.

GRILLED BANANA CUSTARD SHAKE

1	blender	1
2	milk shake glasses	2

VANILLA BEAN CUSTARD

1	vanilla bean pod	1
8	egg yolks	8
½ cup	sugar	125 mL
1 tsp	tapioca starch	5 mL
1½ cups	Heavy 35% whipping cream	375 mL
½ cup	whole milk	125 mL

GRILLED BANANAS

2	ripe but firm bananas, peeled	2
	Nonstick cooking spray	

THE SHAKE

1	blender	1
4 big scoops	really good vanilla ice cream	4
1 cup	chilled vanilla custard	250 mL
2 oz	Gentleman Jack Rare Tennessee Whiskey	60 mL
1 oz	chocolate liqueur	30 mL
Big squirt	chocolate syrup	
2 tsp	chocolate shavings	10 mL

Grilling the bananas gives a little char flavor to this shake which blends well with the charcoal flavor notes in the Gentleman Jack Rare Tennessee Whiskey.

• Separate the vanilla pod from the gooey inside by slicing the pod in half with a small knife, opening up each side and scraping the inside out with the knife. Keep the skin (pod) and the insides separate.

• Whisk together the eggs, sugar and tapioca starch and set aside.

• Over a double boiler, bring the cream, milk and vanilla seeds and pod to a low boil. Remove from heat and whisk into the egg and sugar mixture. Continue to stir this mixture over double boiler, with a wooden spoon, for 10-12 minutes or until the mixture begins to thicken and you can "blow a rose" on the back of the spoon. Remove from heat, strain through a fine sieve and allow to cool.

• Place in the refrigerator and allow mixture to set.

GRILLED BANANAS: Preheat grill to medium-high heat, 450-550°F (230-280°C).

• Spray bananas lightly with nonstick cooking spray.

• Grill bananas for 2-3 minutes per side until lightly charred.

• Remove from grill and allow to fully cool.

THE SHAKE: In a blender, add the grilled banana, vanilla custard and ice cream and blend until smooth.

• Add the Gentleman Jack, chocolate liqueur and a big squirt of chocolate syrup. Then blend a little more.

• Pour into milk-shake glasses.

• Garnish with chocolate shavings and serve immediately.

MAKES 2 BEVERAGES

• Serve with The Billion Dollar Burger on page 122.

Gentleman Jack is a registered trademark ©2010
A gentleman knows his limits. Drink responsibly.

BERRYLICIOUS SMOOTHIE

½ cup	fresh raspberries	125 mL
½ cup	fresh black berries	125 mL
½ cup	fresh strawberries	125 mL
4 scoops	frozen yogurt	4
Drizzle	honey	
2 oz	Southern Comfort	60 mL
2 oz	Chambord Black Raspberry Liqueur	60 mL
6	ice cubes	6

This is the healthy alternative to a milk shake with a bit of a kick.

• Place the berries evenly spaced onto a parchment-paper-lined cookie sheet.

• Place in the freezer until frozen, approximately 2–3 hours.

• Place frozen berries, frozen yogurt, a drizzle of honey, Southern Comfort, Chambord Liqueur and ice cubes into blender. Blend until smooth.

• Pour into large frosty glasses and serve immediately.

MAKES 2 BEVERAGES

• Serve this with the Blueberry Venison Burger on page 186.

BUGS BUNNY LEMONADE SLUSHY

1	blender	1
12	ice cubes	12
1 cup	fresh carrot juice	250 mL
½ cup	orange juice	125 mL
3 oz	Finlandia Vodka	90 mL
1 oz	orange liqueur	30 mL
2 Tbsp	honey	30 mL
2 sprigs	fresh thyme	2

This is an extremely delicious summer cocktail. Icy cold and not too sweet it not only quenches, it refreshes.

• Place the ice cubes in a blender. Add carrot juice, orange juice, vodka, orange liqueur and honey. Blend until smooth.

• Pour into a pitcher and place in the freezer and allow to freeze for at least 1 hour to allow the mixture to become slushy.

• Pour into chilled glasses and garnish with a sprig of thyme and a drizzle of extra honey. Serve immediately.

MAKES 2 BEVERAGES

• Serve this cocktail along side of the Sweet and Sassy Ultimate Chicken Burger on page 197.

Finlandia Vodka is a registered trademark ©2010
Keep your senses pure. Drink responsibly.

Chambord and el Jimador are registered trademarks ©2010
Please Drink Responsibly.

EDIBLE COCKTAIL 2: BOOZY BALLOONS

1	melon ball scoop	1
24	6 inch bamboo skewers	24
24 pieces	red, green or concord grapes	24
2 oz + 3 oz	el Jimador Reposado Tequila	60 mL + 90 mL
1 oz + 1 oz	Chambord Black Raspberry Liqueur	30 mL + 30 mL
1 ripe	pineapple	1
1 ripe	cantaloupe	1
½ tsp	red chili flakes	2.5 mL
2 tsp	fresh cilantro, chopped	10 mL
1	lime, juiced	1
¼ cup	brown sugar	60 mL
	Sea salt and freshly ground black pepper, to taste	

I love the edible cocktail. Alcohol marinated fruit skewers with a boozy dipping sauce. Try this with a variety of firm fleshed fruits. Grill the pineapple if you want too!

Serve this at the beginning of your burger party. A fun edible cocktail that will have your guests moaning . . . mmm!

• In a bowl, combine the grapes, 2 oz of el Jimador Reposado Tequila and 1 oz of Chambord Liqueur. Toss to evenly coat. Place in freezer and allow grapes to just freeze for at least 2 hours.

• Meanwhile using a sharp knife, cut the top and bottom off of the pineapple and cantaloupe. Then cut a 3-inch thick slice across the pineapple. (Note: This is so you can then scoop out a fruit bowl and use it to hold the dipping drink part of the recipe and have something for your skewers to stick into.)

• Stand on one of the cut ends and then cut the rind from the flesh of the remaining chunk of pineapple and the cantaloupe using a curving angular motion. Discard rinds.

• Using a melon ball scoop, cut uniform-sized balls from the cantaloupe and pineapple. You will need approximately 24 balls of each. Place cantaloupe and pineapple balls in bowl. Drizzle with a little el Jimador and Chambord, mix and refrigerate.

• Cut up remaining pineapple and cantaloupe and place in a blender and purée until smooth. Strain and reserve ½ cup, drink the rest.

• Skewer one ball of each of the three fruits onto each skewer.

• Place skewers of fruit in an event layer in a 3 inch deep pan. Add 2 oz of el Jimador, 1 oz of Chambord, red chili flakes, cilantro and lime juice.

• Sprinkle with brown sugar, pour in ½ cup of reserved fruit juice, turning to coat evenly cover and refrigerate to marinate for 30 more minutes.

• Remove marinated fruit skewers from refrigerator, season to taste with sea salt and freshly ground black pepper.

• Pour left over marinade into the pineapple bowl. Push the marinated fruit balloon skewers into the edges of the pineapple bowl.

• Dip boozy fruit balloons into marinade.

• Slurp and enjoy.

MAKES 24 SKEWERS

GENTLEMAN'S MALTED MILK SHAKE

4 scoops	vanilla ice cream	4
2 Tbsp	maple syrup	30 mL
3 tsp	vanilla malted milk powder	15 mL
½ cup	evaporated milk	125 mL
2 oz	Gentleman Jack Rare Tennessee Whiskey	60 mL
Drizzle	chocolate syrup	
4	Whoppers Malted Chocolate Balls	4

The flavor of chocolate adds a fun twist to this beverage.

• In a blender, combine vanilla ice cream, maple syrup, malted milk powder, evaporated milk and Gentleman Jack. Blend until smooth.

• Pour into milk shake glasses, garnish with Whoppers and drizzle with chocolate syrup.

• Serve immediately.

MAKES 2 BEVERAGES

• Serve this with the In-N-Out Burger on page 55.

Gentleman Jack is a registered trademark ©2010
A gentleman knows his limits. Drink responsibly.

Southern Comfort is a registered trademark ©2010
Start and end things right. Drink responsibly.

SOUTHERN PEACHES AND CREAM SHAKE

4 scoops	vanilla ice cream	4
3	peaches, peeled, pitted and cut into chunks	3
½ cup	cold tangerine or orange juice	125 mL
2 oz	Southern Comfort	60 mL
3 Tbsp	condensed milk	45 mL
4	peach cream filled cookies, coarsely crushed	4

A drink for your favorite southern belle. Make sure you use fresh, ripe peaches to get that full, sweet, peachy flavor.

• In a blender, combine vanilla ice cream, peaches, tangerine or orange juice, Southern Comfort and condensed milk. Blend until thick and smooth. Add in crushed cookies and pulse to just mix.

• Pour into glasses and garnish with an extra drizzle of Southern Comfort.

SERVES MAKES 2 BEVERAGES

• Serve this with the Turducken Burger on page 224.